Laboring to Play

Laboring to Play

Home Entertainment and the Spectacle of
Middle-Class Cultural Life, 1850–1920

MELANIE DAWSON

THE UNIVERSITY OF ALABAMA PRESS
Tuscaloosa

Copyright © 2005
The University of Alabama Press
Tuscaloosa, Alabama 35487-0380
All rights reserved
Manufactured in the United States of America
Typeface: Minion and Goudy Sans

∞

The paper on which this book is printed meets the minimum requirements of American
National Standard for Information Science-Permanence of Paper for Printed Library
Materials, ANSI Z39.48-1984.

Library of Congress Cataloging-in-Publication Data

Dawson, Melanie, 1967–
    Laboring to play : home entertainment and the spectacle of middle-class cultural life,
1850–1920 / Melanie Dawson.
        p.   cm.
    Includes bibliographical references and index.
    ISBN 0-8173-1449-0 (cloth : alk. paper)
    1. Leisure—United States—History—19th century. 2. Middle class—Recreation—United
States—History—19th century. 3. United States—Social life and customs—19th century.
I. Title.
    GV53.D39 2005
    790.1′0973′09034—dc22

                                                                        2004019086

Contents

Illustrations

Acknowledgments

I am grateful to many individuals for their guidance, conversation, and general encouragement of this project. I also owe thanks to various institutional sources of support. At the dissertation stage, a yearlong grant from the University of Pittsburgh, the Nancy Anderson Doctoral Fellowship, meant sustained and focused work. Later that year, a summer research grant at the Winterthur Museum Library enabled me to gather materials and to collect many of the images reprinted here. I also owe thanks to the staff at Hillman Library, University of Pittsburgh, particularly Special Collections, where this project began and to the interlibrary loan system there, which proved essential in gaining access to a broad range of home entertainment guide manuals, for many of the items I discuss were not systematically collected in libraries.

For reprint permissions, I thank *Reader: Essays in Reader-Oriented Theory, Criticism, and Pedagogy*, where an earlier version of the Wharton discussion in chapter five appeared as "Lily Bart's Fractured Alliances and Wharton's Appeal to the Middlebrow Reader," *Reader* 41 (Spring 1999). Additionally, parts of the Alcott analysis from chapter four appeared in "A Woman's Power: Alcott's 'Behind a Mask' and the Usefulness of Dramatic Literacies in the Home," originally published in *ATQ*, Volume 11, No. 1, March 1997. Reprinted by permission of The University of Rhode Island.

Among those individuals whose support has been invaluable over the years are Jean Ferguson Carr and Susan Harris Smith, who saw the early potential of this work, challenging and encouraging me at the dissertation stage and well beyond. In addition, Joe Harris (responsible for the *New Yorker* cover I mention in the epilogue) and Paula Kane provided probing questions and critical insights. I am also appreciative of those readers who offered advice during periods of transition and revision, among them Nancy Glazener, Steve Weisenberger, and Steve Carr, who offered crucial, candid insights, provoking a necessary turning point in the text's design. I also owe an intellectual debt to William Gleason for his enthusiasm for the text's project and for an especially enabling response to an earlier version of the manuscript, one rich in intellectual rigor. My thanks also extend to the anonymous reader for The University of Alabama Press, whose insights made the project stronger. At The University of Alabama Press, Daniel Waterman's commitment to the project made the final phases of work a seamless and rewarding experience.

There are also those who have made it possible for me to carve work time out of busy days, or rather, to define work time and life time usefully, among them my parents, Edwina and Edelyn Dawson; my grandmother, Hilton Dawson; and neighbors Loretta and David Nunn. Finally, to my spouse, John Nichols, who knows that time is a gift and who has always been willing to bestow it, even on the days when the products of my labors weren't readily visible, I owe my greatest debts. For his insights, his willingness to read a page at virtually any hour of the day or night, and for his necessary sympathies, unflagging interest, and continued support, I can only hope to repay him in kind.

Laboring to Play

Introduction

Here we have at once a very important point: even in its simplest forms on the animal level, play is more than a mere physiological phenomenon or a psychological reflex. It goes beyond the confines of purely physical or purely biological activity. It is a *significant* function—that it to say, there is some sense to it. In play there is something "at play" which transcends the immediate needs of life and imparts meaning to the action. All play means something.

J. Huizinga, *Homo Ludens*

Home entertainments occupied a specialized, unique position in nineteenth-century American cultural life. They reflected the interests of an increasingly affluent population of middling Americans, a group confronted with genteel expectations, preoccupied with social status, and driven by a desire for professional accomplishment.[1] Without invalidating the larger parameters coming to define middle-class life, home entertainments challenged middling ambitions for polite manners, for streamlined professionalism, and for genteel living, showcasing visions that extended beyond the comfortable circumference of everyday life to celebrate displays of exaggerated, unsocial bodies. Despite their presence in the parlor, the social sphere, and, in later years, the society pages, the various genres of home entertainment upheld ideals of personal agency and authentic work, reacting against a social complacency rooted in even the most moderate modes of affluence. From physical, boisterous games to theatricals to tableaux vivants to commemorative recitations, home entertainments articulate a set of complex responses to the boundaries encircling middling lifestyles.

As they developed across the nearly seventy years from roughly 1850 to 1920, home entertainments helped to clarify, critique, and question the everyday activities of their participants. In this sense, the activities, which varied greatly over time, functioned as an elaborate, interactive sounding board for examining trends in middling lifestyles. Thus, as I treat it, home entertainment provided not only diversion, a relief from ennui, and an occasion for behavioral expansiveness, but it also served as a forum for examining developing middling lifestyles. Home entertainment's activities, among them imperialist play and best-room "stunts," formed a set of extravagant, bodily, and performative practices that were as much a cornerstone of the American cultural experience as piety, sentiment, and the intricacies of etiquette. Hence, for the moderately affluent families, upwardly striving middling hopefuls, social young ladies, groups of young adults, households of holiday revelers, flirtatious youth, and for the gracious host and hostess who participated in home entertainments, these activities defined an individual's conscious awareness of the social sphere's demands and how to take part in them.

Although located within middling lifestyles, home entertainment practices nevertheless showcase a surprising degree of ambivalence regarding comfortable status. The "Museum" game, which appeared in *Godey's* of 1864, for example, reveals a double engagement with genteel social life—a position to which participants in play ostensibly aspired. Like many parlor activities, the game is at once a vehicle of social life and simultaneously a critique of ambitious enactments of middling sociability. It begins with the premise that the company should form a "collection of curiosities" that will be sold one by one; the participants are to prohibit themselves from smiling during the transactions, or must pay forfeits for their lack of self-control.[2] The "museum's" director then proceeds to describe the "curiosities" before him, creating purposefully ridiculous narratives intended to cause the "valuables" to smile. In the example provided in *Godey's*, the director makes the following speech: "Here . . . is the celebrated mummy of Cheops, brought from Egypt at an enormous cost originally as a plaything for one of President Lincoln's children; but the poor little fellow being frightened by the expression of its hideous countenance, it was sold at auc—"(375). The "mummy" smiles and the director moves on to the next "object" for sale. Ideally, the game produces laughter, which the winning director provokes.

Such games present the most obvious object of play as transforming "posed" or genteel persons into living, laughing ones. By encouraging a break in a customary social facade, the game circumvents one of etiquette's codes by overturning an ideal of facial composure. Those players who don't laugh, who remain the most poised, win the game, but the real fun, clearly, derives from breaking genteel behavioral conventions.[3] A similar "don't laugh" game in the same series, "A Few Friends," is entitled "The Picture Gallery." Entailing the presentation of tableaux, vivants, or "living pictures" on various subjects, the object of the game is "to make the obdurate pictures laugh." The text then describes the ways that the "profiles" and "portraits" can be made to come, mirthfully, to life.[4] The tension here—between the means of winning (acting genteel) and the pleasure of the game (breaking into laughter as well as causing others to do so)—attests to the way that many parlor guides represent the activities of entertainment as overlapping with etiquette's conventions, even as the enactment of play encouraged individuals to overturn polite behaviors for the duration of entertainment.

The game, which creates tension by relying on, then suspending polite standards, nevertheless maintains a dialogue with ordinary social expectations. Deconstructing poised, facile exteriors, the game nevertheless positions gentility as a goal that should be embraced, albeit cautiously and self-consciously. Indeed, complex understandings of pleasure characterize domestic play time, particularly the challenge in looking past the pleasure of the immediate contest, with its seemingly straightforward appeal, to leisure enterprise's deepest articulation of belonging (what Pierre Bordieu terms The Game). This was a type of fun that indulged escapism and apparent rule breaking in the immediate sense, but which privileged the pleasures and tensions of belonging above all else.

Primarily played in domestic settings (until the 1890s or so) by families and groups of company, home entertainments were widely available and were dispersed to genteel as well as aspiring consumers. According to guide books on home entertainment, magazine accounts, and fictional depictions of entertainment's activities, leisure activities' participants would have included urban and rural players, women and men, white and black players, adults and teens, plus society matrons, governesses, the unskilled as well as the supremely talented, bankers, clerks, shop girls, merchants, and housewives. All would have been invested in self-uplift, in the power of culture, and possessed of some degree of a disposable income and discretionary free time. While, in reality, most participants were likely white, middling Americans, narratives of home entertainment in both fictions and guide books remind us of the upwardly mobile individuals—lower-class workers, moderately affluent turn-of-the-century blacks, and the economically deprived—who attempted to use their cultural experiences to claim middling lifestyles for themselves—and to articulate their social aspirations through discretionary leisure. Novels such as Emma Dunham Kelley's *Megda* (discussed in chapter seven) and Pauline Hopkins's *Contending Forces* (discussed in chapter five), for example, shed light on the entertainments popular among the northern black middle classes near the turn into the twentieth century, but such depictions are notably unique in nineteenth-century literature. Largely, however, the hopeful narratives attached to home entertainments depict leisurely practices as social equalizers where skilled participants could triumph over traditional privileges such as money, status, and connections. This democratic idealism serves as one of home entertainment's most compelling self-justifications.

Other idealizing stories surrounding entertainments upheld the values associated with individualism. They stressed the value of individual work, unique ability, and personal agency during a time when the proper etiquette governing everyday life called for an increasingly codified, circumscribed social arena filled with polite manners and vestiges of old-time social privilege. In such a context, entertainment's emphasis on individual opportunity (and, often, triumph) as well as competition held an obvious appeal for entertainment's primary votaries, whose entrée into the social sphere was frequently cast as less intimidating through entertainment than through other social interactions. In addition, by highlighting individual abilities, home entertainments provided a powerful and enabling illusion that individuals (even those just entering the social sphere) could shape their social worlds, rather than merely respond to established behavioral codes.

Trends

The changes that I chart through home entertainments depict a narrative of an emerging sense of a group identity, not crystallized around a single event, but through textual trends that signal shifting modes of self-representation. Narrative depictions of the individual's relation to a broader social spectrum —in both home entertainment manuals and literary texts—portray individuals who attempt to claim a loose class affiliation through skills or talents. Characteristically, these figures deploy everyday talents that become, somewhat paradoxically, markers of distinction. Early in this story (1850 or so), there is a greater emphasis on individualism; later, by 1900, the narrative emphasizes affiliation through class structures, but treats them as debilitating and confining. In the beginning of this narrative, individuals can be identified with a distinct social sphere in spite of themselves, for their attitudes toward class are demonstratively ambivalent; later, their consciousness of their social position is much greater, to the point of becoming overwhelming.

Making sense of the varied traditions and practices encompassing home entertainment, for me, has meant considering these practices historically, as a dynamic, shifting set of enterprises. Together they reveal some of the most profound changes, tensions, and uncertainties attending the expansion of middling American life. Because entertainment's forms coincided with the marked development of an American middle class, they reveal one vehicle through which the goals and anxieties associated with class-based identity could be articulated—visibly, repeatably, and socially. In addition, I have attended to the narratives that guide texts and other accounts of play offered their readers, not with the notion of taking such claims at face value, but examining the popular stories that encircled entertainment forms. As I chart the changing history of home entertainment then, I attempt to trace why participants played and how the activities of leisure time defined middling Americans, fusing the work of recovery with a polemical reinterpretation of middle-class cultural life.

The texts guiding entertainment trends provided participants with ways to understand the breadth and consequences of their own social desires and, more importantly, how to think about, test out, and perform their relation to the larger structures of nineteenth-century life. Hence the changing rules of play point to subtle, yet deeply significant shifts in how middling-class goals were redefined and performatively articulated. In making such claims, I seek to extend existing scholarship on middle-class culture in two ways. First, I insist on the political efficacy of entertainment practices as vehicles and reflections of a class rapidly coming to a consciousness of its growing influence, including a self-awareness of its boundaries (rather than, say, a respectful incorporation of borrowed practices). Second, and perhaps more importantly, I chart a deep ambivalence with middling status itself. That the production of grotesque spectacles (producing severed heads) and genteel practices (taking tea) coexisted in mid-century domestic life suggests that both etiquette and entertainment functioned as part of an ensemble of practices characterizing their participants, even as these acts were mobilized differently and assigned varying (if not divergent) social meanings. Of these practices, one set—the mannered behaviors—would rise to dominance in everyday life, even as entertaining activities continued to proliferate in specialized social interactions and as occasions to complicate the image of middling culture life played out in a social forum.

As dynamic forms of social practice, home entertainments inflected topics of ongoing debate in nineteenth-century America. Activities such as parlor games intersected with the varied concerns inflecting middling social life, including anxieties about national development, particularly concerns about genteel, European influences. Other forms of play such as domestic dramas allowed for the portrayal of women as powerful cultural agents controlling domestic spaces. Tableaux vivants and other sumptuously staged spectacles reveal the ways that pervasive impulses toward consumer culture affected various strands of domestic life. Across such variations in entertainment's activities, then, we see a story of how entertainments allowed participants to reflect on the tensions affecting their lives. As I argue in chapters one through three, entertainment forms entailed a recurring critique of genteel life during the mid nineteenth century, when a growing middle class was struggling to find an authentic means of inhabiting a genteel social world. Later, the narrative inflecting home entertainments would change as relative affluence, a nostalgia for lost stability, and, finally, a push toward communal, nationalistic homogeneity infused play time.

Reading for how these variations in play intersect with the history of the largest group of participants in leisure enterprises, I emphasize various developments in middling social life, including a trajectory from competition to assurance, from social initiation to cultural (but not economic) dominance, and from rural individualism to suburban communalism. Such developments entailed claims for an almost unlimited economic ascent, then the emergence of a more defined, limited middling tier, capped by an elite group of investors and entrepreneurs. In addition, there were significant shifts in the middling demographic, from groups of white workers, self-promoters, and middling managers to a more ethnically and racially diverse population including immigrants and affluent blacks, whose entrée into a secure middling economic tier occurred largely toward the end of the nineteenth century. Another major shift in characterization of entertainment's participants involves their relation to various social spheres; at the mid century, participants filtered the world primarily through their homes, whereas in later decades club, church, and beneficent groups, along with commercial entertainments at the theater, nickelodeon, and cinema, increasingly influenced entertainment's votaries.

Devoid of this context, the broad array of nineteenth-century home entertainment practices presents a dizzying spectacle, revealing such diversity and apparent idiosyncrasy that the activities may appear little more than vestiges of the Victorians' propensity toward collections of oddities. Indeed, playful presentations of grotesque bodies, with their twisted features, inverted forms, elongated shapes, and severed heads, appear all the more incongruous when grouped with other home entertainments such as tableaux vivants of sumptuous scenes or respectful recitation pieces, which can seem to appear indiscriminately culled together under the descriptive "home entertainment." Yet in considering the larger swath of home entertainment's practices, including how fashions of play developed and changed over a seventy-year period, I offer a narrative of how a set of shifting, eccentric, and often spectacularly weird social practices represented the goals and tensions infusing the rise of a middling American culture.

Popularity and the History of the Entertainment Book

Described in didactic guides, magazine columns, personal histories, journal articles recording actual performances, short stories, fictions, journals, and occasional letters, the practices of home entertainment circulated widely. Drawing from a dimension of book history rooted in the circulation of popular texts, I examine how entertainment books shifted their parameters over time, as well as how they were part of a publication market characterized by both popular novels and didactic publications. Beginning at around 1850, self-help guide books on entertainment indicate a broad, mass audience for entertainment's activities.[5] At this time, narratives about home entertainment, which began to appear frequently in periodicals, guide texts, and popular fictions, form a richly detailed, extended description of entertainment's practices, providing such details as numbers of participants, types of accoutrements, how personalities and leisure roles could be understood in regard to one another, and how to use a knowledge of entertainment's conventions to better interpret fictional complexities.

One sign of a dawning interest in advice on entertainment can be seen in mid-century periodicals, which increasingly devoted their pages to home entertainments, often anticipating trends in book sales and helping to establish a market for books on the topic. During the 1850s and '60s, magazines such as *Godey's* and *Harper's Monthly* published substantial series devoted to the latest trends in home entertainment; one of the earliest was a June 1846 personal account of tableaux vivants, entitled simply "Tableaux."[6] In addition, and as a sign of the growing popularity of home entertainments, two exceptionally lengthy series, "Ella Moore's Letters From the City" (1860) and "A Few Friends" (1864) appeared in *Godey's*, running six months and nine months, respectively.[7] Opening with an account of a hostess's horror at a disastrous gathering, the narrative of "A Few Friends" revolves around the moment when guests at a party initiate parlor games, which are met with such enthusiasm that the same company agrees to meet every two weeks for subsequent entertaining diversions. Over the course of the series, various games are described in great detail, with the length and prominence of the series attesting to a growing niche in the publishing market.

Such series, while initiating readers into the practices of home entertainment, were ostensibly written by participants in play, presented as personal letters, but also published for the edification of many readers. Indeed, the function of published personal stories and didactic texts often overlapped, blurring the lines between public and private spheres, advice and experience. Such accounts, we may posit, could well have been rooted in actual events, but are greatly and obviously enhanced by their wealth of expository detail. The rules for play are clearly outlined. Long accounts of quoted passages or of original dialogues between participants in the entertainments appear. In addition, as the series "Ella Moore's Letters from the City," "Tableaux

Vivans [*sic*]" (*Harper's Monthly,* 1863), and "A Few Friends" attest, the introduction and development of individualized characters suggests that much
of the interest surrounding such pieces exceeded mere explanation; the
drama lay in contextualized accounts of how various individuals dealt with
the challenges of play time. Because the texts trace who is gifted, who is vain,
who discovers hidden talents, and who falls in love (as well as how the court-
ship progresses over the course of leisure employments), such accounts take
on many of the same functions as fictional accounts of home entertainment's
practices. At the same time, such pieces carefully provide broad, instructional
knowledge, cast with the flavor of personal experience. On the subject of
"Impromptu Charades," for example, Ella Moore writes, "Now, Susy dear, if
you wish to have impromptu charades, you can take these for a model, and
act out countless words. It is rare fun for the performers, and if your audience
tire, change places, then let them perform while you look on. After each one,
let some one of the actors ask the audience for the word."[8] And on the topic
of "Moving Tableaux," Moore confidentially cautions her reader, " . . . these
scenes take a longer time to act than to write out for you, Susy, and four are
as many as are wanted in an evening; they are tedious, if you give too many
of them."[9]

These types of personal accounts filtered into the public representation of
home entertainment, continuing up through the century's turn, when glowing accounts of high-society tableaux vivants involving the most fashionable
New Yorkers appeared in journals such as *Cosmopolitan*. These accounts,
along with those in guide books and accounts of play in nineteenth-century
fiction, are lavishly detailed. Indeed, their wealth of information often outshines references to home entertainments in private letters and journals.
From private letters and journals, we know, for example, that the William
Dean Howellses, the Bronson Alcotts, the Samuel Clemenses, and the Harriet
Beecher Stowe family participated in home entertainments, usually without
documenting the events of play closely.[10] We may learn from private accounts that entertainments took place on a particular night, within a certain
group of company, but not who played what roles or how the participants
understood the links between their leisure activities and their everyday social identities.

Public texts of play (notices, reviews, informative articles, didactic guides,
and fictions) typically articulate recurring concerns about inhabiting social
goals, concerns not limited to a family or neighborhood, but made available
to a number of consumers and participants. Much of my evidence stems
from published texts that circulated images of entertainment for a large

marketplace of readers, thereby situating domestic leisure as a discursive, public topic. Rather than viewing instructional publications as merely theoretical (especially since many also functioned as reviews), I treat these explanatory models of entertainment as artifacts illustrating entertainment's relations to an array of surrounding practices and ideals. These texts attend to the consequences of participating in leisure enterprises, contextualizing entertainment in relation to other personal interests and desires. Both personal accounts of entertainments among specific social groups and period fictions, for example, attend to issues of character development, narrating entertainment's enactments alongside portraits of individual abilities, specific family backgrounds, and fully articulated social desires.

Many such accounts of home entertainment could be classified as "popular" texts in the sense that they were widely dispersed. Additionally, entertainment guide books were mass produced, modestly priced, and somewhat formulaic. The similarities among vast numbers of entertainment guide books powerfully assert the recurrence of narratives about entertainment, for their ubiquitousness in columns in ladies' magazines such as *Godey's* and *The Baltimore Olio,* in children's materials such as *St. Nicholas,* in less expensive weeklies such as *Harper's Bazar,* and in an array of book-style manuals bespeaks a market saturated by references to entertainment.

As is the case with other cheaply produced books, guide books on home entertaining reveal signs of piracy, for they frequently sound much like other contemporary books on the same topic, or closely—even exactly—resemble columns on entertaining in the popular periodicals of the time, many of which appeared some time after the books were published. Some of these visual and textual repetitions appear across multiple guide books issued from a single company, such as Dick and Fitzgerald, a major producer of home entertainment guides. *The Sociable,* for example, is composed of many sections, which were later reprinted in other guide books from Dick and Fitzgerald that were attributed to an array of authors. In addition, whole sections of popular entertainment guide books reappear in texts from various companies. Anonymous guide books are among those from which most material was borrowed, either because of joint or company ownership or because of the generic nature associated with texts without authors. The works of a few successful individual writers, however, also show signs of self-borrowing. A prolific Dick and Fitzgerald writer, Sarah Annie Frost Shields, wrote multiple books of plays for home production; she also wrote for *Godey's* during the 1850s and '60s and for Beadle and Adams's *Dime Dialogue* series, a line devoted to inexpensive publications of parlor plays.[11]

Across these texts, it is possible to encounter various renderings of a popular topic such as "Bluebeard's Closet," which is included in multiple tableaux, charades, and theatrical books. From parlor operas to melodramas to farces to a rather grisly pen-and-ink illustration by Winslow Homer of the "Blue Beard Tableaux," Bluebeard is only one of a number of subjects represented by multiple writers. Other recurring themes include "There is no Rose without Thorns" (which often appears in the form of a proverb in a charade or theatrical) and "Court-ship" (which most usually appears as a charade), as well as multiple plays about hasty marriages to fortune hunters and incidents that indict pretentious behaviors of all sorts. Versions of these themes occur in the vast majority of entertainment manuals.

Which of these versions of play is the "original" or most authentic is a moot question. It is impossible to provide exact figures for the number of times a game appears in entertainment guide books because most texts alter some aspect of the game—the title, the accoutrements, the description— slightly. In addition, there are no accurate records for the market of cheaply produced guide books.[12] A key issue here is that conventional authorship or even a Foucauldian notion of "author function" is, for the most part, inapplicable to this market. Many entertainment books were published anonymously or under obvious pseudonyms such as "Joshua Jedidiah Jinks" or "a Descendant of Cleobulina." The point is not that one guide book author was inspired by a particular advice book from an earlier age, but that a larger textual market could sustain the circulation of a mutating but recognizable set of intertwined social and textual practices for a period of seventy years, suggesting their viability within nineteenth-century culture.[13]

Hence, I have chosen to focus on the broader historical narrative of home entertainment in nineteenth-century U.S. culture rather than its complicated, transnational origins.[14] Many guide books were published in both England and the United States, and a number claim to have been translated from the French (as the earliest appear to be). My working theory has been that many descriptions migrated from France to England to the United States, yet the exact origins of these texts fails to account either for their popularity among Americans or among the developing middle class. There is also the rather vexed question of the age of players, since many games played at mid century by adults first appear in British and American entertainment guide books for children, some dating a half century before the adult game guides became popular at the mid century. Issues of authorship, company policies, transatlantic migrations of play, as well as the relationships between adult and child players offer a compelling potential for future study.

Self-Representation through Leisure

When discussed critically, home entertainments have been treated as anomalies, except in rare studies, such as Karen Halttunen's *Confidence Men and Painted Women*, J. Jeffrey Franklin's *Serious Play*, and the work of Mary Chapman.[15] Marginalized by their presumed privateness and by their supposed adherence to codes of feminized, domestic gentility, the activities of the parlor have received little extended attention.[16] Although it is difficult to pinpoint the genesis of a received portrait of the emerging nineteenth-century middling classes, there are subjects that have set the general tone for such discussions, among them manners and conventions. I aim here to disrupt the centrality attributed to the elaborate daily ceremonies of life a hundred and fifty years ago, or discussions of ritualistic tea taking, card circulating, and making calls. An emphasis on conventions, on ritual, on everyday behaviors makes it difficult to envision middling types as doing anything other than adhering to—or by contrast, breaking—the rules of daily life. Based on entertainment's internal contradictions, however, I characterize a culture of play as more than a reaction against everyday life, situating home leisure activities as a set of practices where rules were manipulated, elided, extended, and, on occasion, suspended.

In their diversity and complexity, home entertainment trends help us to imagine a dynamic nineteenth-century social landscape where testing out one's relation to cultural life constituted a significant dimension of entertainment's appeal. In addition to providing patterns for behavior, parlor games and other forms of home entertainment promised to measure individual progress, reward winners, and reveal unexplored talents; they staged moments of exertion, decision making, and competition, thereby granting participants opportunities to imagine a tangible and immediate control over their lives. They also propelled their participants—individuals who may not have cared to see themselves as affiliates of any particular group—to identify and act out their allegiances in playful, provocative ways, testing out behavioral boundaries, social codes, and the possibilities of rethinking them.[17]

Entertainment's forms, then, allowed for participants' social goals to be acted out within a physical social forum, where competition and individualism were accepted as social behaviors. Through their competitive scenarios, home leisure activities promoted an unusual sense of an individual's ability to shape his or her own successes. By rewarding individual decisions, preferences, and talents, home entertainments (in their various manifestations) charted the place of personal action within a broader context of social belonging, and in so doing, offered participants much more than immediate, temporal successes. These activities offered a vision of active players whose ambitions and successes overlapped. Supporting the image of dynamic players, the guide books, novels, magazines, newspaper columns, and fictions devoted to home entertainment redefine entertainment as a grounds for labor-intensive personal successes. This attractive portrait of entertainment's active, self-actualized participants offers one likely reason for the popularity of the practices.

The texts that feature entertainment's practices reveal the flattering vision of self that middle-class individuals worked to bring to life: the drama of self-representation. Rather than viewing themselves as normative or middling, participants in home entertainment represented themselves as risk takers, as possessed of rich lives through which to distill competitive abilities, and as self-aware performers who turned a critical eye to their own participation in developing markers of class affiliation. Through competition and play, through a performative engagement with entertainment's forms, they were able to assert the immediate values of individualism, the value of seeing themselves as wielding vast powers of personal agency.

In varying ways, home entertainments encouraged participants not only to face expectations of normative social behaviors but also to inhabit those norms through personal innovation—no easy task surely. This was, then, a notion of participation that held personal subjectivity in check with visible, enacted customs, permitting an unrelenting contest between self and society. By recovering such discussions, I have considered what it meant for a dominant culture to come into being—self-consciously, uneasily, and unevenly—breaking and rewriting traditions. It was a culture that displayed a deep respect for gentility, for advice, and for established forms of cultural authority, even as it visibly and dramatically acted out against these forces. This continual negotiation, reminiscent of Edward Said's discussion of cultural affiliation, reveals an enactment of leisure permeated with what Said terms an "awareness—a self-situating, a sensitive response to the dominant culture" that leads not just to "conformity and belonging" but situates the individual as "a historical and social actor" within the larger culture.[18] If we consider the larger body here to be a class, the narrative asserted by entertainment guide books as well as fictions featuring entertainments encouraged readers to affiliate but also to see themselves as individual agents, as self-aware, deeply connected participants in a larger culture.

Through their unusual demands upon participants, forms of home entertainment showcased the labors surrounding specialized transformations, the elaborate preparation and participation. For many activities, particularly those of the more theatrical sort, participants were expected to clear out spaces in everyday life for performances of games, pantomimes, tableaux, and parlor theatricals, which required curtains, stages, and room for maneuvers. All this required a block of leisure time apart from everyday concerns and activities.[19] In addition, specialized preparations were called for in regard to memorizing lines, preparing scripts, costuming various displays, and arranging parties where games would necessitate elaborate staging. The work of participating in home entertainment, like the exacting ideals of acculturation announced by etiquette guides, allowed participants to assimilate unfamiliar roles and to try on models of behavior, marking these transformations as labor-intensive, whether for the immediate purpose of a grotesque display or for the long-term goal of familial advancement.

As Thorstein Veblen noted in 1899, after a leisure culture's practices had been in place for over a half century, the pursuit of leisure is itself a sign of belonging, for "the habit of distinguishing and classifying the various purposes and directions of activity prevails of necessity always and everywhere; for it is indispensable in reaching a working theory or scheme of life." The visible work of entertainment served the crucial purposes of what Veblen terms "the grounds of discrimination" for the mid-to-late nineteenth century.[20] Because entertainment practices connoted elective, discretionary forms of work, they distinguished their participants from genteel mothers, housewives, and professionals, who engaged in necessary daily labors. The labors of accounting and assembling and overseeing and cleaning and cooking and sewing and mending, as important as they were, didn't identify individuals as striving toward a lofty goal. As entertainment texts call attention to playful "employments," they implicitly acknowledge the ways that extending oneself beyond the necessities of everyday life had become a requirement for defining oneself socially. Claiming acculturation and doing so in a congenial, social arena became visible as a valuable and self-defining form of work.

Across the varied trends in home entertainment, the texts surrounding entertainment's activities voice a self-conscious argument about the value of leisure that grew into an extended and strategic deployment of structured diversions. The entertainment guides of the mid century through the next seventy years implicitly argue that how one used leisure time was just as significant as how one earned a living. Thomas Schlereth has used the terms "playing" and "striving" to describe the interdependent impulses surrounding leisure time in nineteenth-century America. This study, however, begins with an era when playing and striving were not yet separate enterprises, dwelling on a moment when leisure time's possibilities for ambitious Americans (who may not have even imagined that they were ambitious) were only beginning to be recognized.[21] At this moment, entertaining activities borrowed heavily from the recreational forms associated with children and with aristocratic Europeans.

Gradually, these forms were remade as emblems of a middling American experience, one that, over time, would be cast as authentic. This study, then, accords with William A. Gleason's characterization of leisure in America as "the culture's most vital work" as it focuses on the rising awareness among nineteenth-century Americans that leisure activities offered them extraordinary opportunities to claim (as well as hone) dynamic, hopeful, and transformative experiences.[22] Across the 1850–1920 period and through various types of guide books, novels, stories, illustrations, and cartoons, the textual artifacts surrounding home entertainments reveal a growing awareness that it was play—and not just work—that allowed for the measure of its participants.

Texts and the Enactment of Entertainment

Because the practices of play were recorded and circulated textually, they host rich inscriptions of class-based goals through their explanatory narratives, their historically specific rise (including the prominence of particular trends within the larger field of home entertainment practices), and their presence within the didactic textual market. In an attempt to recognize these various dimensions of home entertainment, I refer to readers as well as participants in play, often with the notion that the two cannot be separated from one another with absolute certainty, since we have few reliable records of how readers enacted the directions found in entertainment guides. Certainly entertainment manuals were constructed so as to facilitate participation, situating the ideal reader as one who read, then took part in entertainments. Yet it is not likely that all games were enacted by all readers or book buyers, nor is it likely that readers and participants were always aligned. Some readers merely read about play, for example, and some participants played by rote. My allusion to players and participants, then, acknowledges that home entertainments involved both the enactment of play as well as the textual inscription of play as significant cultural phenomenon.[23]

In analyzing entertainment's call for readers to become dynamic participants, I have been influenced by theories of social practice. One plausible approach to entertainment texts would be to assert that guide books on home entertainment (like other didactic guides) set in motion a technology of regulation that bent participating individuals to the machinations of a larger system of behavioral control. While we can never forget the power of directive inscription, even in regard to play time, an investigation of what play offered its participants is essential in attending to home entertainment's changes and permutations. Of the theoretical voices I invoke (among them Pierre Bordieu, Michel Foucault, Mikhail Bakhtin, Edward Said, and Nancy Armstrong), Michel de Certeau offers an inviting theory of practice that allows me to emphasize the show of active, engaged activity associated with play. Writing of the dispersed, tactical, and makeshift creativity of groups or individuals already caught in nets of "discipline," de Certeau suggests that even a highly regulated individual could exercise a degree of personal agency.[24] Furthermore, de Certeau's theory highlights the ways that multiple appearances of entertainment could host opportunities for both liberation *and* conscription, depending on their particular manifestations.

Nineteenth-century textual representations of home entertainment repeatedly complicate the ease with which social regulation and individual release may be severed from one another, for texts about home entertainment claim individual agency for play's participants, arguing that through the mechanisms of amusement, participants could shed gentility's customary conventions. By suggesting that games were pleasurable, in part because they allowed participants the opportunity to view themselves as active individuals, I don't claim that such goals were realized, but rather, that they formed a central aspect of home entertainment's appeal. Noting the claims made by entertainment guide books, moreover, helps me to articulate the importance of the unique social conditions that guide books and fictions about entertainment seek to represent, that is, a set of practices where voluntary, competitive play and rules-bound expectations coexisted. Much of my analysis, then, revolves around moments when the rules of play could be enacted so as to produce the impression of profound personal agency, even as the larger institution of performative leisure created clear patterns of social belonging, including behavioral conventions.

As forms of play changed, so too did the balance between individual actions and collective social expectations. Whereas agency and individualism characterized parlor games at the mid century, later, during the 1880s and beyond, highly presentational forms of domestic entertainment lessened individual participants' competitiveness and instead emphasized social relations, communal connections, and a pronounced reverence for a collective past. Both types of cultural practices are important to my understanding of home entertainment's development, for both posit a different balance between individual accomplishment and social belonging and with it, a shifting sense of how to come to terms with modes of affiliation linked to emerging class structures.

Changing Styles of Play and the Arrangement of Chapters

From the 1850s through the 1920s, home entertainment practices were continually reconstituted, and while the shifts from games to scripted theatricals or from tableaux to group pageants (to provide but two examples) are compelling in themselves, the context that helps explain these trends is the changing narrative of belonging to a middling social tier. In charting a narrative of entertainment's changes, I highlight entertainment texts' invitation for participants in play to engage with public representations of middle-class identity, even while revising those definitions as they participated—just as individual players individualized scripted dialogues. As I make this claim, I treat the "evolution" of the middle class in a nonteleological sense, describing this development as less a culmination of the best and most aggressive social qualities than a product of various events arranged in a history.

In tracing changing fashions of home entertainment, I refer to a chronology of entertainment trends that I have divided into four parts, based on fashions of play that emphasize varying types of skills and changing roles for participants. These categories are not absolute, for there were types of play that overlapped, varying fashions in regard to urban and rural practices, and, of course, reprises of older trends. Yet, roughly speaking, entertainment guide books and fictions provide a sense that various identifiable approaches to home entertainment succeeded one another in popularity.

During the first twenty-year epoch of interest in parlor guide books, appearing approximately from 1850 to 1870, games, tableaux vivants, theatricals, and acting charades stressed the value of a vernacular and skills-oriented mode of play. Such activities contrast with forms of parlor play popular during the early decades of the nineteenth century, which tend to be dominated by textual play (in the forms of word play, rhyme, and figurative language), all markers of an aristocratic education. The more noticeably modest activities of the mid century challenge literary elitism with their competing emphasis on physical skills rather than educational privileges. Emphasizing action and the reading of the body, play forms highlighted everyday skills, disrupting the monolithic textuality of earlier entertainments, pointing to the value of "real," enacted experiences. These mid-century, skills-based forms of play assert, in miniature, a narrative wherein ability and diligence lead to social success. These are the types of leisure activities that I explore in chapters one through three.

Chapter one, "Labor, Leisure, and the Scope of Ungenteel Play," begins with the entertainment forms popular at the mid-nineteenth century and addresses a mutually symbiotic relationship between gentility and play, exploring the rules-bound nature of both activities, even as these distinct forms of cultural expression offered two very different goals in offering participants manners (through etiquette) and skills (through entertainment). Chapter two, "Dramatic Regression: The Borrowed Pleasures and Privileges of Youth," explores the invocations of childhood obvious in mid-century boisterous play, and chapter three, "The Social Body and the Severed Head: The Cultural Work of Grotesque Play," investigates the most physical, outrageous, and ungenteel games of the parlor, situating them as part of a skills-based culture where the work of producing effects was of greater value than the effects themselves, even in the case of a severed head or an outrageous "nondescript." These three chapters examine an unease with borrowed and reinvented social practices, along with a desire to display what mid-century participants in entertainment were urged to uphold as a vernacular, authentic mode of culture, one situated in relief to genteel practices. Ultimately, however, this was a mode of culture that we can see as staging dramatic spectacles of individualism rather than providing players with radically new and lasting identities.

Chapters four and five, "Skills Rewarded: Women's Lives Transformed through Entertainment" and "Staging Disaster: Turn-of-the-Century Entertainment Scenes and the Failure of Personal Transformation," explore how entertainment scenes in novels inflected representations of entertainment with narratives about class warfare, interjecting a profoundly important narrative of personal transformation into conversations about entertainment's social significance. I explore Charlotte Brontë's *Jane Eyre* as a European precedent to American renderings of entertainment (among them Alcott's "Behind a Mask"), reading a narrative of entertainment as promoting a vision of permeable class boundaries, where upward ascent is furthered by an individual's unique abilities, made visible through entertainment. Attributing great importance to competition and skill as strategies of articulating self-worth, I argue that mid-century texts gradually give way to more cautious narratives about developing skills to accomplish social goals. Issues of interpretive prowess figure prominently in fictions such as Norris's *The Pit* and Wharton's *The House of Mirth*, where the skills associated with entertainment appear as tragically misleading, outdated myths of social ascent.

As the novels I study also illuminate, the personally transformative mid-century genres of play gradually gave way to a second phase of entertainment, one beginning in the mid 1850s and continuing through the 1870s. Unlike the competitive games also popular at the time, the display-oriented activities of this later era are less combative with the concept of gentility, reflecting a push toward a refined sense of culture. Initially, entertainments such as the allegorical and inspirational displays of tableaux vivants suggested narratives of sentimental pathos, which I discuss in chapters four and five. Emerging in the 1880s and continuing through the century's turn, a subsequent, third phase in entertainment takes this interest in tableaux vivants and ushers in more elaborate props and materialistic settings. The parlor play of this era combined ideals of beauty with unmistakable shows of economic privilege (often exceeding middle-class material possession), marginalizing individual skills and, with them, possibilities of personal ascent.

In the final chapters of this study, I explore argumentative, historical, and nostalgic trends in entertainment forms, which blossomed to include recitations, performed readings, and group pageants—all inheritors of the parlor play market. These were not necessarily forms of play, but cultural performances that continued to be defined under the rubric of home entertainment. Emerging in the late 1880s and enduring through the 1920s, this final, fourth stage of "home" entertainment involved a narration of past events and a profound respect for previous generations, often situating speakers as dutiful ventriloquists. As the most pervasive genres of play, recitation pieces and dramatic readings mark a return to a textually emphatic and nonspectacular mode of entertainment. Additionally, children are frequently situated as performers, for many of these activities attest to an infantilizing of nineteenth-century entertainment forms in the face of a modern and technological world, a world that is often contrasted with a complacently insular, but supposedly simpler, past. Notably, too, such forms of entertainment migrated from the home to the school, church, and club, resulting in an increased institutionalization of play activities and, with them, marked communal and nationalist sensibilities. I detail these developments in chapters six and seven.

Chapter six, "Old Games, New Narratives, and the Specter of a Generational Divide," focuses on questions surrounding participants' agency in entertainment forms at a time when nostalgic recitations begin to replace more active forms of entertainment, with such recitations focusing on the perceived problem of generational dislocations. In chapter seven, "Imagined Unity: Entertainment's Communal Spectacles and Shared Histories," I explore tensions addressed by communal and individualistic forms of entertainment, particularly narrative "memory pieces" that create a contrast between past and present social practices. These pieces call for a moment of benevolent reflection, celebrating and containing the nineteenth-century past while evoking a formative period of middle-class development. Such texts rewrite older ideals of individual achievement, positioning skills as emblems of retrograde beliefs and as impossibly individualist pretensions unsuited to the modern world.

This study, then, follows a trajectory of home entertainment from the mid-nineteenth century through the opening years of the twentieth, covering a swath of undeniable social and economic change, not only in how a middling social sphere developed, but in how its participants envisioned themselves. In this sense, entertainments served as a performative, reflective space, a place to test out visions of a culture in the process of (trans)formation. Through the physical, temporal, spectacular, and, ultimately, self-conscious practices of home entertainment, leisure practices conjured visions of social identity so that middling Americans could perform their new postures, attitudes, and behaviors—during their leisure hours and in the everyday scenarios that followed.

Along the way, I have had the temerity to write about fun while keeping the many complexities accompanying home entertainments in view, including the elaborate, social production of measurable enjoyment. Even when considering games consisting of stolen kisses, phallic candlesticks, bark-like-a-dog forfeits, and displays of incongruous nondescripts, I have eschewed the narrative of pure pleasure for an understanding of contextualized social practice. To be sure, I have attempted nothing as aggressively clever as fashioning anagrams out of chapter titles or posing conundrums, complete with answers. Indeed, the conundrums are already there, in terms of questions about how home entertainment's activities rose to social and textual prominence and why their fashions changed over the decades of the mid-to-late nineteenth century. Borrowing from the well-known narrative idiom, then, I invite you, Dear Reader, to find pleasure in the pleasantly textured details of play: the scripts, the characters, the costumes, the moments of outrageous rule breaking, the foolishness of regressive, childish play, but also in the intricacies, the contradictions, the unresolved and perhaps unresolvable tensions infusing home leisure enterprises.

1
Labor, Leisure, and the Scope of Ungenteel Play

"What is the key-note to good breeding? B natural."
a conundrum
Parlor Entertainments, or Evening Party Entertainments (1885)

Repeatably, performatively, mid-nineteenth-century home entertainment texts and the practices they outlined defined themselves against the excesses of genteel living. Play's votaries were asked to push aside the social ideal of politeness, and along with it, parlor furniture, breakables, carpets, and draperies as they engaged in various forms of competitive entertainment. By focusing on what lay beyond genteel postures, these activities, with their collective attention to the facade of polite interaction, exposed the labor-intensive realities of middling (and, on occasion, working-class) life, privileging competition, inventiveness, and visible work—operatives that were often concealed beneath etiquette's social niceties.

Because of the unique behavioral licenses surrounding play time, the tensions between the immediate goals of entertainment and the larger project of genteel acculturation were magnified during leisurely play. In responding critically to pretentious gentility, entertainment texts present two types of activities that countered perceived elitism and sought to inculcate a common-sense spirit of social behavior. Worker games, which mimic scenarios of labor, showcased and celebrated what were primarily manual forms of work; theatricals that mock gentility, a second type of play, directly confronted mannered pretension and sought to expose its contradictions, arguing its unfittedness to middling family life. Both types of leisure pursuits countered expectations that home entertainment games were, like mannered behavior, imitative and elitist.

As seen through the lens of entertainment texts and through games such as "The Genteel Lady," social individuals could be exposed as ridiculous figures—beaked, horned, and befeathered creatures who cawed forth predict-

ably materialistic drivel. While exemplifying the middling privileges of leisure moments and expendable incomes, such activities heralded a dissonance
within a middling social sphere where genteel status was a ubiquitous goal,
but one fraught with overly stylized, pretentious, and materialistic interests.
Although a game such as "The Genteel Lady" purports to uphold something
labeled "gentility," it aggressively questions the fittedness of genteel ambitions to the game's participants, most of whom will in fact lose the title
"Genteel Lady" and will become "Horned Ladies" instead.[1] To earn the right
to be called "genteel," players must perfectly repeat a complicated text gen-
erated by the game: "Good morning, Genteel Lady, always genteel: I, a genteel
lady, always genteel, come from that genteel lady, always genteel (pointing to
player on left), to tell you that she owns an eagle with a golden beak."[2] Subsequent players add descriptive phrases such as "silver claws" and "lace skin,"
"diamond eyes," and "purple feathers" when describing the "ladies'" possessions.[3] When players fail to repeat the text exactly or to incorporate all the
necessary cues, they receive paper horns, which resemble "a lamplighter or a
curl paper."[4]

Mocking gentility, even while retaining genteel status as the best players' reward, the game never entirely overturns gentility's value. Emphasizing
skills such as the retention and repetition of an exact and lengthy text, as
well as the quick integration of visual cues (for each player must be identified
by changing the number of horns in her hair, which indicate her progress in
the game), the activity exposes many "genteel" players as horned players, or
as young women physically bearing the remnants of their toilettes. Along
with the game's warning that one cannot presume to attain a secure social
status without sufficient preparation, it also voices the larger question of how
to inhabit gentility, mimicking genteel conversation with a simpering repetition of "Good morning, Genteel Lady," while the lady's accoutrements
(gold, silver, lace, diamonds, and feathers) are cast as outrageously elaborate
trappings. Stressing the "gossipy" nature of mannered behavior, the game
also contains a basic untruth, for the "genteel lady" is not "always" genteel,
just as a three-horned lady is not "always" three-horned; the game in fact
revolves around the importance of charting fluctuations in social standing.

Yet by heightening gentility's rarity, games such as "The Genteel Lady"
reveal their dual alliances. Although positioned as the object of critique, gentility nevertheless remains the game's ultimate reward, even as genteel status
is exposed as fragile and hard-won. Here, gentility appears as the product
of great effort, a reward for the best and most practiced workers, or those
with the most visible skills in manipulating the game's complicated text. At
such moments of duality, home entertainments' ambivalence toward mid-

dling social ambitions becomes visible. Although retained as a value, polite sociability inspires criticism as well as doubt, hence the game's efforts to re-craft gentility so as to make the category more representative of the modest, everyday lifestyles claimed by many participants in leisure entertainments.

Highlighting Gentility's Contradictions

During the mid-century decades, Americans purchased record numbers of etiquette books, which codified their social interactions into elaborate ritu-als characterizing mourning, introductions, and social calls. At the same time that this array of guide books directed readers to submit to behavioral, financial, and sexual codes of conduct, a rising category of entertainment texts detailed the "rules" for play time.[5] Entertainment texts clearly furthered the cultural pursuits characterizing the middling home, but they also created a unique market niche by exploiting their perceived differences from eti-quette.

Although clearly comparable to other didactic texts marketed to middling consumers (etiquette guides among them), guides to home entertainment display an unusual hybridity in their message to readers. They upheld the possibilities of gentrification, dispensing advice that would help families and hostesses create admirable leisure spectacles. Simultaneously, they countered the ideal of a behavioral and bodily facade by promising to expose labor and celebrate unsocial attitudes, implicitly promising that reacting against gen-tility's boundaries constituted a pleasurable response to the laborious pro-cess of becoming affluent.

Yet it is clear that more than the pursuit of pleasure was at stake. As book buyers and purchasers of instruction, consumers were treated as individuals who invested in the textual representation of social ideals, that is, as readers possessed of a willingness to envision themselves as representatives of a so-cial tier in the process of determining its boundaries. Yet as participants in play, they were invited to act out against the conventions that would ordi-narily mark their status. Hence, the progression from reading idealizing texts to transforming them into a practice marked a richly suggestive moment—at least on the level of individual experience. More broadly, based on the popu-larity of entertainment practices, this moment—when the activities that marked a class-based ideology collided with leisure activities that mocked markers of status—was a moment signaling a deep ambivalence with the ways that genteel living was realized.

The whole category of genteel social life was problematized by entertain-ment texts, as they exaggerated the perceived inauthenticity of genteel interaction. The tensions surrounding gentility's enactment in mid-century social life permeate texts such as Emerson's *The Conduct of Life* (1860), which attempts to theorize etiquette, advancing ideals of mannered interaction that were frequently cited in popular guides to manners. Although in the chapter entitled "Behavior" he seeks to invest social forms with meaning, he nevertheless reveals a deep and, ultimately, unresolved conflict surrounding gentility as Emerson struggles to reconcile formulaic behavior inherited from Europe with the nature of the American middle class.[6] Emerson declares that

> manners are the happy way of doing things; each one a stroke of genius or of love,—now repeated and hardened in usage. They form at last a rich varnish, with which the routine of life is washed, and its details adorned. If they are superficial, so are the dew-drops which give such a depth to the morning meadows. Manners are very communicable: men catch them from each other.[7]

Situated near the opening of the essay, such a passage stresses a contrast between "natural" and learned behaviors. Emerson asserts that each mannered act was, at one point, "a stroke of genius" or a spontaneous and "natural" act, which then "hardened" into an accepted "routine." Indeed, the notion of manners as convention alone appears distasteful to Emerson as he stresses the "genius" of gentility rather than its continuance, treating good manners as products of spontaneous reinvention.

As a philosopher of behavior, Emerson is most interested in the usefulness of manners to the self-made man, examining the work involved in attaining a secure social status. At the same time that Emerson values genteel traditions, his message to middle-class hopefuls remains conflicted, for Emerson values both spontaneous acts of naturally generous persons and, simultaneously, signs of a "centuries' long" tradition. Stressing the uplifting goal of becoming genteel, Emerson examines the accumulation of manners by the "natural" individual who has managed both to retain individual identity and to absorb the intricacies of mannered behavior. This idealistic marriage of individual nature and codified manners is nonetheless accompanied by obvious tension, as revealed by Emerson's statement that

> the power of manners is incessant,—an element as inconcealable as fire. The nobility cannot in any country be disguised, and no more in a republic or a democracy than in a kingdom. No man can resist their influence. There are certain manners which are learned in good society, of that force, that if a person have them, he or she must be considered,

and is everywhere welcome, though without beauty, or wealth, or genius. Give a boy address and accomplishments, and you give him the
mastery of palaces and fortunes where he goes.[8]

Emerson highlights the larger question as to whether or not manners innately define the upper classes or function as ambassadors for democracy.
Although the passage argues for manners as a democratic tool among the
ambitious individuals who cultivate them, the language of the passage also
recognizes the historical "nobility" of manners. Mannered behavior thus appears as a "hieroglyph," one of Emerson's favorite terms for a complex (and
often, internally conflicted) idea. Manners are not only signs of status, but
they also serve as a means of acquiring and claiming distinction.

Further complicating the legibility of mannered behavior is Emerson's
assertion that aristocratic "nobility" seems "naturally" mannered, having
seemingly absorbed conventions of conduct into their blood. In the terms of
the dual invocations of "nature" operating here, the "natural" manners of
the aristocracy run counter to the "natural" abilities of untutored but generous persons. According to Emerson, genteel social interaction represents
two different and competing classes. To further illustrate this complexity,
Emerson contends that manners can be conquered (or acquired) if there is
a "capacity for culture in the blood," harkening to inheritance, while also
claiming that "the basis of all good manners is self-reliance," presenting a
more democratic interest.[9]

Emerson attempts to resolve these contradictions with a short narrative on the history of manners. In this "history," a democratically oriented
individual at one point in an amorphous and unhistoricized past acts so
thoughtfully that nearby aristocrats imitate the gesture, disseminating it as
a sign of genteel civilization, with the behavior eventually "harden[ing]" into
the empty shell of custom. Emerson is thus, and somewhat fancifully, able
to claim that the middling classes could rightfully reclaim the manners that
sprang from their generous hearts, since manners are an expression of innate
nobility later co-opted by the elites. The illogic of Emerson's assertion is
striking, highlighting the degree to which he, like other writers about polite
behavior, struggles to naturalize gentility, resorting to the creation of an absurdly generic tale championing some unnamed and ostensibly ordinary individual.[10] By creating elaborately convoluted logic, along with a flattering
portrait of the middling tier, Emerson creates a resolution that rests on a
double meaning of "nobility" as both aristocratic and as indicative of the
qualities of a democratic heart. Emerson's text was hardly alone in its convoluted attempts to reconcile gentility's goals with everyday, middling lives.

This essay, along with the many etiquette books that referenced it, attests to the fact that producing acceptable versions of genteel behavior was a difficult task, given the seriousness associated with manners and with the pursuit of social standing.

Ultimately, the contradictions facing Emerson (and, more generally, the practices of mannered behavior) are more significant than the fanciful resolutions he provides. There is an obvious paradox at work in American etiquette books, as Emerson suggests; genteel ease can only be achieved through great effort, for mannered conventions demanded that individuals appear to be the thing that they were continually working to become. Yet gentility was difficult to explain as "naturally" possessed by persons actively engaged in acquiring it through the acquisition of manners. Ideally, upward strivers were to assume gentility as a mechanism of their ascent to a place where gentility itself was presumed. That is, the act of striving toward a genteel goal could reveal an individual's distance from gentility itself; hence there was virtually no way, via etiquette's logic, to labor in order to become a social being characterized by an absence of visible effort.

Writing of the "unselfconsciousness that is the mark of the so-called 'natural' distinction," Pierre Bourdieu notes that attempting to belong to a group can mark an individual's status as an outsider: "they [the social agents] merely need to be what they are in order to be what they have to be, that is, naturally distinguished from those who are obliged to strive to distinction."[11] In the instance of etiquette, trying to achieve gentility had the curious effect of negating the goal of embodying distinction, for striving to appear genteel would only increase the jarring discontinuities of acquisition within a realm of behavior where the seamless adoption of gracious behavior was valued. In addition, etiquette books present the ideal of "good breeding" as paradoxically denoting mannered behavior rather than an actual bloodline. If, as John Kasson has argued, etiquette books "deflected the pressures and inequities of the society back on the individual," then entertainment forms individualized the social realm even further by granting players the ability to claim competitive skills.[12]

Sarah Annie Frost's parlor play "Refinement" (1866) illustrates some of the problems infusing the social ideals attached to mannered behavior. It also provides insight into the ways that entertainment texts frequently critiqued the pretensions and contradictions they associated with the practice of etiquette.[13] In the play, the recently wed Kate Stanley is constantly criticized by her husband because of what he sees as her social flaws, among them colloquial speech, unceremonious dress, blatant demonstrations of affection, inappropriate discussions of domestic arrangements in the presence of company, and invasive personal questions. Although Kate is said to be kind, cheerful, and loyal, these qualities are not always visible, for her terrible manners (which are demonstrated in detail during the play) all but obscure her positive qualities. At the end of the play's initial scene, Kate's vexed and embarrassed husband describes the potential she possesses, exclaiming, "Was ever a man so annoyed! . . . with Kate's kind heart and natural talents, she would be perfect with a good address, but her whole manner is so terribly counterfeited it seems almost impossible to refine it."[14] Hope for Kate lies in her kind heart and generosity, in short, in her "nature" as her husband recognizes the untutored but potentially felicitous "natural" gifts that Kate already possesses. Yet the question of "nature" becomes increasingly problematic as Kate's husband refers to her *untutored* behavior as "counterfeited," for in his eyes, this behavior runs counter to the socially constructed roles that are widely accepted as natural. Ironically, the husband believes that mannered behavior serves as the most "natural" expression of Kate's personality.

The play's conflation in terminology (a lexicon borrowed from etiquette books) also portends a confusion in values as Kate's husband leaves for three years. In his absence, Kate studies etiquette, hoping to please her husband upon his return. When he eventually arrives, Kate conceals her joyful emotions behind dignified conversation, exhibiting a marked emotional restraint and consequently distressing her husband, who begins to believe that she has outgrown her love. The play ends with the husband's entreaties for Kate to drop her genteel facade and resume her "natural" behaviors. Although apparently condemning refinement, the play allows for the speculation that Kate's future will entail some compromise between her "natural" sympathies and a mode of social interaction that *appears* natural to individuals who have internalized genteel practices (among them Kate's husband). But because the play concludes at precisely the moment when Kate's efforts to refine herself are finally visible, the text's final position on genteel behavior remains unresolved, especially regarding the question of "nature." Can refinement be forgotten, once acquired? Is it now second nature to Kate? Is there a way to value both "natural," individualized qualities and mannered forms, which should be produced so as to appear natural, as well? Here, as in many of the directives announced by etiquette books, the fissures between "nature" and refinement remain visible, largely because there are two types of "naturalness" described by the play, both explained according to the same rubric.

In addition to highlighting the complicated value systems surrounding "natural" social behaviors, the text engages in a common representation of gentility as officiously pretentious. In his study of middle-class professionalism, Burton Bledstein argues that "naturalness" in Victorian culture was a concept that encompassed contradictory ideals.[15] In resolving the contradictions infusing both individual competition and social pressure, Bledstein contends, Americans focused on the concept of "nature," for "every person was bound by his 'nature' in the everyday world."[16] The category of the natural, moreover, encompassed abilities as well as limitations, so being aware of one's nature, Bledstein argues, meant being "aware of the boundaries that circumscribed common abilities and talents."[17]

A daunting conceptual problem pervading the textual representation of genteel behaviors, as Frost's play illustrates, lay in the implied promise behind mannered, stylized behavior: the promise that an emerging American middle class could assume the behaviors already associated with an European aristocracy by reinventing these forms as signs of a unique cultural identity. One of the central difficulties attending this transformation was, as Bushman claims, that "gentility was essentially aristocratic and America was not," resulting in "the anomaly of aristocratic gentility exercising vast influence in a democratic, middle-class society."[18] Given this inherent contradiction, a genteel culture appeared fraught with numerous internal dissonances.

Distancing themselves from such an irresolvable quandary, many entertainment guides critique the perceived problems associated with gentility as they assert the importance of the skills-based value system, one perpetuated by entertainment. Books such as *Parlor Entertainments* (quoted in the epigraph to this chapter) make pointed reference to etiquette, situating predictably genteel behaviors as a source of amusement and as an enterprise distinct from home entertainment. The answer to the joke, "What is the key note of good breeding?" treats etiquette as a system of transparent mechanisms, for etiquette bears the brunt of the ensuing pun about being "natural" (488, 501). Alluding to a system of musical notation, the joke's directive to "be natural" exposes gentility's most conflicted ideal, hinging on the recognition that acting "natural" requires intensive labor. Play, by contrast, is inscribed as intuitive, as enhancing the abilities already possessed by players, and hence, as a dimension of an authentic, everyday—and therefore suitable—middling social identity.

Individualism and the Didactic Idiom

In addition to supplying a wealth of practical information, entertainment guide books broadened the reader-text relationship set up by many didactic texts. Within an instructional idiom that often positioned readers as subjects requiring advice, home entertainment books offered readers a compelling self-image as they emphasized individual decision making, skill, and competition—in short, individual agency—situating individualism as congruent with a social setting. At the mid century, when entertainment books for adults emerged as a new, popular category of text, they competed with etiquette books for market space, but more significantly, they launched a portrait of playful social behavior that was very much at odds with the constrained genteel interaction promoted by manners guides. When the Historical Publishing Company issued *How to Behave and How to Amuse* in 1895, this uniquely bifurcated guide book highlighted the separate histories of entertainment and etiquette, a separation rooted in the mid century. Indeed the text reveals how distinct these two social traditions were, for one half is devoted to etiquette and the other to entertainment.[19] While the guide book assumes that its audience is invested in a broad ideal of acculturation and how to achieve it, the etiquette and entertainment sections of the book make no reference to one another. In this sense, *How to Behave and How to Amuse* is characteristic of the larger publishing field (including the earlier decades) as it suggests a complicated relationship between the complementary and, for a time, competitive practices of etiquette and entertainment, which were similar enough to be sold to a single audience and housed under one book jacket, but notably divergent in terms of directions for behavior.

Entertainment guide books typically claim that entertaining in no way overlapped with etiquette, asserting that there was a recognizable license to play that permitted the participants in leisure activities to step outside of gentility's behavioral parameters. The carefully severed textual traditions of etiquette and entertainment thus invited readers to imagine entertainment as an escape valve in the machine of social life. Whereas etiquette books produced an image of middling Americans as demure beings whose greatest pleasure was in participating tastefully and inconspicuously in social rituals, by contrast, entertainment guides promised "amusing" evenings when genteel conversation was replaced by bouts of competition, characterized by the taking of forfeits, the granting of transactional kisses, and the creation of grotesque, ungenteel bodies.

Despite entertainment guide books' claims that they created a unique social environment, we can nonetheless see that the rules governing parlor play were not as distinct from the conventions of gentility as entertainment manuals suggested. Entertainment books claimed for themselves a unique behavioral tradition, based on an invitation to suspend the codes of mannered interaction. Yet they are essentially books of rules, encouraging the idea that acting in response to defined rules could be enjoyable and that the participants in such activities could be dynamic, outrageous, and competitive. In this sense, entertainment manuals overlapped, elided with, and complemented other guide books inscribing middle-class behavioral ideals. By insisting that middling Americans already possessed the necessary tools for accomplished social life, entertainment texts sought to differentiate their practices from other genteel interactions, thereby exempting readers from anxieties about acquiring new, labyrinthine traditions. In short, home entertainment was textually presented as an authentic mode of cultural expression, one ideally suited to everyday, middling Americans who possessed an inclination for playful amusement, but who also required instruction on specific fashions of play.

Given the carefully maintained separation of etiquette and entertainment, it is tempting to assemble the two practices into two combative groups, to imagine that genteel and grotesque activities were as oppositional as were their immediate spectacles of genteel and competitive, active bodies. Despite their external differences, the activities of the genteel parlor and dynamic forms of parlor play supported deeply congruent social visions. In both etiquette and entertainment, specific rules governing the body and its presentation allowed for the recognition of success, whether or not that success was marked as accomplished social work (in the case of etiquette) or as playful victory (in the case of entertainment). In terms of their ideological investment, it is clear that manners and skills were related phenomena, united in the common social pursuit of upward mobility that each furthered.

By highlighting the contiguous social vision encompassing both gentility and play, I am not dismissing the uniqueness of leisure activities in nineteenth-century America. Claiming that these activities were countercultural, or in conflict with gentility (as entertainment manuals would have us believe), would mean pointing to their failure, for certainly etiquette did not wane in the Gilded Age and beyond. In the end, we see proof of entertainment's lasting impact on nineteenth-century life if we see it as an innovative means of representing social participation at a time when entertainment forms allowed participants in play to cling to ideals of individualized abilities and accomplishments. If we imagine such a scenario, we see in parlor play the great potential to insinuate an allegiance to a notion of class-based belonging, even in the most boisterous players and the most skilled competitors.

Making Abstract Labors Representable

During parlor games, middling Americans donned the roles of the coachman and the gravedigger, the butcher and the fish merchant as easily as they would wear a new garment for an evening in company. By invoking workers' roles, the games of the mid-century parlor frequently borrowed from the kinds of occupations that were, by mid century, becoming less common among the middling classes, incorporating images of manual labor. References to manual forms of work, then, focused on labors that were no longer daily realities in the lives of the readers/players who would have participated in mid-century games. This exercise in what Bourdieu would term "symbolic capital" allowed for the invocation of preprofessional forms of work, or activities that at first appear incongruent with the ideals and aspirations of a rising professional class in their obvious distinction from the labors being mimicked.[20] Hence, it becomes clear that worker games were deeply symbolic renderings of work, recast through their context in the genteel parlor and betraying a discomfort with gentility's relation to visible, tangible work. As Stuart M. Blumin has argued, a deep ambivalence about inhabiting class structures was interwoven in prevalent nineteenth-century attitudes. Samuel Haber similarly contends that mid-century Americans embraced both egalitarian ideals and professional distinctions, despite the obvious dissonances between them, revealing conflicted responses to emerging social hierarchies.[21]

The nineteenth-century working classes, from all accounts, didn't engage in entertainment forms that directly mirrored their everyday lives; they instead frequented local festivals and fairs, drinking amusements, and both street and public theaters.[22] Hence, there is no real evidence to suggest that the work-based games of the mid century had lower-class roots. Rather, playing at manual and, at times, forms of archaic labor appears as a distinctly middling interest. The very act of placing manual work on display was, in part, proof of readers' and participants' distance from it, for leisurely displays make light of what were for actual workers the grinding, inescapable hardships of life. In this sense, playing at work situated participants in play as significantly distanced from the bodily labors of the working classes. Home entertainment's invocation of preprofessional labor nevertheless served as part of an elaborate effort to represent genteel work to genteel types, and to broadcast an image of work that was dynamic and, at the same time, reflective of middling ambitions.

Leisure practice's borrowing from forms of work appears as a function of the particular distinction between visible, physical work and dynamic, social entertainment. The parameters of leisure, however, allowed for some fluctuation between normally defined modes of activity, some interchange between activities, but not to the extent of erasing boundaries between the two.[23] Given the division of work and leisure that worker games presuppose, we can see work-based games appearing to recapture the moment when work and play operated in a much more fluid relation to one another. Ultimately, however, leisure games make use of work, rather than create an interstice, thereby increasing the distance between spheres of comfortable leisure and arduous work.

As mid-century games dramatically invoke images of labor, they also actively engage the tensions and uncertainties surrounding shifting notions of how everyday labors defined social beings. In part because of their marketing to the middling classes, home entertainment guides critique narrowly focused forms of success, arguing that material comfort alone does not provide social ease. Hence, home entertainment guides argue for their own potential to diversify life and extend success into the social sphere, as they address the unspectacular nature of business and the life of the middling worker.

Hinting broadly that businessmen and their families are narrowly defined through their moneymaking and consequent spending, guide texts attempt to persuade readers that they require social instruction. Article series such as "A Few Friends" (*Godey's*, 1864), ostensibly written about a group of actual friends, portray the socially adrift businessman, making an example of his regrettable inattention to social interaction. Although successful, a Mr. Simmons described in the text appears a "subdued, feeble-looking man," or less than inspiring, once out of his economic habitat. "He moved like the family ghost," the article continues, "in loose slippers and a tight coat, a counting house bend in his back, and a ghastly smile upon his countenance that seemed the very inspiration of wretchedness. What wonder! His whole life had been given to money-making. . . . He would no more have dreamt of really enjoying himself, than he would of reading any of the gilded books upon his marble and ormolu centre table."[24] As the evening progresses, the socially bereft Mr. Simmons will come to life as he hosts an evening of parlor games; more significantly (especially for *Godey's* readers), the successes of the evening include his daughter's companionable play with a young man who will become her husband. Without sociable play, the article suggests, both she and her family may well have remained socially adrift. Moreover, the article's emphasis on the benefits of defined play exemplifies how families like the Simmonses benefit from specified tasks in entertaining, as they do in their daily lives, where specialized labors signify their status and provide opportunities for individual distinction.

While professional modes of work were gaining a momentum born of industrial progress, they were problematic in terms of their visible dynamism, as with the physically feeble Mr. Simmons. The ambiguous and, at times, conflicted attitudes toward work visible in parlor games are reminiscent of Michael Newbury's account of uncertainties in representing professional authorship in antebellum America, when literary figures still looked to physical work as an ideal form of labor. Authors such as Hawthorne, who expressed a discomfort with their intellectual pursuits, revealed what Newbury describes as a "cultural anxiety" about the expansion of "nonmanual work and material nonproductivity."[25] Arguing that this anxiety can be seen as a larger condition of middle-class intellectual work, Newbury contends that professionals and nonmanual laborers of the 1840s and '50s strove to identify themselves with the "residual virtues of manual labor," even as the middle class "worked to re-unite in rhetorical terms middle-class occupations with traditional valorizations of manual work."[26] Whereas middling work was problematic in mid-century representations, those games that feature manual work also highlight a complexity infusing a historical transition joining types of labor.

Because championing the authenticity of manual labor presented something of a problem, at least when considering manual labor's distance from the everyday experience of middling types, entertainment guides sought to create an authentic form of leisure enterprise, ideally suited to an amorphous, fairly diverse middling social tier. Within the scope of mid-century games, trying to inhabit the rules, attempting to win, and striving for success all appear as self-legitimating behaviors that articulate the affiliations of their participants. Through such spectacles, entertainment forms facilitated a definition of middling cultural labors as distinct from both aristocratic gentility and working-class manifestations of labor, for they emphasized a mode of skilled sociability, or a proficiency in leisure enterprises that served as the basis of a livable, and what Richard L. Bushman has termed a "vernacular," version of gentility.[27] In addition, games situated the competition connected with sociable play as an exciting, new, and argumentative cultural phenomenon at a moment of pronounced social reinvention, when an American taxonomy of class was steadily emerging.[28]

While encouraging the pursuit of a more refined social milieu, wherein entertainment's participants could claim status through leisure enterprises, home entertainments reveal a deep ambivalence about representing the pleasures of discretionary time. In this sense, they reflect a contentious mid-century debate over class and status, which overflowed into uncontrollable spectacles in various American cities. A concerted rise in urban populations of the 1840s and '50s, along with the class divisions that resulted from widespread industrialization, had created marked divisions between suburban aloofness and the poverty, pollution, and the labor unrest that increasingly characterized cities.[29] Combative events such as the Astor Place Riot of 1849, which involved the contest between Europhilia and Americanism as well as tension between elite and lower audiences, was only one of a number of events that dramatized divisive class stratifications. On the cultural front, too, divisions of class and acculturation resulted in increasingly hierarchical public entertainments, which privileged feminized, respectable theatergoing audiences over more vocal, active and rowdy attendants associated with the lower classes.[30] That middling forms of home entertainment reveal an interest in markers of status suggests a considerable interest as well as anxiety in interrogating vertical social hierarchies, an endeavor that extended into middling homes, where those uncertainties were enacted and broadcast.

During the course of play, entertainment forms situated referential pantomimes of physical work in the undeniably genteel context of the parlor, asking participants to acknowledge the kinds of labors that they did not ordinarily enact, but simultaneously, to consider themselves as genteel social beings whose labors included the pursuit of organized leisure. In the context of comfortable, middling lives, entertainment's borrowing from nonprofessional images of work, incongruous as they may initially seem, reflects an interest in examining and reconsidering what counted as work. Through games that pantomimed work-based scenarios, participants in leisure entertainments were encouraged to confront the linkage between participants' social aspirations and what would have been (for the middling classes) older forms of labor. For an increasingly professional social tier, then, playing at physical forms of labor meant looking beyond genteel enterprise to modes of work that yielded clear, visible references to corporeal work. Whereas professional forms of employment were abstract and aloof, manual labors could be represented as unambiguous and straightforward. In contrast to images of working bodies, professionalism may have resembled contemplative leisure (at least outwardly) more than physical work.[31] Hence, on the most practical level, home games point out that it was much more satisfying to pantomime the work of the coachman than that of the bookkeeper; similarly the labor of the cook appeared more dramatic than the work of the factory manager.

This difficulty in representing professional work was as significant as it was unresolvable. How could middling Americans make compelling references to their labors when those labors were little understood, physically unimpressive, and visibly undynamic? References to manual labors did not supplant invocations of professionalism, but they did invite participants to translate the dynamism of physical labor into an enriched understanding of what were becoming characteristically middling occupations. Hence, many games allude to the roles of the merchant and the stagecoach driver as well as those of the lawyer and teacher, interweaving references to professional and manual forms of work and suggesting loose parallels between them.

These images of manual work, once connected to professional references, helped to create a conceptual translation that defined middling labors as legitimate, challenging, and dynamic forms of employment.

Part of the anxiety about representing professional employment centers on the capacity to represent hard work, since there was no immediately striking physical rendering of demanding professional work, as there was with arduous manual labor. Gradually, the ideal of competition helped redefine arduous labor as demanding enterprise. Inscribing middling labors as forms of work, entertainment guides sought to isolate the skills that they attributed to professional accomplishments, thereby defining the inhabitants of a middling social tier as both able and competitive. The preface to *Family Pastime* (1855), for example, asserts that home entertainment can "stimulate the faculties, quicken the apprehension, arouse the wit, and under the disguise of pleasure, develop and exercise the mental functions."[32] In many didactic guides to entertainment, games are similarly categorized according to levels of skills, where they are grouped according to the type of knowledge called for during play. In addition to highlighting games of geography, spelling, composition, history, and science, there are categories devoted to games of the inventive faculties as well as activities requiring a "knowledge of society" or a "knowledge of the same kind" (or comparative knowledge). Other parlor entertainment texts organize play by situating skills according to "wit," "memory," and "learning"—terms that appear frequently. Through such categories of play, mid-century entertainments attempt to make work, of both manual and genteel forms, visible, but in facilitating a representation of work, they also implicitly supply a narrative of how various forms of labor relate to one another. Although manual labor served as an effective evocation of work, it was by no means an ideal for ambitious Americans. By the mid century, a general understanding of middling work constituted a paradigmatic shift away from what Blumin terms the "myth" of the "respectable worker," or an appreciation for the manual laborer, whose previously uncontested claim to "labor" was disrupted by a broadening professionalism.[33] Hinting at a history that placed manual labors as the precursors to professional ones, guide books on entertainment implicitly argue that middling, professional types are indeed laborers, though of a new and more evolved sort, thereby creating a historical trajectory of imagined and somewhat self-congratulatory progress from manual labor to genteel living.

As in parlor games, the task of interrogating the nature of mid-century work—of various sorts—was widespread throughout the mid century. Textual investigations of work range from representations of factory work (Mel-

ville's "The Paradise of Bachelors and the Tartarus of Maids," 1855) to agri-
cultural as well as literary labors (Hawthorne's *Blithedale Romance*, 1852)
to the life of the writer (Fern's *Ruth Hall*, 1854, and Hawthorne's "Custom
House" introduction to *The Scarlet Letter*, 1850) to the work of pioneering
(Kirkland's *A New Home, Who'll Follow?* 1839) to Whitman's celebration of
the common worker (in *Leaves of Grass*, 1855) to the work of a free black
house servant (Wilson's *Our Nig*, 1859) to examinations of Southern slaves'
work by Jacobs and Douglass (*Incidents in the Life of a Slave Girl*, 1861, and
Narrative in the Life of Frederick Douglass, An American Slave, 1845).

Entertainment's commitment to representing both manual and genteel
forms of work, and of creating conceptual segues between them, however,
remains distinct from the arguments made in period fiction, which attends
to stark, uncomfortable chasms between types of labor and other related
modes of living. A concern for a growing chasm between physical and professional work, taken up by authors such as Rebecca Harding Davis, focuses
on the middle class's need to broaden its sense of humanity and to recognize
the latent, frustrated desires of workers. When addressing the separation of
laboring and genteel worlds, fictions such as "Life in the Iron Mills" (1861)
assert the disastrous consequences of class division as the tale's narrator
notes that "Not many even of the inhabitants of a manufacturing town know
the vast machinery of system by which the bodies of workmen are governed, that goes on unceasingly from year to year."[34] The narrator commands
readers to enter the Dantean world of work, announcing "I want you to
hide your disgust," and continues with, "take no heed to your clean clothes,
and come right down with me,—here into the thickest of the fog and mud
and foul effluvia. I want you to hear this story . . . I want to make it a real
thing to you."[35] Having separated genteel reader from industrial subject, the
tale documents the trials of mill worker Hugh Wolfe, who has crafted a
woman made of korl, a waste product at the mill. Her appearance drives
home Davis's point, for the figure would seem to combine genteel and laboring interests and, as such, point to some ease of movement between points
of status. Representing a pale, unclothed woman, the sculpted figure initially
appears as an aesthetic object, but it is also ungainly and crudely fashioned
out of a worthless material.

As a hulking, indecorous symbol of the deep divisions between genteel
and laboring worlds, the korl figure in Davis's story represents something of
little value to either realm, for she and her creator exist in a liminal space;
the figure, like its sculptor, evokes amusement and, ultimately, dismissal from
the mill owners who encounter it. Dramatically inscribing the distance be-

tween genteel and laboring experiences, Davis's story severs a sympathetic or conceptual pathway between labor and leisure in an effort to garner sympathy for the unrecognized plight of thwarted menials such as Wolfe.

Clearly, representing polemic portraits of the gulf between classes and evocations of the misunderstood manual laborer lies outside the scope of home entertainment, yet games' allusions to representable work underscore a real and significant cleavage between forms of work. If the larger project of embodying gentility suggests a class devoted to the outward signs of social elitism, parlor games emphasized the uncelebrated realities of everyday life.[36] For a class born in the context of the industrial revolution, everyday life meant a comfortable removal from physical labor, a degree of distance from demanding and potentially degrading employment, even as genteel living demanded an apparent denial of even the most modest labors of everyday life: the domestic upkeep, the work of tending to home, hearth, and horse, for example. The conceptual difficulty surrounding genteel life stemmed, as Bushman has argued, from gentility's incongruency with the lives of "smaller merchants and professionals, ordinary well-off farmers, successful artisans, schoolteachers, minor government officials, clerks, shopkeepers, industrial entrepreneurs, and managers."[37] Thus while a life of relative social ease served as a social ideal, it was very much an image that demanded the careful cultivation of leisured appearances.

Taking up the difficult task of making middling labors more representable, home games worked against an image of complacent gentility, for they effectively redefined leisure pursuits as highly evolved forms of cultural work. This meant that parlor games not only reasserted a connection between laboring bodies and genteel people, but they also redefined work as visible through intellectual and competitive tasks, not just corporeal ones. Valorizing middling work, while remaining mindful of the roots of their labors, games such as "The Trades" set forth the scenario in which "The shoemaker sews his shoe. The washerwoman soaps. The painter takes a portrait. The cook tastes a sauce. The locksmith beats the iron on the anvil. The spinner makes her wheel turn round."[38] As in "musical chairs," a leader begins the game by selecting a trade for himself, while the other players take up various occupations, which span a range of manual and professional positions. When the leader suddenly changes occupations, the player whose job has been usurped must in turn take up the trade discarded by the leader. Although requiring no more than a basic familiarity with various occupations, the game highlights a more important aspect of labor by pointing to the instability of work and the need to adapt to a changing environment in order to remain a "player."[39]

Other games stress the supposed simplicity of manual labor and the uncomplicated relationships among workers (pointing to small communities with one baker and one coachman, for example). They also portray controlled, communal contexts for work. Thus, images of sociable, communal labor contrast with a common characterization of professional work as overly competitive as well as unsocial, with references to past forms of labor suggesting that middling occupations should more closely resemble their sociable predecessors. Focusing on the vocabulary of work, Burton J. Bledstein contends that "the middle-class person was relentlessly competitive. He took pride in being 'on his own hook.' In his own words, he could 'go it along,' 'go it strong,' 'put himself into' his work, 'see' his opportunity, 'skunk' the opposition, 'spread' himself, and 'shine,'" identifying the middle-class professional as "self-reliant, independent, ambitious, and mentally organized."[40] This lexicon highlights the ways that competition was paramount in the economic sphere; yet in the context of home games, playful competition (via entertainment) and economic individualism (via work) were made to complement one another, thus neutralizing the negative connotations of cutthroat competition.

Competition, while cast as playful and disruptive, was nonetheless complicated by its genteel context and by gentility's valorization of nondisruptive, uncontroversial interaction. As they mimicked physical labors, many home entertainment games allowed their participants to claim cultural striving as a goal, whether those individuals won or lost a particular game. Pierre Bourdieu might contend that we can see the actual game as that of middle-class belonging, which supplies a "direction, an orientation, an impending outcome" for the contests of play.[41] Within the walls of the mid-century parlor, as Bourdieu's theory suggests, it seldom mattered who won or lost, for the elaborate and ongoing work of justifying middle-class lifestyles was intricately interwoven into the context of home entertainment. A narrative of cultured development set forth by entertainment texts, then, points to the humble, reliable nature of preprofessional work (defined as manual, menial labor), while struggling—albeit uneasily at times—to make links to a newer, complicated professionalism.

Because of these layered nuances, the comment about labor made by parlor games is initially difficult to parse. Both teleological (implying professionalism's highly developed status) and faintly nostalgic (treating manual labor as unambiguously authentic) representations of labor appear at a moment when the transition between physical and professional work signaled the broad dispersal of genteel lifestyles. As a consequence, some games appear conflicted in their interests; they ask participants to recognize an authentic past and simultaneously attribute value to the professional's modern employment. One such hybrid game is "The Family Coach," which takes as its subject the work of the coachman. Somewhat incongruously, the game becomes both physically representative and evocative of abstract concepts such as job-based hierarchies of power. Preprofessional forms of labor are transformed into worker/manager scenarios reminiscent of middle managers and industrial overseers. As a "division of labor" game, the activity exemplifies the consequences of an industrial system in the proliferating jobs that allowed for the rise of the professional. Here, a leader (a kind of manager) narrates a brief story in which various "items" are called upon. When the leader calls for a player's item, that individual must take some action (standing up, moving, or speaking); the object of the game is for the speaker to narrate the story in such a way as to distract players from their assigned duties. This activity, also known as "The Stage Coach," required players to act as representatives of the harness, the horses, the coachman, the pole, and the whip, and to fulfill their roles as the journey is narrated. In "The Traveling Soldier," another division-of-labor game, the soldier's equipage is represented by participants, and in its feminized counterpart, "My Lady's Toilet," the lady's grooming articles and accessories are brought to life.

The hybridity infusing such popular activities suggests the ways that entertainment forms made use of manual work as a referent, and, at times, as a conceptual shorthand for authenticity, but not necessarily as a social model. Most notably, the above game involves only the faintest gestures toward physical work, such as standing up or pretending to raise a whip. It is, then, the desire to *represent* work that is on display, in a performative rendering. Despite the game's allusions to preprofessional labors in "The Coachman," players' participation is bound textually by the game's structuring narrative, with the manipulation of an elaborate text ensuring the players' genteel status. Through their responses to the narrative, players are subdued, penalized, or rewarded.

A similarly superficial invocation of manual labor appears in forfeits, including the common scenarios of "Going into Service" (or acting the role of a servant) and "The Postman" (which required being heaped with bundles). Such games suggest the limitations of nonprofessional work; notably, these scenarios of manual labor appear as penances—a sign of a teleological class narrative infusing play, one that situates gentility as the sign of social evolution.

From our historical standpoint, we can clearly see gentility as a form of labor, but one that was, and indeed remains, difficult to quantify in relation to manual work. Based on their invocations of manual labor, entertainment books remind us that, for mid-century Americans, physical work epitomized not only dramatic, sociable work, but also authentic labor in a way that intellectual and social striving did not. Moreover, an ambivalence toward genteel forms of labor (as physically unimpressive and potentially hostile in ethos) points to the mid century as a period when the middling classes were only beginning to adapt to the problematic public representation of themselves *as* genteel, hence the texts' repeated attempts to situate genteel living as both insulated from sustenance-based struggles and as disconcertingly abstract.

"Tormenting you" with Competitive Skills

Especially in light of the complexities infusing physical, worker-based games, home entertainment guides' claims to straightforward diversion exceed the simplicity they claim for play, but instead remind us of the ways in which attractively simple references to pleasure could be used to articulate the grounds of group affiliation. In contrast to continuing dilemmas surrounding genteel behavior, an alternative culture of play, as constructed by home entertainment texts, invoked a simple claim to unfettered pleasure. Under the category of pleasure, games that emphasized action, skill, cunning, and spontaneity allowed participants to break from some of gentility's most onerous demands on bodies and behaviors.

Presented as repeatable, exhibitory gestures, the skills of play could take varied forms, even as they consistently challenged the ideal of seamless bodily control associated with mannered behavior. In many games, skills emerge as oppositional to gentility. An amusement similar to "The Genteel Lady," entitled "I've Come to Torment You," counterpoises the rules of play with the common laws of mannered behavior, deconstructing the social ideal of making oneself pleasing for company. Involving skills such as the rote repetition and memorization of a text, the game begins with a leader who announces that he has come to torment someone.[42] The player on the left asks, "What with?" The leader then retorts, "My finger and thumb," and proceeds to snap his fingers in a steady rhythm. Subsequent players add other annoying (and socially taboo) actions such as stomping their feet, wiggling their elbows, nodding their heads, "hitching up," or half-rising from their seats. Each player is to enact these movements while verbally repeating an expanding list of "tormenting" actions. In contrast to the game's wiggling, gyrating, and undignified movements, "genteel" behavior is presented as bland and boring. Tormenting another person (skillfully), the game suggests, is much more entertaining. Like "The Genteel Lady," "I've Come to Torment You" unflatteringly exposes social conformity, for both round games (or games played in a circle) mimic the "social circle" of society, undermining conventionality and delineating the skills of play as pleasingly refreshing. The novelty of skills here, in fact, stems from their unsocial dimension, their obvious deviance from ordinary social behaviors. These skills, moreover, appear as the impetus for claiming a vernacular level of culture for the participants, a type of status that could be seen as congruent with ordinary behaviors.

As both "I've Come to Torment You" and "Museum" (discussed in the introduction) reveal, the leisure culture's ambivalent attitude toward mannered gentility appears in a number of activities that interrogate the value of gentility to the middling sorts, who are redefined as democratically individualized via play. Even as games encourage socially deviant acts, they simultaneously recognize a middling culture's investment in genteel decorum, and in large measure, they build upon its importance as an ideal as well as subject of debate.

Whereas etiquette texts offered behavioral conventions as a model, home entertainment guides stressed the value of individual abilities and promised to reward them, however modest, both during the immediate scenarios of entertainment and, on a larger scale, in the instantiation of a skills-based reward system. These assertions assured readers that they could become active participants in shaping their own destinies, in operating by rules that reflected their lifestyles. More so than most instructive texts, entertainment guide books encouraged readers to become doers, to make a performative transition from aspirants guided by texts to active agents who exhibited their abilities through elaborately prepared scenarios of play. In this sense, entertainment guide texts promised to help readers identify and hone the skills that would lead to immediate competition (via play) and social success (through the social contexts created through play).

Presenting skilled behavior as deliberately broad, or as encompassing such activities as memory games, physical tricks, and the memorization of lengthy texts, the guide texts outlining parlor activities highlighted players' mechanisms for achieving measurable, definable victories. Those players who mastered the elaborate scripts of play could be defined as clear winners, thereby erasing the many nuances and subtleties characterizing genteel interaction. By permitting individual distinction (especially winning), leisure activities suggested that abilities were unambiguous and would therefore be recognized.

According to the narratives presented through forms of entertainment, skills (like manners) could be studied and acquired, privileging the diligent student. Yet unlike mannered behavior, skills attested to the value of "natural" abilities for drawing, singing, spelling, storytelling, reciting poetry, or history. By suggesting that some individuals were, by nature, good actors, musicians, spellers, scene painters, memorizers, or punsters, parlor entertainments offered a conceptual balance between inherent and learned behaviors. Characterizing a rising middle class as both able and competitive, entertainment books circumvented many of the complications facing etiquette manuals, which evinced difficulty reconciling ability with polish, competition with graciousness.

A prevalent lexicon of etiquette revolved around the "heart," focusing on the importance of creating "natural" or authentic appearances (as Frost's "Refinement" attests), transcending intricate rules so as to render them second nature. Entertainment texts, however, avoided the perennial problem of bourgeois authenticity; instead, they left the language of authenticity to etiquette books, dwelling on the competitive ethos already attributed to a growing professional class, now repositioned as the source of delightful, edgy entertainment, once competition could be harnessed in the context of the social sphere. In these ways, the texts of home entertainment distinguished themselves from etiquette's apparent contradictions by embracing skills such as imitation, mimicry, memorization, and adapting to obvious roles—activities that were so offensive within the world of etiquette.[43]

Portraying the cultural work of leisure time as a liberating experience of individualism and a display of ordinary, day-to-day abilities, entertainment guide books also studiously avoid the uncomfortable question of cultural antecedents. Whereas etiquette books often uphold European precedents, they also reveal anxieties about pretentious (and nationally inflected) imitation.[44] Gentility's numerous critics were quick to indict the unnatural, stiff, and constrained behaviors that they associated with imitation, arguing that these behaviors were unsuitable for a nation where class was said not to exist. Entertainment texts, however, appear much less invested in encouraging Americans to emulate Europeans, even though they, too, reference continental precedents.[45] Appearing as more than the continuation of European aristocratic practices claimed by the landed gentry of a previous century, the types of games popular during the 1850s were not the types of lavish spectacles represented in the elite worlds of Austen's *Mansfield Park* or Maria Edgeworth's *Vivian,* for example.[46] By contrast, the games characterizing the mid-century American parlor implied a wide gulf between visibly elitist traditions of home amusements and democratically competitive forms of play, uniformly condemning elitism and stressing vernacular alternatives to pretentiousness.

Home Theatricals and a Vernacular Sociability

Rather than explain domestic work through invocations of manual labor, parlor theatricals, as a popular genre of mid-century home entertainment, upheld the value of domestic, middling labors by contextualizing gentility within a middling social sphere. While they, too, frequently mocked the genteel enterprise as unappealingly excessive, theatricals scrutinized the daily life of middling figures who struggled with the gap between individual intention and social custom. Repeatedly, such plays emphasized the ways that contextualized, modified skills allowed individuals to claim a secure social status in unpretentious ways. In example after example, mid-century plays suggest that cultural accomplishments and not merely social desires herald middling status. Moreover, accomplishments are represented as authentic, individual, and frequently, as overlooked in the pursuit of genteel imperatives. Often, these scripts detail scenarios of direct confrontation, pitting everyday skills against extreme, mannered gentility; in such contests, characters who display a strategic and tempered realization of skilled behavior triumph over those who display a more superficial social identity.

A number of plays from the late 1850s and '60s, particularly those by playwright Sarah Annie Frost, highlight the absurdity of pursuing an extreme version of genteel life.[47] Frost's scripts relentlessly critique gentility's superficiality as she elevates the qualities of self-restraint, or an elaborate self-monitoring based on individual skills rather than predictable, transparent desires for distinction. By treating most invocations of gentility as absurdly elitist, these texts cast home entertainment practices as more accurately exposing the central concerns of a developing middle class as they take up a range of subjects, including self-improvement, leisure reading, and domestic felicity. Frost's parlor play entitled "Slang versus Dictionary," for example, features characters who serve as obvious foils for one another. One can only converse in slang, while the other sounds like a dictionary.[48] A third player represents a happy medium. Another script, "Novel Readers," continues Frost's depiction of pretentious and unnatural persons as the short play depicts a young novel reader, who in her eager grasp for sophistication, misuses large, descriptive words. In such plays, characters have not yet refined their skills to usable levels. They instead appear as caricatured strivers who sacrifice true knowledge for outward show. Much like skills-based parlor games, these scripts suggest that practical compromises should be made when pursuing social distinction. Rather than supplanting gentility with skills, however, parlor plays attempt to temper gentility, scaling down mannered interaction to a level suited to its middling participants.

Stories of genteel pursuits gone awry appear in a number of other period plays, among them those by Mrs. Russell Kavanaugh (*Original Dramas, Dialogues, Declamations, and Tableaux Vivans,* 1867).[49] In "The Mechanic's Daughter," for example, a mother is horrified to discover that her son has proposed to a manual laborer's daughter, only to discover that the young woman in question accepted a respected senator instead. Similar stories depict women who are reluctant to marry the men whom they love for trivial reasons (one is a poor speller while another uses prepositions incorrectly). Indicting the corrupting effects of social pretension, these scripts depict a skills-based culture as signaling a return to a more realistic and tempered value system, if only individuals can match their existing abilities to everyday social scenarios.

Kavanaugh's "The Pea-Green Glazed Cambric," for example, offers a skills-based critique of hypergentility as a young woman unintentionally alienates her lover by appearing to dress too extravagantly. Nellie, the young woman, lives with her grandmother and can't afford new finery for an upcoming party, but discovers a piece of pea-green glazed cambric in an attic trunk. Because Nellie makes up the fabric into a formal dress pattern, the ordinary fabric creates the illusion of a much finer silk, an illusion that is especially successful when Nellie trims the garment with recycled lace and velvet. Although impoverished, Nellie is of "aristocratic blood"; because of her family's elevated reputation, she is widely considered to be the very incarnation of good taste, and, presumably, would never pretend to possess items that she does not. Also blessed with a good deal of cleverness, Nellie is so successful in her dress-making that the town belles are jealous and her lover repulsed by her apparent extravagance. Yet when Nellie's secret is discovered, she is considered by her lover to be resourceful, sensible, and ingenious. Ultimately, the play positions the lover's suspicions (themselves signs of an anxiety about genteel values) as less valid than Nellie's clever economy. While his fears of genteel excess fuel a set of irrational anxieties that threaten to blight the heroine's happiness, her skills are eventually situated as proof of her fittedness for a modest life that will be characterized by economy, restrained ambitions, and a somewhat ambitious attitude toward her family's place in the larger social spectrum. Moreover, it is not until traditional notions of gentility (and the inconsistencies accompanying them) are pushed aside that Nellie's practical talents can be appreciated.

By positioning the skills of play as antithetical to the pretensions of mannered behavior but as congruent with social goals, entertainment guide books helped to dramatize a rift between genteel and skilled behaviors by somewhat unexpectedly positioning entertainment on the practical end of that divide. This was, in essence, a debate about imagining the definition of the middling classes that parlor plays visibly staged before vast numbers of participants and viewers across middling households, in part as an effort to perpetuate and legitimate home entertainment. In doing so, however, the texts also recast an understanding of the middling social experience as attractive, authentic, and as characterized by untapped skills. George Arnold's short play "There Is No Rose without Thorns," from *Parlor Theatricals* (1859), aggressively questions what the play exposes as a veneer of mannered behavior.[50] The play, which is an "acting proverb" illustrating a common saying, features a petulant young woman named Rose Thorne, who verbally lashes out at her closest companions, especially her father and her maid. Ordinarily, Rose adopts an angelic guise before her fiancé, Jack. Even though Jack is warned that Rose possesses "a most ungovernable temper" and is a "regular virago," he sees only her sweet-tempered wiles.[51] To convince Jack that he is making a grave mistake, Rose's father and maid conceal the young man, letting Rose assume her usual tendencies. As anticipated, she soon threatens to box the servant's ears, berates her father, and calls her fiancé "good-for-nothing," "hateful," and "odious."[52] Jack, rather understandably, breaks the engagement. Based on the proverb "There is no rose without thorns," the play indicts the thorny underside of mannered behavior. While the play appears to argue for good manners, it also points to a larger problem inherent in the pursuit of gentility, where manners can be deployed independently of good intentions. Thus, the play claims to expose the everyday behaviors operating beneath deceptive facades. Yet, while the play argues for the value of skills, it upholds a livable form of gentility—one rooted in skills and modeled by the act of putting on the play.

Play scripts (like the other activities presented in entertainment guide books) offered their readers models for inhabiting a vernacular level of culture, positioning entertainment itself as a means of honing significant, individual, and effective social skills. Parlor plays appeared in texts that allowed participants to try on a vernacular sociability, a skilled, yet socially competitive form of interaction. Situating common talents as usable skills, theatrical scripts presented accomplished leisure activities as a significant step toward social belonging, for many mid-century theatricals, like parlor games, bolster the methods associated with acquiring mannered behavior by stressing memorization skills, "conversational" skills, physical discipline, and the integration of visual clues—abilities also necessary for the acquisition of polished manners. At the same time, they offered a critique of blatant social ambition by offering play's votaries a way to hone, enact, and evaluate their behaviors in immediate and practical contexts. In this sense, theatricals, arguably the most fanciful form of leisure in the nineteenth-century home, advanced a complicated understanding of labor and an assessment of the work of creating a commonsense sociability.

* * *

The recognition of labor, the internalization of class markers, and the development of a class-based social appropriateness all constituted the most challenging and least tangible tasks within which the various labors of home entertainment converged. Through games and theatrical scripts, entertainment guide books entered a broad conversation about individuals' abilities to inhabit a modest and scaled-back form of gentility. Repeatedly, they demonstrated that cultural striving constituted a real form of work and that part of the difficulty surrounding it lay in recognizing the activities and accoutrements that were appropriate to middling life. Those leisure activities that so vividly displayed middling fashions, mannerisms, and domestic concerns more significantly demanded arduous preparation, a willingness to question genteel conventions, but most of all, a careful and unrelenting self-assessment rooted in a notion of individual skills. Hence, learning the lines of a parlor play or cleverly manipulating the text of a round game displayed immediate, dramatic forms of skilled social work, even as the impetus fueling such activities suggested that the essential forms of middling labor—contestable, vague, and amorphous as they may have been—were only in the process of becoming visible.

2

Dramatic Regression

The Borrowed Pleasures and Privileges of Youth

All work and no play makes Jack a dull boy.
What Shall We Do Tonight? (1873)

The task of representing growth, maturity, and ambition—ideals that were hailed as central to a developing middle class—had its narrative risks. Those same activities that could appear, on the one hand, as examples of dedicated self-improvement, could also be viewed as ambitious posturing. Self-awareness or self-obsession? Ambition or aggression? Nineteenth-century authors faced the difficult task of representing development in a positive light and of countering the apparent unnaturalness of pursuing upward mobility—an unnaturalness that mid-century entertainment guides sought to correct by permitting the display of "authentic" modes of social interaction. Just as worker games brought ideals of bodily authenticity to the social arena, so entertainments revisited childhood, along with its combination of playful release and developmental drama.

Both entertainment guides and period fictions invoked the child in ways that permitted a discussion of natural progression (whether realized or thwarted) as well as regulation (and, at times, freedom from it). The ubiquity of childhood in mid-century popular texts can be seen as a measure of the concern surrounding development and how it was understood in relation to a class of middling Americans. The children who erupt from the pages of nineteenth-century popular texts—novels as well as parlor games—represent striking parallels to middling adults. Encouraged to seek out a uniquely individualized role based on personal traits and abilities, the child is also expected to take up the customs and forms characterizing a larger group. This was a combination of tasks laden with the difficulties of imagining the developing self as situated within a powerful group identity, within a social context composed of elaborate rules and directive instruction. As adults appropriated a peculiar and carefully constructed vision of childhood, they enacted moments of playful release, and, in a delicate balance, adherence to a rules-bound social system, taking up the project of group affiliation that home entertainment, throughout its variations and trends, both invited and demanded.

Invoking vestiges of childhood, popular entertainments broached questions that readers confronted in their daily lives as individual behaviors intersected with the public ideals articulated through various regulatory genres and voices. In the conflicting opinions that resulted, there arose the question of whose vision of development mattered. At what point and by whose estimation was a given phase of development complete? How could individuals claim success when an advice culture continually inscribed new levels of refinement? In the context of the formation of the middling social tier, these questions took on sweeping significance. As figures fashioned in conjunction with widespread concerns about development, children allowed for the ideological project of perpetual self-improvement to be viewed sympathetically; in particular, the Enlightenment's ideal of the child as tabula rasa helped naturalize the quest for self-improvement in children as well as in adults fashioned in the guise of children. And although gradual development could appear natural in the child, issues of regulation and governance, as applied to exceptionally mature, child figures became more problematic. As hybridized constructions of the child suggest, youth became a site within mid-century popular culture through which to interpret elaborate and often dissonant processes of personal reinvention.

Moreover, the image of the child at play united theories of personal development as well as gestures toward the developing and untapped potential of a broad, middling tier. The use of the child as a reference point for adult concerns appears striking in light of deeply discrepant images of the child marketed to and, eventually, embraced by middling adults. Whereas period fiction focused on the oppressed, regulated child, whose development was vociferously charted by adults, games of the mid-century parlor involved scenes of celebratory revelry, where adults acted the role of the carefree youth, without apparent concern for developmental models. If mid-century fiction reminded its readers that purposeful instruction was a necessity, the games of the same era assured them that childhood was a natural state, ideally free from regimented expectations; in the first scenario, childhood was measured in relief to carefully charted maturity, while in the second, youth was a uniquely individualized experience.

This configuration of childhood allowed for one of leisure's two possible freedoms: the "freedom to" act out fantasies and experiment with one's identity. But, just as clearly, there was no real "freedom from" external, regulatory forces. Hence, the figure of the child operated in specific and limited ways so as to sanction leisure pursuits, specifically to render the pursuit of leisure "natural," when, in fact, it was operating as a highly organized, assiduously guided enterprise.[1] This version of childhood, then, furthered the peculiar role of leisure practices as reflecting the tensions of a society where ideals of individualized behavior conflicted with the codes and expectations structuring social life.

Many of the conflicts surrounding ideals of individual development are visible in Susan Warner's *The Wide, Wide World* (1850), the first in a series of prominent mid-century novels that depict a difficult childhood. The novel dwells painfully and at length on the helplessness, submission, and injustice characterizing Ellen's highly regulated youth. As the object of criticism and censure, Ellen is compelled to act out a continually reinscribed youth, a role she repeatedly confronts as she moves from household to household, adapting to new expectations and varying rules at each juncture. In Warner's vision, submission indicates Christian restraint; despite such explanations, the oppression facing Ellen is markedly virulent. Warner's text celebrates Ellen's eventual compliance to these expectations, but beyond that approval, the novel also attends to the necessities and difficulties of performing a prolonged childhood for multiple authorities, among them a biological mother and father, a suspicious and penny-pinching aunt, an adopted "sister" and "brother," assorted friends, and finally, newfound relatives in Scotland.

Issues of deference, respect, and obedience confront Ellen at every abode and hideaway. When, late in the novel, Ellen's new guardian, Mr. Lindsay, tells Ellen that she must bend to his will in everything, he, like other adults, insists on Ellen's deference to his authority, just as Ellen seems to be progressing into adulthood. He also realigns her national and class affiliations (for she is now considered by her guardian to be one of the Scottish aristocracy), commanding, "Forget that you were American, Ellen,—you belong to me; your name is not Montgomery any more,—it is Lindsay;—and I will not have you call me 'uncle'—I am your father;—you are my own little daughter, and must do precisely what I tell you."[2] Here, as elsewhere in Ellen's life, harmony can only occur as "little" Ellen renounces an interest in controlling her life, deferring (as she will again and again) to her guardian's judgments.

Ellen finds it necessary to accept guidance from those adults who manage her life, even through she often appears more mature than they. Territorial as well as greedy for Ellen's attention, the adults around her produce strikingly arbitrary judgments. Ellen's performance of an extended childhood, which is gratifying to her protectors, however, is particularly trying as Ellen is repeatedly transferred to new families, each operating under idiosyncratic rules. On one occasion, Ellen goes through the motions of learning to ride a horse to please her adopted father, even though she is an expert horsewoman already. For Ellen, performances of regression, played out to please authority figures, are necessary exercises in self-preservation. Rather than being evoked as the platform for neutral performances of the contest between self and societal convention, childhood serves as a site where discontinuity, tension, and the lack of resolution overtake real growth.

Ellen's trials, it is worth noting, resonated powerfully with mid-century adults, who were the primary purchasers of the best-selling novel as well as purchasers of gaming manuals that promoted versions of child's play.[3] In both the texts and practices that allude to childhood, adults, much like Ellen Montgomery, were encouraged react to calls for governance, to defer to the authority of those forces and texts that expressed behavioral ideals for them, yet, at the same time, to enact the deeply individualized experience of personal development. Like the child, the adult of the middling sorts was, by 1850, undergoing a "rite of passage," a transition into another phase of being.[4] This was a period when expressing class-based affiliations through the child became possible because the child offered a site where outrages, petty humiliations, and demands for accomplishment converged.

Whereas the child in the novel could be used to depict the dangers of a development overzealously charted, the games of the parlor invoked a carefree vision of childhood characterized by kissing forfeits and physical versions of "Blindman's Buff" and "Pin the Tail on the Donkey," now converted to games for adults. The playful vision of interaction that they constructed was free from all visible regulations and emblematic of the supposedly natural expression of youthful vigor. In popular games borrowed from childhood, "Shadow Buff," for example, participants cast exaggerated shadows onto a white curtain, attempting to prevent onlookers from guessing their identities as they crept, hobbled, and charged across a lit expanse of curtain, with the goal of the game being the obstruction of everyday identities. As in games such as "Museum" or "The Genteel Lady," the object of play encompasses the ability to manipulate the mode of identity useful at a given moment. Here, however, the game involves a backdrop, against which players' outlines are projected. The most obvious symbolism of play invokes a background of "blank," customary social interaction, against which individual identity will be measured, manipulated, and skillfully disguised. Encouraged to blur their outlines, participants were to adopt unusual gaits, to don clothing that cast unusual shadows, and to otherwise alter their silhouettes, obscuring their everyday appearances.

With grounds for participation in play resting on a type of release that was situated as childish, adults' borrowing from childhood points to a transitional moment in the self-representation of a class, where childishness was attractive both because of its licensing of ungenteel behaviors and because of its promise of future development. It allowed for behaviors that were at once playfully regressive and an emblem of a more prolonged phase of unfinished sociability.

The Child as Metonym

By the mid century, childhood was a concept undergoing widespread revision as adults' attitudes toward their progeny were reinvented, ushering in what is now visible as a modern version of childhood. This new, Enlightenment-based understanding of childhood, in turn, gave rise to youth's developmental privilege, a sympathetic patience for gradual growth and elaborate social instruction. This attitude distinguished nineteenth-century understandings of childhood from their historical predecessors.[5] Because childhood was recognizable as a relatively new construct, it was eminently useful as a form of cultural shorthand.

As they were invited to identify with, even act out the behaviors of the youth during their leisure hours, adults encountered constructs of the child that uniquely accommodated their own engagements with the boundaries of their evolving middling status, on several levels. Reading the child as a stand-in for adults as national subjects, we may note that the United States was graduating out of its deference to Great Britain, based on the new American prominence after the Mexican-American War, a context that supplies a nuanced understanding of childhood as a rich historical metaphor.[6] If the situation announced by mid-century allusions to childhood can be read as analogous to the international scene and to U.S. efforts claim to metaphoric adulthood in the global arena, then we see the complexities infusing claims to broadly imagined social and economic maturity. The more immediate context through which to interpret maturity is the more localized attention to developing identities, namely the image of a rising class.

As Philippe Ariès has shown, the emergence of childhood as a distinct phase of development is linked—socially, ideologically, and economically—to the rise of the European middle classes.[7] Similarly, I look to the status of the mid-nineteenth-century American middle class to make sense of its production of and identification with the purposeful construction of a metonymic childhood. Through the games of the parlor and in the period's best-selling novels, modes of entertainment offered adults the opportunity to act out youthfulness, to appropriate the behavior of children whose obvious contradictions reveal their very constructedness.

Notably, mid-century invocations of childhood highlight a marked self-consciousness about youth who fail to develop. The child also figures as a sympathetic stand-in for middling adults who pursue a course of uplift, even as the child suffers from flawed, self-interested advice. Focusing on the prevalence of youth in nineteenth-century fiction, Leslie Fiedler articulates a dissatisfaction with the American novel's focus on young people. Invoking the privileges of aesthetic judgment, Fiedler laments the immaturity of the American novel and its subjects, writing that, ". . . our novels seem not primitive, perhaps, but innocent, unfallen in a disturbing way, almost juvenile. . . . The great works of American fiction are notoriously at home in the children's section of the library," lamenting the novel's "incapacity" to develop, along with the text's return to a "limited world of experience, usually associated with childhood."[8] This attention to childhood can also be seen as a consequence of a metonymic construction, where the constructed, artistic rendering of childhood overshadows the possibility of realistic development.

When read as neither simplistic nor celebrated, the child characters of the mid century appear as elaborate invitations for middling adults to identify with the child's experience of the world. But by identifying with childhood, these adults weren't to *be*, in a metaphoric sense, children, or to be *like* children, in the terms of a simile, or even to possess the heart of a child, as synecdoche might imply. Instead, adults were invited to see themselves as characterized by youthful qualities. As Wai-Chee Dimock has explained metonymy, which she positions as a significant trope in nineteenth-century writing, the concept allows for a "telescoping" effect, or the magnification of a set of characteristics useful in inviting the identification of a specific group of readers.[9] The carefully constructed children of the 1850s thus appear as children in a conceptual fun-house, shaped and reflected as a nineteenth-century print culture for adults found it useful to fashion them and situated at the reflective center of popular entertainments.

Unnatural Hybridity and Staged Development

Problematizing development as more often dictated than it was realized, popular mid-century fictions reveal hybrid child figures who combine knowledgeable insights and social inability, but who face expectations for continued social progress. Though notably mature in some dimensions, the protagonists of mid-century literature live out a youth extended by powerlessness, lack of agency, and a submission to external regulation born of continuous external assessment. As they experience vicissitudes of authority figures who chart their development, child figures participate in a series of staged exhibitions of development, accepting startlingly regressive roles so as to *appear to* develop, an experience that highlights their hybridity.

The acting out of childhood is especially problematic because unusually mature children are subjected to generic forms of regulation, or modes of conditioning grafted onto them. Hence, the individual's marked and unusual maturity is subsumed under the presumed characteristics of a larger, less accomplished group. In this way, youthful engagements with generic expectations become yet another way that home entertainments dramatized the problematic aspects of affiliating with a larger group and, here, of being made to sublimate personal distinctions so as to conform to less flattering, more conscriptive behaviors. By portraying youth who are exceptionally mature in their conviction, insights, and deportment, but are nonetheless hindered by a childhood that their loved ones demand, mid-century fictions reveal regulatory gestures as preserving long-standing forms of authority. In mortifying detail, the stories of the mid-century child illustrate the didactic impulses that converge so as to rob individuals of decision making and self-determination.

For child characters, the difficulties of growth are linked to the processes of remaking identity and to questions about the authorities overseeing that reformulation. Both Hawthorne's *The Scarlet Letter* (1850) and Stowe's *Uncle Tom's Cabin* (1852), for example, portray characters who encounter instruction, regulation, and advice as part of a gradual, linear model of growth projected onto them.[10] *The Scarlet Letter*, like *The Wide, Wide World*, problematizes the assessments of authority figures, who ludicrously attempt to impose a narrative of growth onto a character as individual as Pearl. A hieroglyph in the form of a child, Pearl possesses an intuitive understanding of the world that allows her to sense passionate motivations, such as Dimmesdale's interest in her mother and herself. Seemingly worthy "to be the plaything of the angels," Pearl is instead possessed of a "wild, desperate, defiant mood," and subject to "gloom, despondency, and flightiness of temper" (49, 52). With her violent mood swings and fervent emotions, Pearl causes her mother to wonder whether she is in fact a human child. When Hester removes her hated adornment and attempts to live outside of the social inscriptions of Puritan society, Pearl refuses to approach her mother, causing Hester to exclaim, "Was ever such a child!" (116). With a phrase reminiscent of one that would appear again in Stowe's *Uncle Tom's Cabin*, Hawthorne points to the fact that there indeed never was or could be a child like Pearl, highlighting her as a stylized creation, an obviously constructed rendering of childhood.

Through Pearl's unusual hybridity, Hawthorne calls attention to the impossibility of inscribing growth and development. Focusing on the way in which order is maintained through punishment in the small Salem society, Hawthorne positions Pearl at the apex of politicized contests of compliance and rebellion. The most startling aspect of Pearl's constructedness, however, stems from Hawthorne's allusion to a child-rearing conflict, or a contest of discrepant authorities that pits Hester against the elders of Salem, situating the authority of the state against what the novel portrays as the natural right of a mother to determine the appropriate course for her child. In an attempt to prove Hester an unfit mother, the governor and church fathers, relying on a linear pattern of development congruent with their understanding of moral discipline, attempt to position Pearl's moral training as backward and unsuitable. Governor Bellingham informs Hester that he is concerned about the child's need to be "disciplined strictly, and instructed in the truths of heaven and earth" (61). In the following inquisition of Pearl, on which the child's custody depends, the men attempt to determine "whether she hath had such Christian nature as befits a child of her age" (61). When asked about her origins, Pearl, responding bad-temperedly, "announced that she had not been made at all, but had been plucked by her mother off the bush of wild roses that grew by the prison door" (61).

While the governor is shocked that a three-year-old cannot announce that God made her, the scene stresses the ways in which progress is the vehicle not of disinterested moral guidance, but of an egoistic exercise of authority, especially when one of the ministers involved is the child's recalcitrant father. What is problematic here is not Pearl's development, which appears in the novel as strangely charming, but the means by which the authorities are endowed with the responsibility, the privilege, of charting and measuring development by hypocritical and inept authority figures.

As a symptom of the lack of fit between lives and laws, between passions and the customs that seek to subdue them, Pearl remains in a state of suspended development, an elfish creation in which the text delights and a measure of a widespread moral and political inertia, a sign of the split and irreconcilable patterns of authority arresting the development of the New World. As Pearl's suspended hybridity is symptomatic of the confusion that results from competing types of authority in her world, so too is Little Eva's suspended childhood, which points to the problem of an adult society that has shirked its moral and religious duties toward slavery, with the child supplying a moral precocity. By suggesting that adults have abdicated their true responsibilities, *Uncle Tom's Cabin* (1852) indicts the supposed social progress of the South and of the larger nation as suspect, critiquing any mode of progress that does not begin with the clarity of vision that Eva possesses. Adult society, Stowe contends, has allowed itself to circumvent the most significant steps of growth by privileging social and economic concerns over spiritual and Christian truths. The text's central irony, then, makes obvious the discrepancy between Eva's physical frailty and her fully developed moral clarity.[11]

Like other child characters of the mid century, Eva embodies the apparent contradictions of her development, or from her combination of adult and child characteristics. While her particular brand of maturity is doubted by her mother, who despairs of Eva's "ever get[ting] along in the world," the novel upholds St. Claire's position that Eva will "get along" supremely in heaven, that her blending of worldly simplicity with mature insight is the only mode of growth that matters (277). Eva's reaction to slavery highlights her serious involvement in the complex moral and political issues that confound adults. Upon hearing the violent history of the escaped slave Prue, Eva "did not exclaim or wonder, or weep, as other children do." Stowe particularly stresses Eva's reaction as "her cheeks grew pale, and a deep, earnest shadow passed over her eyes. She laid both hands on her bosom, and sighed heavily" (325). A second time the narration addresses Eva's unusual behavior as Dinah exclaims that the story "isn't for sweet, delicate young ladies . . . it's enough to kill 'em!" (327). But, Stowe insists, this story is for Eva and for others of tender years who exert a morally directed influence over others.[12] Arguing that the child is the "only true democrat," and that adults can learn from the untarnished eyes of a child, Stowe insists on Eva's uniqueness, on her unusual melding of child and adult qualities, with the narration asking, "Has there ever been a child like Eva?" (383).

Remarkably similar to Hawthorne's comment about Pearl in *The Scarlet Letter*, this question directs readers to Eva's symbolic status, to her unique possession of adult insights and childlike innocence. Perishing rather than fulfilling her caretakers' notions of growth, Eva appears as a divinely sanctioned model of resistance to immoderate and impersonal conditioning. She makes inscribed notions of growth appear as the product of faulty measurements and authority figures' regulatory fantasies, for forcing Eva's conformity to these expectations would destroy her moral center, her uniqueness.

Overly regulated growth also appears in the tutelage of Ellen Montgomery, who prompts widely discrepant responses. While reviled by Aunt Fortune as an unruly brat, she is accepted by Alice and John Humphreys as unusually mature. Later in the text, she is termed "too childish for her years" by her worldly Scottish grandmother, but appears appropriately dutiful to her adopted father (548). Despite these varying opinions, Warner encourages readers to note the accomplishments that Ellen possesses—good sense, tact, delicacy, and religious confidence—despite the means through which she has acquired these practices—by being abandoned, then orphaned, left to the whims of a hostile aunt, then separated from an adopted sister by death, and finally, pried from her chosen home to become the plaything of proud and worldly Scottish relatives. Whether at the fabric shop or on a ship, Ellen is judged by varying standards. The common experience of such child figures across mid-century fiction suggests that an insistence upon charting the child's development can only be fulfilled if the child is surrounded by elaborate and regulatory forces that seek to mold her to idiosyncratic ideals.

Regulation, Readers, and Didactic Texts at 1850

In part, the hybridity of childhood suggests the complexity of representing the social and developmental double bind facing upwardly mobile, middling sorts. Just as children were assiduously guided and tutored, so too, mid-century adults faced calls for social conformity of the type outlined by an omnipresent didactic popular press. At this juncture, various types of mid-century guide books drew attention to adult Americans' social immaturity, despite economic security. Hence, in their pursuit of professionalism, better manners, and elaborate social forms, middling Americans of the mid century faced a barrage of advice through an explosion of print materials that sought to inculcate a desire for continued acceleration.[13]

Directed by a wealth of guiding texts, middle-class consumers purchased visions of themselves—both as they were (in need of instruction) and in light of what they wanted to be (accomplished, knowledgeable, and possessed of cultural finesse). While advice texts rarely narrated the difficulties of receiving instruction, of participating in culture as the objects and recipients of advice, such difficulties are articulated in other middle-class arenas, including those leisure pursuits presenting metonymic children. In concert with those directive impulses that promised to guide and reflect them, a middle-class readership turned to diversions—games and popular novels— that directly addressed the complexities of instruction and the attendant issues of cultural authority.

Readers' responses to such advice appear deeply ambivalent. A dramatic rise in guide books addressing etiquette, domestic management, child rearing, and home entertainment positioned the middling reading public as an audience propelled into inhabiting a circumscribed social identity attainable through directive advice. In propelling readers toward self-improvement, such texts hosted deep and potentially troubling contradictions. As John G.

Cawelti notes, advice authors ". . . dwell at great length on the temptations and dangers facing the ambitious young man. . . . In somber but glowing, almost loving detail they set forth the awful degradation which awaits the young man who unwarily sets his feet on the primrose path."[14] As Cawelti points out, advice texts construct boundaries around readers' experiences, coaching readers on how to avoid the "forbidden" experiences that the authors of such texts treat knowingly.

While we might expect didactic guides to display an insider's worldly, astute knowledge as a sign of the texts' value, these texts also positioned readers as bereft. Shaped as ideal recipients of advice, readers were described as figures whose desires were far more sophisticated than their habits. In order to become culturally empowered by advice, the readers of such texts needed to accept their initial place among the faulty and inexperienced. Judy Hilkey has described the tone of advice texts as "ministerial and declarative," even though, as she contends, success manuals themselves rarely provided practical advice.[15] Indeed, there is much less usable advice in such texts than what Nancy Armstrong has referred to as "pure ideology," or the outlines of an ideally constructed lifestyle.[16]

At a historical moment when readers were expected to encounter a succession of guide books and (more pejoratively put) a cacophony of advice, the marked increase in instructional texts radically affected ideas of any form of agency during this golden age of didacticism. Typically, advice books asked readers to suspend all judgment, casting readerly resistance to the text as unreasonable, uninformed, or—worst of all—antithetical to progress. Others repeatedly portray readers as characterized by defective training and an elementary cultural capital. Like Ben Franklin's "empty sacks" waiting to be filled, common readers are portrayed as potential hazards to themselves, facing imminent social danger at every turn and requiring corrective intervention.[17]

In their justifications for their own existence, entertainment guide texts lay bare their "organizational didactic," providing instruction for the very activities that seemingly would be among the most spontaneous and natural.[18] They also portray the challenges inherent in entertainment guides, as they transform children's activities, previously considered "playful" and naturally expressive, into normative practices for adults. To sanction their own existence, entertainment manuals needed to position their readers carefully, invoking them as capable of playful leisure, but also as lacking a knowledge of social appropriateness. In order to neutralize such contradictions, authors of entertainment manuals invoked a developmental logic, reaching for the figure of the child, for whom directive advice had been naturalized.

Advice texts on entertainment risked exemplifying the most ridiculous contradictions inherent in nineteenth-century didactic manuals, for they promised expert, organized advice about the seemingly simple, natural activities of play. Yet because they strategically fashioned their imagined readers in the guise of children, didactic texts took on a parental voice. By treating adult readers as if they were children, entertainment guide books attempted to naturalize the various burdens of refashioning the self. In their portrait of hybrid adult-children, such guides nevertheless alluded to the figure of the child for two distinct and apparently oppositional reasons. First, the figure of the child suggested a lack of development that enabled advice givers to imply a particular deficiency on the reader's part, one related to inexperience rather than inability. Second, the child figure usefully suggested a natural, unconstructed relation to play that promised to empower adults. In entertainment texts, then, readers could be constructed as possessing a "natural" interest in play, but at the same time, as deficient in particular knowledge about the minutia of organizing and implementing social amusements. Parlor play thus combined the spirit of unfettered play with expectations for highly structured social time, resulting in an unlikely blending of childhood's privileges with adult social imperatives.

Reframing the Privileges of Play

For adults who encountered infantilizing advice and regulatory overtones, playing out a particularly carefree version of childhood—a boisterous, escapist childhood—meant resisting advice and implicitly arguing for a supposedly natural course of development. Emphasizing play and apparently eschewing external monitoring, guide books about social entertainments stress childhood's playful agency as a counter to advice givers' directiveness. Moreover, games appear to draw attention to individuality, privileging personal abilities, individual competition, and personality (games such as "Marriage and Divorce" assess personal qualities, for example) rather than demographic expectations. Whereas for the child figures of mid-century novels, inhabiting childhood means accepting regulatory and, often, infantilizing advice, entertainment guide books invoke idealized images of active, energetic children who fully and enthusiastically exercise their developmental privileges through play. Such games assert that adult concerns can wait, that growth and development should not be attempted too early or with worrisome regulation.

The startling aspect of home entertainment, however, lies in the way that leisure activities were remade, for the games that were newly marketed to adults at 1850 had been played for decades—by children. Indeed, the emergence of the home entertainment guide book is a curious artifact of an adult-based, mid-century print culture. It is distinguished from other guide materials by its tone, references, and refusal to mention manners. Setting out the rules for parlor games and encouraging adults to participate in activities such as "Blind Man's Buff" and "Hunt the Slipper," guide books on parlor play were markedly unusual in that they were not precipitated by a new invention, say, in printing technologies, or by an advance affecting distribution, as rural free delivery would transform the periodical market at the turn into the twentieth century. Furthermore, the activities outlined by entertainment guide books—among them round games, brain games, and forfeits—were already part of an established social practice. Instead of outlining new forms of play, home entertainment books attempted to reinvent entertainment's audience.

Child's play, as borrowed and redeployed during home entertainment, became a place to reconsider notions of individual development, for play time connoted both a "natural" state of innocence and, in the social context, a precocity for adopting social forms. A more mature audience for entertainment meant also that leisure had to be explained and sanctioned in radically new ways, or rationalized in the context of adult interests. With an appropriation of children's forms of play, adults could perform new and spectacular identities as they publicized their relation to childhood resulting from a purposeful engagement with child's play. Adapting paradigms from child's play, home entertainment guides treat activities such as "Blind Man's Buff" as opportunities to act out against social pretentiousness, to escape dreary conversation, and to pursue members of the opposite sex, literally and bodily. Among marriageable young people, for example, "Blind Man's Buff" and other tactile games offered the opportunity to engage in overt sexual pursuits in the company of other boisterous adults.

As Gabriel Furman noted of his experiences in early nineteenth-century New York, various types of forfeits demanded that players engage in "kissing back to back, kissing through bars of chairs, and in every other grotesque way imaginable."[19] Furman's emphasis on kissing is notable, particularly its prevalence during play, as represented in his description of "Love's Ladder." In this activity, he writes,

> A lad selects his lass, stands up in the room and then kisses her. Another couple come on, and in passing under the arms of the first they are caught around their necks, and the girl is kissed by the lad who caught her, and the lad who is caught kisses the girl who caught him;

then the second couple take their station by the side of the first and so
the couples continue coming on getting caught and kissed by and kissing every couple that went before them until "Love's Ladder" is complete. (13)

Lamenting what he sees as the emergence of a more sophisticated brand of
sociability, Furman nostalgically contends that in "fashionable parties" of
the present "every thing must be cold and unnatural or else it would not be
fashionable, which, nowadays, with some persons, would be a most dreadful
affair. They would rather sacrifice all the real pleasure of life than forfeit their
claim to fashionable rank" (13). His account, which casts kissing as a "real
pleasure," details a notable level of physical contact among youth. Moreover,
it implies that the behavioral excesses of play were necessarily cast as childishly innocent and, significantly, as outside the social sphere of "fashion."

In their remaking of an audience from children to adult players, entertainment guides of the mid century reveal an elaborate strategy for borrowing and reinflecting existing cultural practices. In particular, they assign a
developmental logic to adults' invocations of children's play. Whereas borrowing gentility (with its European and elitist precedents) remained an unresolved source of tension for mid-century Americans, entertainments such
as "Blind Man's Buff" appropriate vestiges of the less sophisticated and supposedly less troubling province of childhood. Play forms thus stage spectacles
of regression back to what appeared as a carefree phase of life. Engaging in
childish play, however, did not encompass the suggestion that adult Americans were backward; indeed, their maturity was made clear by playing at
childhood, just as their separation from manual work was made manifest by
playing "working" games. Within the scope of mid-century evocations of
childhood, the playful activities of the parlor emerged as behavioral correctives to the prescribed and regulatory version of childhood problematized by
the mid-century novel.

Dramatized during the parlor's social hours, home entertainment's spectacles of play reveal what Michel Foucault has described as the flexibility of
a dominant culture interested in reformulating itself. Revealing a "chain" or
"system" of power relations, reconstitutive acts are, according to Foucault's
theory, essential to maintaining a cultural dominance, for at moments of
their incorporation, new materials reveal what Foucault terms the "effects of
cleavage that run through the social body," or the fault lines of change.[20] The
social fissures surrounding mid-century parlor games reveal such a "cleavage," as a sign of a shifting social terrain in the attitude toward individualized pursuits. Home entertainments harnessed the apparatus of social be-

longing as a means of articulating individualized desires; in this sense, the child promised to unite class and individual interests, but at the expense of casting identity as a dangerously hybrid state.

By stressing the sexualized dynamics of social interaction, moreover, home entertainments not only remade child's play in the guise of innocence, but the very act of situating adult, sexualized preferences in an acceptable, permissible context highlighted the operation of strong, personalized preferences. In her discussion of desire in the nineteenth-century British novel and the didactic literature governing period social behavior, Nancy Armstrong posits that individual subjectivity (articulated through personal, sexual desires) facilitated the portrayal of the individual consciousness that came to characterize a middle class, defined in part through the woman's experience. Similarly, forms of sexualized play allowed for an acceptable expression of deeply individuated desires within the specter of a world of rules that could be manipulated, remade, and inflected by an individual under the influence of personal desires, which could overwhelm official codes (here, codes of play). Manipulating the parameters of play was not only possible but pleasurable, these games suggested, as the child became a vehicle for inviting adults to view behavioral freedoms as signs of individuated desires.

Borrowing Childhood's Innocence

Like the competitive games of the mid-century parlor, the "innocent" games of physical interaction borrowed from child's play would have entered domestic circles as boisterous spectacles, enlivening genteel leisure. In guide books, such practices are described as correctives to dull gentility. Childhood's forms of play offered a new and adoptable "tactic" for social participation, for mid-century parlor games posit, at least in theory, that the same rules apply to children and adults.[21] These activities borrowed a liberating innocence from childhood, thereby cloaking mid-century adults with a special license to play, a license that virtually remade mid-century social life.

As adults colonized children's games, the cultural importance of game playing, heretofore associated with youngsters, gained a newfound significance through an adult using audience. Home entertainments were additionally invested with new nuances, stemming from their context in an adult social milieu, although guide books do not generally acknowledge this fact, since the disjunction between borrowed activities and a new audience for them appears as a liberating complexity characterizing leisure pursuits. Previously, books such as *Youthful Recreations* (1810), *Remarks on Children's Play* (1819), *The American Girl's Book* (1831), and *The Girl's Own Book* (1832) instructed young players on the rules for round games and pantomimes. The same activities were later circulated to adults through texts such as *The Book of Parlour Games* (1853), *Family Pastime* (1855), and *The Sociable* (1858), along with their textual descendants during the next fifty years.[22] These texts encouraged "mature" participants to relinquish their genteel, composed facades so as to indulge in physical, overtly aggressive activities, countermanding the demands of etiquette books.[23]

As presented by guide books, parlor entertainments alleviated discord, ennui, and a longing for the unwholesome pleasures lurking outside the home by turning attention to the relatively "safe" diversions already associated with a domestically sanctified childhood, that is, a version of childhood congruent with the middling classes and their attention to moral and social development. With an appropriation of children's forms of play, adults performed new and spectacular behaviors as they publicized their own relation to childhood, resulting in claims to childhood's unique privileges, among them physical aggressiveness and cultural initiation. Thus, childhood served as a means of voicing concerns about modifying and augmenting personal identity, particularly as that identity was being inscribed by popular mid-century texts. Playing at childhood, players could step outside of an arduously constructed ideal of social maturity, even as they obviously molded their behaviors to meet the expectations of a particular game.

Adult game players, guide books suggested, were to appropriate childhood's behavioral license. But it does not necessarily follow that parlor manuals' invocations of childish innocence resulted in a convincing mimicry of juvenile interests, even when adults played games such as "Blind Man's Buff" or "The Postman." Instead, guide books for adults borrow the playfulness attributed to childhood, applying it to adult interests, in essence, invoking childhood's outward appearances and associations. As might be expected, entertainment guide books characteristically assert that adults are merely engaging in "innocent" behaviors, relying on a rhetoric that seems calculated to counterbalance the images of sexualized, physical play pictured in the texts. Manuals also refer to their adult readers as "children of larger growth," as does the 1855 guide book *Family Pastime*, which also encourages players to be "sensible enough not to be above being amused."[24] Other entertainment guide books remind readers that "All work and no play makes Jack a dull boy," a sentiment that is to apply to those in "the sedate gravity of their years," who should bring themselves down to "the youthful level of Jack and Gill," and recognize that there is "nothing more delightful than, laying aside all stately dignity and unnecessary restraint, to devote the whole or part of an evening to some social amusement, pure and simple."[25] By invoking ideas of behavioral simplicity, such texts direct readers to rationalize forms of play that clearly violate the ordinary boundaries of adult social interaction.

Although borrowing childhood's association with innocent diversion, parlor games made visible and frequent allusions to adult libidinal interests. Sexual desire, flirtation, and titillation permeate mid-century game playing, suggesting that the version of childhood performed by adults supplied only a thin veneer of innocence, cloaking otherwise unmentionable impulses. While borrowing the supposed innocence associated with childhood, including mirthful attitudes, obedience to accepted rules, and disinterested sexuality, parlor play, as realized by adults, ushered a physical permissiveness into the social parlor. As represented by entertainment guides, parlor games express an interest in sexual expressiveness as participants are ever ready to exploit situations for kisses, embraces, and errant touches. In most of these games, "Blind Man's Buff" among them, there is no guiding narrative that sanctions libidinous interaction (as there would be in home theatricals, with their courtship stories). By contrast, mid-century games display the impulsive, ungoverned, and unsentimental dimensions of adult sexuality, or a set of impulses severed from framing explanations.

Even while operating under the supposedly simple "rules" of children's play, adults' games were mobilized very differently. Games of touch such as "Blind Man's Buff" allowed for a particularly adult type of license as the Blind Man attempted to identify players by touching and groping. It is instructive to look back to earlier versions of the game, such as Eliza Leslie's *The American Girl's Book* (originally printed in 1831), a text that preceded an adult game-playing textual market.[26] In this text, preadolescent girls play a sedate, controlled, and same-sex version of the activity, seated complacently on small stools. But with the introduction of a mixed company of adults, the nuances of the game are altered dramatically in later entertainment guides. Based on the illustrations of groping "blind" men (fig. 1), who come dangerously close to the bosoms and buttocks of the women who flee from them, the physical contact of the game becomes notably titillating, with curvaceous women typically eluding groping men. In these kinds of illustrations, the sexes pursue one another in front of representatives of both the older and younger generations. With the older and younger figures cast as viewers, young adults are left to interact with one another.

Similarly focusing on titillating contact between the sexes, a popular game entitled "Marriages and Divorces," when played by adults, could take on a significance impossible among children, for the game focuses on compatible traits in couples, with a tribunal debating which of the players should be

Fig. 1. "Blind Man's Buff" as pictured in *The Book of Parlour Games* (Philadelphia, 1856). The Elizabeth Nesbitt Room, University of Pittsburgh.

"married" or "divorced." Here, the overlapping of the real and the playful worlds, complete with provocative pairings and communal judgments about desire and compatibility, posed a level of interaction that was more real than imaginative and more reflective of individual, subjective desires.

Parlor play's evocation of a symbolic childhood (one enacted by adults) obviously did not erase players' adult interests. Kissing and other contact games make clear the ways that libidinal urges were infused into the play forms inherited from childhood. Two illustrations of "Crying the Forfeits" make clear the cleavage between the adult's and child's realizations of the activity. The first, from *Parlour Amusements* (1824), depicts an adult, possibly a mother, and children; the adult figure holds one of the children's personal possessions, which the kneeling boy will attempt to redeem (fig. 2). With its sedate setting, its solemn figures and pronounced, almost neoclassical sense of order (one furthered by the adult-child hierarchy of power), this rendering of forfeits contrasts with a later, flirtatious scene involving adults. In the adult version of forfeits from *Parlor Amusements and Evening Party Entertainments* (1885), two young people are poised as if participating in a romantic interlude, an interlude in which the man's redemption of his belonging overlaps with a pose reminiscent of the "bended knee" of a marriage proposal (fig. 3).

Described in one parlor manual as a means to "give somebody a lawful excuse for kissing someone else without offense," kissing forfeits, one of the most common forfeits, took precedence in many texts for adults in mid-century manuals and their later descendants.[27] Most forfeits, for example, would have begun with a narrative stressing the exchange value of a kiss, with the keeper of forfeits crying out, "Here is a pretty thing, and a very pretty thing; what shall the owner do of this very pretty thing?" To retrieve the item, players publicly enacted a penance, with the game highlighting the pleasures as well as the pitfalls of mature social interaction, whether with the bestowing of kisses or via other ungenteel actions. As representative of the "lawful" excesses of play, these forfeits were most often assigned to female players in elaborate scenarios that enabled male players to receive kisses. In such activities, libidinous attitudes predominate. The illustration "Wooden Face" (fig. 4) depicts a young man receiving his social punishment (essentially the aim of forfeits) by kissing the wall, while another couple (described as part of a line of youth who alternate by sex) pairs off and exchanges kisses. An illustration of "Kiss the Candlestick" from the same text (and in a similarly titillating vein) depicts a young woman who kisses an unmistakably phallic candlestick while a young man interposes himself between the woman and the candle. In the spirit of play, forfeits such as "Kiss the lady you love best without anyone knowing it" created scenarios where a male player would kiss *all* the ladies in a room so as to conceal his preference. While filling the parlor with images of cheerful and compliant lovers who bestow payments for "debts" incurred during play, the physical (and public)

Fig. 2. "Crying the Forfeits" as performed by a mother and
children in *Parlour Amusements* (London, 1824). Courtesy,
The Winterthur Library: Printed Book and Periodical
Collection.

exchanges of play resemble the similar (yet hidden) economies of prostitu-
tion, a topic of fascination for adult Victorian audiences.[28]

These forms of adult play show that mid-century entertainments selectively reinflected children's games, even while insisting on the stability of an
"innocent" childhood. Such attempts to deny any significant change in game
playing highlight guide books' useful tactic of treating social practices as appealingly uncomplicated. Allusions to the "simplicity" of play clearly serve
an important function as they allowed an adult culture to revise the uses to
which the games were put, yet without detailing the full context behind their

Fig. 3. "Crying the Forfeits" as performed by adults in *Parlor Amusements and Evening Party Entertainments* (London, 1885). Courtesy, The Winterthur Library: Printed Book and Periodical Collection.

redeployment. Thus, "childlike" behaviors, when enacted by adults, sanctioned titillating, sexualized, and opportunistic dimensions of play under what was termed "family fun." *Family Pastime* (1855), for example, voiced such an argument by claiming that "Every parent must feel that in the attractiveness, cheerfulness, and pleasures of home lies a great safeguard in the minds of children against the pernicious fascination of vicious and foreign pleasures. . . . " In addition, claims this manual, play will "foster harmony and unity of feeling, and by community of pleasure culturate the generous virtues of sympathy and good feeling."[29] As compelling as the goal of family participation would seem, most entertainment guide books invoke references to families based on an idealized portrait of the congenial family, not

Fig. 4. "Wooden Face," a forfeit from *The Book of
Parlour Games* (Philadelphia, 1856). The Elizabeth
Nesbitt Room, University of Pittsburgh.

based on enactments of play. Despite claims of togetherness, adults—not
children—are most visible in mid-century parlor play texts; descriptions of
play mention children infrequently and suggest that youth were to remain
on the margins of organized amusements when adults were present.[30]

Most mid-century entertainment books indicate that real children were
expected to exit the parlor so that adults could appropriate and remake children's activities and privileges, thereby taking over rather than complement-
ing children's play. In most entertainment guide manuals, sections of the text
devoted to markedly different activities separate the "young folks" from
adults. Only on special occasions were all family members welcome; Christmas, for example, appears to be a particularly egalitarian holiday, described
as one of the few occasions where adult and child interests could merge.[31]

More usual are signs that children were expected to lend assistance as stage hands (holding props, fetching costumes), or voice appreciation as enthusiastic onlookers, leaving the real fun for adults to enjoy in one another's company.

The popular guide book *The Sociable* (1858) takes up the issue of the child as a participant in "family" play, arguing that children need not take part in order to enjoy parlor play, as the following narrator claims, even as he disingenuously describes parlor play's inclusiveness:

> We have heard many people say, "Oh, he's too young, he can't play." We say not so; no child is too young to join in healthy and innocent pastime. There is no occasion to give a child a prominent part to perform, or to let him perform any part at all; but you can lead him to believe that his presence is in every way as desirable as that of the oldest person present. Not that we advocate deception as a general thing, but we do countenance it where it is used for the purpose of making children happy. We ourselves have, in the game of "Fox and Goose," carried a child on our arm through the whole; he had nothing at all to do with it, but he laughed as loudly and as heartily as any of the party.[32]

The Sociable's allusion to a symbolic child is in many ways emblematic of the social practices of mid-century America, for the child serves as a reminder of the qualities of mirth, innocence, and good humor deemed synonymous with playful release. In the text's illustration to the section on "Parlor Games," two children appear at the margins of activity, either tugging at adults or mimicking their activities (fig. 5). Again here, however, the participating adults (who appear of an uncharacteristically advanced age) enact a kind of public flirtation sanctioned by both the game and by the intergenerational onlookers, with the presence of children superfluous to the countenancing of adult play. At such moments, adults have effectively colonized childhood by borrowing its behaviors. *The Sociable*'s explanation of participation in home entertainment, appearing in one of the most frequently reprinted entertainment texts of the century, suggests the degree to which adults made use of symbolic children, the invocation of whom enabled an oblique announcement of adult desires.[33]

Mid-century inscriptions of child's play both acknowledge the presence of conventional social forms and make light of them by situating those rules as playful and voluntary, thereby situating social rules as uniquely appealing. Staging a regression back to an earlier state of playful childhood, entertainment manuals encourage adults to appropriate childhood's innocence, along with the uncomplicated nature of entertainment's rules, inviting adults to

Fig. 5. Illustration to the section on "Parlor Games," from *The Sociable* (New York, 1858). Special Collections, University of Virginia.

project their own, highly individuated, libidinal desires onto the landscape of childhood. In child's play, individuation and rules-bound behaviors met, but without obvious resolutions, for the expression of individual desire was located in specific, limited, and constructed renderings of childish leisure—a setting where the ideological significance of individual desires was difficult to claim. Yet the activities' adaptability to new interests, adult inflections, and specific pairings of individuals suggested the ways in which even the most obviously directed and organized pursuits could be remade so as to yield personal pleasure. The adult participants of parlor play could act out youthful innocence in a way that situated parlor play as an elaborate mechanism for rewarding players' compliance to external regulation, even as it allowed for and highlighted an exceptional behavioral license. Adult game playing of the mid century most obviously presented participants as spontaneous gamesters, as naturally youthful, even though it is clear that they also appeared as individuals whose desires were crafted so as to intersect with publicly inscribed ideals of age-specific behavior.

Whether acting out childhood's vitality during play or identifying with fictional child characters who wrestle with problems of agency and development, adult readers encountered figures whose presumed group and personal identities remained at odds. As they inscribed development as an unresolved dilemma, the combined representations of childhood at 1850 illustrate the unevenness, the contradictions of a middling identity at a moment when a mature, public image of middling adulthood contrasted with individualized, childish pursuits embraced by the same group during their leisure hours. In this context, the broad enterprise of home entertainment suggests that the spectacular nature of leisure activities stemmed from their intersection with daily behaviors and unresolved dilemmas about charting social growth. Through their invitation for mid-century adults to appear as sociable youth, entertainment guide texts reveal how borrowed, reinvented social practices allowed for the expression of a transitional period, one where a liberal borrowing from childhood announced a self-conscious sense of incompleteness. Neither aligned fully with the proper adult (for whom submitting to external regulation would be a given) nor the boisterous child (for whom pleasure was supposedly unfettered), middling adults were to appear hybrid, provocative, internally contradictory, eluding simple formulations, generic advice, and easy evaluative assessments.

3
Fracturing Genteel Identity
The Cultural Work of Grotesque Play

My whole is significant of dissolution.
Behead me, and I am a school exercise significant of
  construction.
Behead me again, and I denote the place attained by the
  exercise.

Answer: Decomposition, composition, position.
Cassell's Book of Indoor Amusements (1880)

Along with overtly competitive and childishly playful activities, which circumvented genteel expectations, representations of the bizarre, transformed
body rose to prominence in mid-century cultural life, forming another challenge to mannered social self-presentation. Like mid-century freak shows,
miscellanies, and sensationalist museums such as P. T. Barnum's (which
opened in 1841), grotesque forms of play attested to an ongoing interest in
outrageous spectacles. The tradition of the grotesque, which infused domestic entertainments around the mid century, reveals the degree to which
entertainment forms commented on period anxieties about controlling gentility's boundaries. Like other home entertainments, grotesque forms of play
emphasized the work of transforming oneself to fit into a specific social category, but spectacles of grotesque bodies visibly undermined the genteel ideal
by showcasing bodies that disallowed social interaction and instead became
visions prompting horrific delight.

According to entertainment manuals, mid-century Americans were to
gather in their parlors to applaud wild spectacles, waiting for the rise of presentational curtains, exclaiming over displays of distorted figures, and staging demonstrations of corporeal elongation and contraction, abnormality
and exaggeration. The same Americans who made up a professional class,
who embodied domestic motherhood, and who worked toward the easy assumption of mannered gentility were directed to create and to stare un-
abashedly at the delightful horrors of the unmannered, unrestrained, and
aesthetically alarming body. This was not, then, a neutral exercise in corporeal rearrangement, but an elaborate, spectacular performance freighted with
self-awareness, an overturning of standard expectations about deportment.

Fig. 6. "The Severed Head" from *What shall we do to-night? Or social amusements for evening parties* (Philadelphia, 1873). Courtesy, the Winterthur Library: Printed Book and Periodical Collection.

Just as etiquette books detail the most effective means of producing genteel poses, parlor guide books elaborate upon ways to produce startling physical transformations. Such texts, for example, carefully chart the processes of creating the spectacle of the severed head, positioned at the base of a table (fig. 6). They also detail the creation of a parade of dwarves, beasts, and exotic animals. Participants are encouraged to become giants, "midnight screechers," and "nondescripts," displacing carpets, furniture, and even the family Bible for a carnivalesque evening of elaborately prepared revelry. By exaggerating isolated physical features, grotesque displays called into question one of mannered behavior's basic dimensions as they fractured genteel demands upon the body.

Contending that the regulations of the "socially qualified" body organize the world in significant ways, Pierre Bourdieu observes that "the social determinations attached to a determinate position in the social space tend, through the relationship of one's own body, to shape the dispositions constituting social identity. . . . "[1] By altering the most basic platform of social interaction, or the site of the body, grotesque forms of entertainment invited their participants to reinterpret their social sphere, realigning the world from the body outward. Moreover, by releasing the individual from the rigors of everyday stances and reorienting his experience of the world, grotesque home entertainments gestured toward the irregularities of individual bodies as a point of contrast to standardized expectations. Disregarding the customs of bodily conformity and embracing a performance of physical idiosyncrasy and corporeal irregularity meant that the individual body became visible in relief to group norms, if only for consolidated periods of time and within the category of play recognizable through the grotesque.

As in other forms of home entertainment, claims to individuation formed a major part of the allure of the grotesque. Because nineteenth-century social and sexual norms produced a "struggle to individuate," as Nancy Armstrong has argued, then the tradition of the grotesque offered a visible means of altering the physical terms of social uniformity.[2] A significant difficulty facing a rising American middle class, as Armstrong suggests of nineteenth-century England, stemmed from individuals who conceived of themselves as "on the one hand, an array of unique individuals and, on the other, a body of all individuals—an abstract and standardized body, rather than one that was heterogeneous and permeable."[3] Understanding the body as both literal (a plastic form) and figurative (as a metaphor for evolving notions of group identity) highlights the ways in which home entertainments negotiated between displays of individual and collective authority. Because the social body functioned as the site of generalized expectations for deportment, as Karen Halttunen and John Kasson have shown, it was both the site of a visible standardization of bodily conduct as well as the home of individual irregularity and uniqueness. Adding another layer of complication onto the binaries of individual and collective, mid-century home entertainments challenged the standardized body by producing twisted, distorted forms that challenged the conditions of controlled conformity, yet in doing so, offered a new tradition of bodily alignment. This was, then, a practice that harnessed vestiges of an individualism that was, in the end, more idealized than enacted.

Allowing middling Americans to throw off a mantle of minute control and adopt exaggerated poses for specialized moments of play, the grotesque, like games of childhood, rewarded ungenteel behaviors. Even marginally grotesque activities such as "Dumb Crambo," for example, required players to listen to a monosyllabic word and to match that word with a single syllable rhyme and the actions it describes. The challenge lay in deploying "signs or actions" to "clearly express the thing signified."[4] Should the initial world be "bog," and the rhyme "dog" or "hog," the player must "act so very like one of these animals, finishing the picture, perhaps, by a bark or a grunt, that all can recognize the portrait" (6). Encouraging players to suspend the mannered norms of the nineteenth-century parlor, the game rewards the player who most obviously departs from social, genteel behaviors.

Directions for creating bizarre bodily displays filled entertainment guide books from the mid century to the century's turn, although they were particularly prevalent during the 1850s and '60s, the period of gentility's most dramatic rise. In the context of genteel expectations, it is easy to imagine the outrageousness of witnessing young professionals bark like dogs for forfeited personal items. Equally dissonant with gentility would be the transformation of a polite young woman into an object of horror as she combed out her hair, tied it to a suspended hook, stuck her head through a sheet, rolled back her eyes, and slackened her jaw so as to resemble one of Blue Beard's beheaded wives. In their fashionable parlors such young women deliberately, playfully worked against normative poses, transforming themselves into bizarre and unsocial spectacles.

Rather than facilitating the social interaction that is so significant in etiquette books, grotesque figures required viewing from a distance, or staring, which according to Rosemarie Garland Thompson, is an activity that seeks "to normalize the viewer by abnormalizing—indeed, spectacularizing—the body on view, fixing it in a position of difference."[5] It must be recalled, however, that in mid-century entertainment activities, staring was only part of the response solicited by entertainment's work. Grotesque bodies were productions as much as they were spectacles. Whereas staring had the capacity to reinforce social norms, among them the oppositional stances of viewing and being viewed, producing the grotesque permitted entertainment's participants to occupy both the roles of the alarmed, admiring viewer and, in turn, the awful, exaggerated object of that gaze. More broadly, grotesque entertainments encouraged postures that disrupted the very idea of normalcy by privileging both social and unsocial bodies, uniting an interest in manipulating the body with the activities of viewing and being viewed.

In nineteenth-century fiction, particularly that by Edgar Allan Poe, a relation between the normative and strange, the genteel and grotesque, becomes the focal point of a psychological drama. Composed during the decades of grotesque play, Poe's short stories explore the line between the polite and the unmentionable, the social and the unseemly, for as they focus on the grotesque, they expose the fragility of normative, genteel behaviors, revealing them to be appearances that are all but impossible to maintain. In Poe's portrait of cognitive duality, the grotesque appears linked to transformative emotions such as ungovernable grief and unlicensed curiosity, with tales such as "The Oblong Box" revealing the transformations of seemingly ordinary, properly composed individuals who are suddenly propelled into a sea of ungoverned impulses. But while removing his characters from everyday behaviors, Poe nevertheless portrays their consciousness of social norms, interjecting the codes of gentility as significant markers.

"The Oblong Box" (*Godey's*, 1844), one of Poe's curious narrator stories, explores the moment when characters lose their restraint, gradually becoming grotesque caricatures. Part of the tragedy is that they recognize their own transformations, a cognizance that, in turn, plunges them into greater exaggeration and despair. The story is set on a passage at sea, where the narrator encounters a recently married college friend, an artist known for his excellent taste and general fastidiousness. When the voyage commences (after an unexplained delay), the artist becomes "morose," stiff, and "gloomy."[6] He appears to have lost a servant once in his employ and now has a wife who resides in a separate room. In addition, the artist's bride appears "totally uneducated, and decidedly vulgar" (712). Over the course of the ship's passage, the artist frequently weeps over a long crate that is assumed to contain precious art works. In response to these events, the narrator becomes increasingly intrusive, pressuring the artist to divulge the contents of the mysterious box. A shipwreck ensues, and as the boat descends to the sea's bottom, the artist chooses to perish with his box. Later, the narrator discovers that as the voyage began, the artist's lovely and accomplished wife died and was impersonated by a servant; knowing that he would be denied passage if traveling with a corpse, the artist had his wife "partially embalmed, and packed, with a large quantity of salt, in a box of suitable dimensions" and "conveyed on board as merchandise" (719).

The horror of the story stems from multiple types of partiality—both that of the wife's corpse and that of the two male characters, who lapse into unsocial behaviors. Most obviously, the artist's claims to accomplished social interaction unravel as he descends into melancholia. In addition, the narrator himself becomes less socially adept throughout the tale, admitting that "I was, just at that epoch, in one of those moody frames of mind which make a man abnormally inquisitive about trifles: and I confess, with shame, that I busied myself in a variety of ill-bred and preposterous conjectures" (711). Just as the wife's body lies, most unnaturally, between two states, being both embalmed and unpreserved, so too the two men begin to lead dual lives, caught between impulse and propriety. Even as they recognize their increasingly strange behaviors, they have no power to halt these social regressions; they are already outside of gentility's boundaries, which are all the more recognizable to them because of their estrangement. Consequently, the two men struggle to maintain the appearance of propriety, seeking to conceal what has become, even to them, an alarming social grotesqueness. Poe depicts the greatest threat to genteel stability as emerging from an uncontrolled slippage out of genteel behaviors and into a metaphoric half-life. His half-embalmed bride figure, lying partially exposed (and intact) and partially concealed (and decaying), and her socially facile yet secretly obsessed husband represent the horrors of incomplete self-control.

Parlor games present the grotesque as a construct equal to the one in "The Oblong Box," situating it as a stylized self-production in opposition to genteel propriety. Among the most elaborately prepared and physically controlled of nineteenth-century home entertainments, grotesque presentations reveal the genteel and the grotesque as interconnected opposites, or foils that continually threaten to overwhelm one another. By dramatizing a kind of social change that could be prepared and practiced, entertainment guide books suggest that the deliberate transformations into the grotesque are but one example of social self-control. Similarly emphasizing the value of controlled appearances, P. T. Barnum built his empire on the celebration of "the individual's ability to stylize a public persona and assert these artificially constructed identities into the public sphere," emphasizing "the pliant and adorned nature of self."[7] Drawing a line between the grotesque and the genteel, overtly physical forms of home entertainment amplified the meaning of controlled social poses and equally stylized bodies.

At the same time, grotesque exhibitions countered everyday genteel practices by positing that the unmentionable was never far beneath the surface of politeness, thereby challenging gentility's seemingly complete circumference of social life. The grotesque's most daring announcement was that outrageous behavior was no less constructed than everyday, mannered interactions, setting up an implicit comparison between the labors necessary to produce genteel behaviors and those that brought about exaggerated, unsocial ones. The most important work associated with this type of play, then, lay in exposing the conceptual manipulation of identity that undergirded middling social interaction, with its ideal of elaborate self-control.

Throughout literary and social criticism, there is a long tradition of equating physically and behaviorally outrageous forms of play with spectacles of resistance.[8] While such an interpretive approach to bodily spectacles has its salient features, in the context of the nineteenth-century parlor, full-fledged "resistance" is difficult to locate, for the most significant aspect of home entertainment is not the immediate display of the exaggerated body, but, rather, the mechanisms necessary to create it, mechanisms that overlap with gentility's larger goals. Indeed, much of this chapter reorients a discussion of the grotesque away from its corporeal products and instead calls attention to the laborious processes of producing grotesque transformations. The work of production, of remaking genteel bodies into unsocial forms, then, promises to shed light on the place of leisure practices in the greater social sphere, for a complicated exchange between the genteel and the grotesque bespeaks a mutual symbiosis.

Home entertainments, in their studious attention to bodily control, deploy the grotesque as an amplification of an ideal of seamless corporeal preparedness. Yet the grotesque itself was an elaborately prepared effect. Despite the disruptive appearances created during home entertainments, grotesque spectacles more importantly displayed deliberate and extreme corporeal control, which was not unlike the conscious deliberateness necessary for polite social interaction. As grotesque productions required participants to shed genteel identities, then become genteel once more, they drew attention to the work of manipulating personal transformations. The most significant dimension of the parlor's grotesque play was not the creation of exaggerated or physically disruptive social beings, but a showcased performance of exaggerated bodies, revealing the constructions of genteel behavior that, in contrast to the grotesque, became visible *as* representations.

The Production of the Grotesque

Because the grotesque depended on careful manipulations of the body, it required that the work of creating transformations be recognized and rewarded, laying bare the elaborate production normally concealed under gentility's decorum. Grotesque and physical activities of the mid-century parlor expose the conceptual (and, often, textual) invocation of a license to play, or a set of specialized behavioral expectations that inverted social norms, a situation reminiscent of the medieval carnival, as described by M. M. Bakhtin. Describing the serious dimension of the laughter and disorder of carnival, Bakhtin argues that "laughter has a deep philosophical meaning. . . . The world is seen anew, no less and perhaps more profoundly than when seen from the serious standpoint."[9] As applied to the nineteenth-century parlor, Bakhtin's theory of carnival makes visible a spatially specific and temporally limited potential for social disruption. While Bakhtin has in mind a very different mode of spectacle—one that is communal and collective—his formulations are nonetheless useful in articulating the ways that the grotesque spectacles of leisure time challenged the normative postures of everyday life.

As I explore the complicated cultural work of the grotesque and its dual situatedness as contradictory to genteel practices but simultaneously as compatible with a genteel, middle-class ideal of bodily control, I attempt to understand the importance of social transformation to the middling classes. While the grotesque could have many different invocations, taking on radically different meanings in relation to lower-class performers, for example, it is the intersection of the grotesque and middling domestic life that is most compelling. As defined by mid-century forms of play, the parlor appears as an arena where grotesque, and more broadly, carnivalesque play offered middling Americans a means of testing out concerns about the boundaries of an increasingly circumscribed polite society.

In nineteenth-century social life, the grotesque and the genteel were intricately connected, for grotesque forms of play depended on gentility's conventions for their shock value. Alone, the grotesque, as Bakhtin has suggested, has no inherent meaning, but instead depends on relations with other behaviors, intersecting with and gaining meaning from a collision with everyday practices. Rendering the body and its behavior outrageous, the grotesque substitutes illegible bodily signs for recognizable social codes. As the epigraph to this chapter suggests, invocations of the grotesque produced "beheaded" or truncated meanings, in contrast to the composite expressions and gestures characterizing polite bodies.[10] For nineteenth-century Americans, for example, there was great and contextual meaning in a certain gracious inclination of the head, in the haughty rise of a chin, or in the cephalic gesture of dismissal. By contrast, via the production of a decapitated sociability, a grotesque severed head, positioned under a table (the attached body concealed), defied immediate signification. Denying the possibility of socially contextualized meanings, the grotesque focused on a single and, often, unattached body part. A severed limb or a truncated body, a dwarf's figure, or the spectacle of a hairy, crawling "Midnight Screecher," separated from genteel legibility, would be impossible to parse. Abstracted—one might even say amputated—from genteel codes, grotesque spectacles were to supplant the expressions of mannered society, but in so doing, they offered no narrative in return.

Parlor renderings of grotesque spectacles appear as isolated, shocking displays, but they also call attention to the difficulty surrounding their creation.[11] Forms of grotesque play emphasize labor-intensive mechanisms by revealing the methods that produced their displays. Hence, the questions that

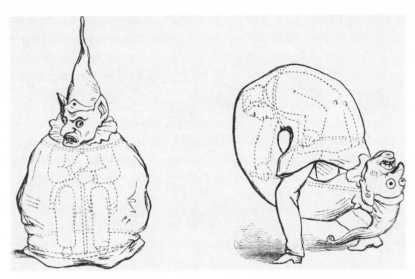

Fig. 7. The "Nondescript" from *What shall we do to-night? Or social amusements for evening parties* (Philadelphia, 1873). Courtesy, the Winterthur Library: Printed Book and Periodical Collection.

entertainment books seek to answer are practical ones: "How does a Nondescript move? How can a grotesque quartet be arranged? How can mature adults become unrecognizable to one another, if only for a moment?" As a partial answer to such questions, many illustrations of grotesque spectacles take pains to expose the methods behind shocking visions, revealing internal movements and unseen tricks behind the displays (fig. 7).

Grotesque bodies—and their resulting transformations back into social, genteel bodies—dramatized the rigors of self-production, stressing adaptability and flexibility, even to the point of caricaturing such abilities.[12] At the heart of the grotesque, then, was a stylized display that was itself a skilled production. In its extraordinary role within the social fabric of nineteenth-century lives, the grotesque offered participants in play an exaggerated response to calls for the middle class to refit, reshape, and reclothe itself according to specific expectations. On the broad scale, such spectacles demonstrated a subject's willingness to reformulate, an attitude congruent with a rising class's assumption of new professional, genteel, and urban identities.

At the moment of a grotesque display, the presentation of an "elongated man," for example, must have seemed outrageous in its departure from genteel ideals of "inconspicuous" appearances. Yet what such an exhibition celebrates is not merely the strangeness of a figure, but the effectiveness of its production. In their unnaturalness, grotesque bodies demonstrated the elaborate labors of rendering the genteel body unsocial, drawing upon the same skills of personal control that etiquette books situated as desirable. With their attention to exaggerated features and magnified physical characteristics, grotesque displays simplified the all-encompassing demands gentility placed on the social body, isolating out a single bodily feature.

In contrast to professional pressures and mannered gentility, which demanded strict adherence to elaborate rules, grotesque transformations appear as voluntary changes for the purposes of recreation. The metamorphoses required by grotesque entertainments offered players a sense that change was a product of design and personal impetus. Setting up scenarios that rewarded adaptability and that encouraged group appreciation, grotesque play presented transformative labors as outrageous, playful, and immediately empowering, countermanding ideals of strictly serious self-regulation.

Severed Bodies and Fractured Identities

While grotesque forms of play encouraged their participants to overturn genteel bodies and postures, it is nonetheless important to recall that within parlors and on specific evenings devoted to entertainment, the invocation of the grotesque was an accepted social trend and hence part of genteel social lives. Disruptive and outrageous forms of play often appear in the context of other narratives guiding home entertainment, in the same entertainment guide books explaining genteel forms of entertainment such as magic tricks and elaborate wordplay.

Many grotesque presentations would have appeared in a kind of circus, complete with a stage, curtains, an announcer, and attendants to arrange costumes for the "actors." Only a few activities called for full group participation, among them "The Grotesque Quartet," which revealed a spectacle of contrasting forms (fig. 8). Here the grotesque is a collective effect, where bodies are assigned contrasting roles representing various "types." In preparing the shock of the display, "grotesque quartets" would have situated audiences as more than appreciative viewers; their bodies were essential to the success of grotesque displays, for such exhibitions were built upon visible contrasts, but not only those among participants. On the most basic level, genteel spectators created relational meanings between a social norm and its inversion, serving as obvious foils for the abnormal, exaggerated extremes that they applauded, particularly the somewhat macabre mid-century fascination with spectacles of decapitated heads.[13]

The story of Blue Beard's Closet, for example, is one of the nineteenth

Fig. 8. How to create a "The Grotesque Quartet," from *What shall we do to-night? Or social amusements for evening parties* (Philadelphia, 1873). Courtesy, the Winterthur Library: Printed Book and Periodical Collection.

century's most common topics of charades and tableaux. According to the illustration of the "Blue Beard Tableau" by Winslow Homer, appearing in *Harper's Bazar* of 1868, the purpose of the grotesque display was to create the effect of actual decapitation, with participants projecting their heads through holes in a sheet, meanwhile adopting alarmingly slack-jawed, trans-fixed, and disheveled poses (fig. 9).[14] Compared to the ordinary positioning of the genteel body (as pictured through the fashion layouts in the same issue of *Harper's Bazar*), Bluebeard's wives boast tussled coiffures, unadorned

Fig. 9. "The Blue Beard Tableau" from *Harper's Bazar: a repository of fashion, pleasure, and instruction* (New York, 1868). Courtesy, The Winterthur Library: Printed Book and Periodical Collection.

heads, and downcast attitudes vastly different from those of *Harper's* complacently fashionable models. In addition to the tale's alarming suggestions of misogyny and domestic violence, the immediate shock of "Blue Beard's Closet" depends on the impact of seeing an intimate or seemingly "unposed" view of the female form.[15] Yet even this revelation is linked to an appreciation of the labor necessary to convert genteel women into alarming spectacles. The relational spectacle of the tableau is further cemented by the story of Bluebeard's last wife, Fatima, the genteel woman at the closet door, who serves as a way to contextualize the second tableau of the severed heads in the closet—an otherwise incomprehensible spectacle.

Other decapitation displays such as "The Severed Head" (*What Shall We Do Tonight?*) sensationalized the display of an apparently unattached head, positioned under a table. This effect, once again, entails the recognition of the elaborate work necessary to convert a social body into a shocking spectacle. Illustrations of this activity, accordingly, emphasize the social impact of the exhibition. By reducing the genteel body to a single and overpowering feature, abstracting and magnifying it, grotesque displays dramatized control of a limited feature, thereby assuring the completeness of transformation. The grotesque shapes of dwarves, "compressed" men, and beasts are based on an amplification of a singular bodily feature, such as height or width. Such spectacles suggest that a focus on isolated features enables radical, shocking change that is at once more immediate and, perhaps, more complete than the gradual adoption of multiple genteel habits. Streamlining the body often meant that exaggerated physical displays were, of necessity, brief. Repeated exhibitions of a severed head, for example, would serve no real purpose after the initial shock and accompanying admiration for the effect; in fact, repetition could reveal too much transformational artifice.

Permitting participants to respond to perceived social imperatives, the grotesque offered nineteenth-century Americans a powerful way to call into question vestiges of an evolving middle-class ideology. Focusing on the myopic nature of an emerging professionalism, Ralph Waldo Emerson invoked grotesque bodily images in order to stress the unnatural effects of culturally determined identities. In the 1837 address, "The American Scholar," Emerson discusses the problem created by an ideal of consolidated professionalism.[16] By deploying images of amputation, Emerson speaks out against the ways that individual identities are streamlined among members of a growing professional class. Emerson begins with an attention to the "whole man," or to the aggregate of "men" who create the social category of "man," suggesting the effects of individualism upon a broad social spectrum. The unity of humankind, Emerson argues, has been challenged by divisions of labor, seen in the lines increasingly drawn between farmers, professors, engineers, scholars, and statesmen.

The creation of separate professions, according to Emerson, allows individuals to define themselves by their individual labors rather than by their collective spirit. "In the *divided* or social state," Emerson contends, "these functions are parceled out to individuals, each of whom aims to do his stint of the joint work, whilst each other performs his" (46). The resulting problem for Emerson is that the "original unit" of man becomes divided, resulting in an "amputation from the trunk" (46). As Emerson focuses on the monstrosities created by a fractured society, he positions the social body as a direct contrast to a severed limb. Professional men, according to Emerson, "strut" about like "so many walking monsters,—a good finger, a neck, a stomach, an elbow, but never a man" (46). This passage, which conjures the grotesque imagery of ambulatory, amputated parts, dwells on the disappointing metamorphosis of man into discrete units, or empty "forms." In a corrective gesture, Emerson redefines the intellectual man not as a professional, but as a "man who thinks," an alternative concept that emphasizes the need to imagine life beyond constructed divisions.

Over the course of "The American Scholar," Emerson rhetorically "decomposes" the social man, only to transform him back into the ideal of the integrated whole, narrating a return back to the restored, meaningful social whole. By linking professionalism to a troublingly fragmented identity, Emerson situates the consequences of middle-class development as unthinkably grotesque. Man has become unsocial or, according to Emerson, severed from his humanity. By contrast, the complete, social man is defined in relation to his greater communal responsibilities rather than his individual goals. Emerson's stringent critique of an emerging middle-class identity as obscenely myopic suggests that we may read grotesque bodily transformations in the parlor as also dramatizing the extremes of narrow self-definition in an age when grotesque bodies were frequently positioned as subjects of public horror, like Barnum's displays of the Fejee Mermaid, Colorado Giant, and George Washington's nurse.[17] Similarly interpreting a mid-century fascination with the grotesque, we see such spectacles commenting powerfully on arguments that urged cultural strivers to streamline their lives, to become professionals, to embrace gentility.

One of the consequences of interpreting the grotesque in relation to the growth of a genteel class is that grotesque transformations cannot be positioned as escapist or anomalous, but neither can they be heralded as moments of complete or lasting disruption. Indeed, these spectacles, which permit inversions for limited periods, break with the most obvious forms of gentility. The resulting transformations appear as deliberate, reactionary attempts to point to limited personal agency in controlling the body, even as grotesque displays granted participants a way to play along, to participate socially and in accordance with a defined set of behaviors, that is, even while appearing to break all social rules.

Spatial Disruptions

While grotesque bodily transformations are among the most startling and dramatic alterations in the nineteenth-century home, there were comparable spatial disruptions in the accoutrements and furnishings of the middle-class home. The material minutiae of the parlor, for the duration of special entertainments, would be pushed aside, along with furniture and decorations, mantle scarves, tidies, fine carpets, etageres, crewel pillows, china and porcelain knickknacks, tables and their coverings—all temporarily removed from the space now devoted to boisterous physical entertainments. For the purposes of play, the parlor could be made to represent a city street, a poor village, a humble cottage, or a faraway land. Just as radical transformations of genteel bodies challenged the legibility associated with the codes of social interaction, so too could physical alterations to the parlor's space disrupt the traditional meanings associated with the room and its objects.[18]

Because a spirit of adventure and experimentation called for by many parlor activities was contingent upon the remaking of the parlor's physical space, many entertainment manuals contain elaborate directions for altering the setting so as to signal the behavioral licenses of play. Caroline L. Smith's *The American Home Book* contends that "some lady can almost always be found who will give the use of her house" for the purposes of private theatricals, as the text asserts that

All the furniture and carpets should be taken from the latter room [the parlor for the stage]. A rough staging should be built (boards can be easily hired), and by boring a hole in the floor, a gas pipe can be run up along the front of the staging, with a sufficient number of burners. Tin shades painted green (as they render the light softer, and more agreeable to the eye), are an addition, for they keep the light from the audience, and throw it directly on the actors. A large floor cloth can be nailed on the stage for a carpet. A drop curtain, so arranged as to be rolled up quickly and easily, by means of a cord pulley at one side of the stage, where the prompter sits, just out of the sight of the audience, is necessary.[19]

These extensive and rather alarming "necessities" for play are hardly unique to Smith's manual. They are frequently associated with presentational versions of home entertainment as preludes to more significant behavioral transformations.

The general theme of transforming the parlor and its guests appears frequently in home entertainment narratives. The *Godey's* series "A Few Friends" asserts the need for social transformation by depicting a gathering that is described as virtually an assembly of corpses. Appealing to a hostess's fears, the text describes the scene.

> There are few refined agonies keener than the sufferings of a hostess who, either in the fullness of her heart or from some conventional necessity, has invited a few friends to spend a social evening at her house, and seen them at last sitting in dismal semi-circle as a result. . . . When she finally turns, in a moment of leisure, to survey the party, she sees with horror that they have disposed themselves in a "cold spread" around the edges of the room precisely, the wrong people sitting side by side, all with ghastly smiles upon their faces, not knowing what to do or say.[20]

A similarly dismal social scene is described in an 1855 entertainment guide book, *Family Pastime, or Homes Made Happy.* Both texts hint at a common desire for a radically reconfigured social life, and for the transformation of hostesses, families, and groups of associates. Based on these accounts, entertaining evenings were to infuse leisure time with dynamic fun and a steady source of diversion, thereby casting participants as attractively energized as well as socially compelling.

The frontispiece to *Family Pastime, or Homes Made Happy* iconographically stresses the carnivalesque potential signaled by a transformed home. The manual, which particularly targets those family members described in the preface as "children of larger growth," builds on a special license associated with transformative play, contending,

> It is not necessary to enter here in any defence of these modes of fireside amusement. Their advantages and even their usefulness are generally admitted. Every parent must feel that in the attractiveness, cheerfulness, and pleasures of home life lies a great safeguard in the minds of children against the pernicious fascination of vicious and foreign pleasures. Every parent should seek, therefore, to render the allurements of home superior to those of the world. These Pastimes, moreover, serve another purpose. They stimulate the faculties, quicken the apprehension, arouse the wit, and under the disguise of pleasure, develop and exercise the mental functions.[21]

While suggesting that pleasure is a facade concealing important social and cultural work, the text, despite its invocations of traditional behavior and

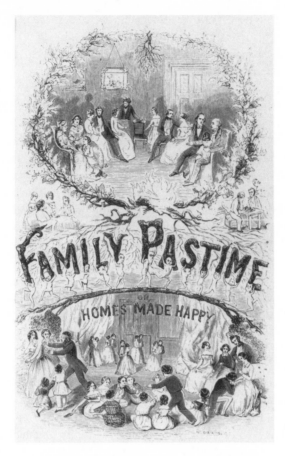

Fig. 10. The frontispiece from *Family Pastime, or Homes
Made Happy* (New York, 1855). The Elizabeth Nesbitt
Room, University of Pittsburgh.

family pedagogy, also points to the behavioral license associated with home
entertaining. In its opening illustration, the guide book presents two visions
of the parlor (fig. 10). The first, which is bound by garlands of greenery, is
inhabited by a semicircle of couples engaged in polite and fairly staid conversation. Each figure interacts with a fellow conversationalist; there is nothing that occupies the attention of the entire group. Additionally, the room is
lit from the front so that the seated figures cast a row of background shadows,
which loom ominously. Well-defined structures of the funereal room emphasize spatial restrictions. Hanging pictures and a large door mark the room's
boundaries.

Heralded by naked, dancing gnomes, scene two, entitled "Homes Made

Happy," displays aspects of carnival, with the customary order of the parlor displaced by active physicality. Instead of being characterized by stark
shadows and dark walls, the room is filled with active figures and billowing
theatrical curtains. In addition, the room's occupants are engaged in various forms of play. In the scene's foreground, youngsters play a round game,
groups of flirtatious adults engage in "Blind Man's Buff," and promenading
couples fill the background. Not only does the scene convey a sense of continuous movement and unlimited space, but it defines the "happy" home as
a site where the traditional propriety of the parlor has been overturned.

A carnivalesque inversion of customary order is also suggested by the
Heaven and Hell contrast implicit in this illustration, and the Hell it portrays
is quite an attractive one. In the iconographic tradition of Blake, the illustration contrasts an orderly social world (ostensibly a peaceful setting for rest
and reward), with a more mirthful underworld, which is a realm of skilled
play and an arena devoid of genteel customs. It is here that ungenteel and
unsocial behaviors will be rewarded, or so the illustration suggests, for even
though the underworld occupies the traditional position of Hell, it is nonetheless the preferred gathering place to a stodgy Heaven. Uniquely, under the
auspices of play, it is the genteel parlor that can be considered socially hellish.

Representing a version of disorder and excess that defied the orderly manners of society, spatial transformations of this type sanctioned the "revers-
ible world" of the carnival, where disorder prevails for specified periods of
time.[22] Reminiscent of the carnival, grotesque transformations invert normal
hierarchies, positioning gentility as negotiable and situating it as a learned
behavior rather than a set of inherent characteristics. But such assumptions
also point out the relational meanings between behaviors, wherein the carnivalesque makes sense only in relation to genteel practices and only as a consequence of an invitation to disrupt that gentility.

Holidays and Carnivalesque Inversion

The kind of settings that made the grotesque possible were those that hosted
the possibilities of marked, uproarious social inversion, where deviations
from the norm were uniquely possible for Americans increasingly likely to
recognize one another in a web of genteel interrelations. Like Bakhtin's annual carnival, elaborate home entertainments such as theatricals and other
rehearsed, planned, costumed, and elaborately staged spectacles were, by all
accounts, infrequent, revealing a "temporary suspension of the entire official
system with all its prohibitions and hierarchic barriers," with the brevity of
the activity allowing for a "utopian radicalism, born in the festive atmo-

sphere of images."[23] Of particular note is the temporally limited disruption of home theatricals, tableaux vivants, and holiday celebrations, where brevity allowed for exaggeration. By contrast, relatively sedate musicals, recitations, and quieter activities such as card games, chess, and enigmas seem to have been fairly common employments, requiring few physical changes in the home. As heralded by entertainment guides, holiday occasions, Christmas included, served as unique opportunities for festive entertaining and for the elaborate work of overturning everyday behaviors. That is to say, entertainment guides invoked Christmas as an occasion that permitted inversion. In addition, such holidays also functioned as an epicenter of domestic caretaking, complete with the work of building sets, creating costumes, and pursuing other time-consuming preparations, hosting activities that promised to occupy and entertain family members and holiday visitors who might gather under a single roof (however modest the dwelling) for weeks at a time.

The link between Christmas and carnivalesque behavior is a rich one in U.S. domestic history, as Stephen Nissenbaum has argued, focusing on the domestication of the holiday near the beginning of the nineteenth century, when it ceased to be associated with outdoor revelry and class conflict.[24] Nissenbaum contends that Christmas gradually metamorphosed into a domestic, family-oriented celebration, a shift that has particular bearing on the grotesque and the physical displays that many entertainment manuals associate with yuletide festivities. At the historical moment when Christmas was ushered into middling homes, entertainment guides challenged the seamlessness of the now-genteel holiday by associating it with an older, more physically demonstrative form of entertainment. In contrast to the domestication of Christmas, carnivalesque forms of play served as signs of older, boisterous, holiday traditions associated with the lower social orders.

Most entertainment manuals present the holiday as a hybrid event, where genteel ease may yet be punctuated with exaggerated spectacles, thereby negotiating between the older celebration of Christmas as a bodily and uproarious event and a newer, socially controlled domestic holiday. From a genteel perspective, Christmas, with its revelry and its disorder, functioned as an extreme event, one heralded by entertainment manuals as a rare opportunity to embrace disorder. *The Sociable* (an enormously comprehensive entertainment manual of 1858), was marketed to "family circles, schools, picnic parties, social clubs, and in short, for all occasions where diversion is appropriate."[25] The text calls attention to games at "Merry Christmas-time," which contrast with activities "on a wet day in the country or . . . a winter's evening," occasions where "young folks are often at a loss, and their elders too, sometimes, to know how to amuse themselves" (172). Like *The*

Sociable, Lydia Maria Child's *The Girl's Own Book* notes its appropriateness for the holidays.[26] Invoking a seasonally specific version of carnival, some texts allude to Christmas as a justification for more active, outrageous games and theatricals, as in the entertainment manual that links Christmas revelry to "the Saturnalia of the Romans."[27] *The American Home Book* (1873), by Caroline L. Smith (inscribed with the message "Merry Christmas / for Hattie from Mama / Dec. 25, 1874"), contains a chapter titled "Amusements for Christmas Holidays," a section of the text that contrasts with surrounding chapters devoted to sedate activities such as conundrums, enigmas, memory games, games of "head work," and quiet amusements; the Christmas section contains directions for theatricals, charades, proverbs, and tableaux vivants—all activities that invoke the license of a holiday spirit.[28]

Alfred Eliott's 1868 *The Playground and the Parlour,* an entertainment book specifically for boys, invokes a holiday spirit, calling for "A right-down merry romp—'under the holly'" (220). These renderings of Christmas as carnival make it clear that the traditions of Christmas, particularly those that were disruptive and boisterous, required an overt explanation, or a reckoning of the ways that social disruptions were part of a holiday that had become both sacred and domestic. Overt explanations of this behavioral license reveal the care with which genteel ideologies were maintained, primarily through the expression of deep and punctuated contrasts to everyday life.

Grotesque Imperialism

In their various manifestations, grotesque transformations created foils to social bodies, presenting momentary disruptions in the decorum of genteel life. Similarly, spectacles of otherness, while pointing to the cultural primacy of genteel bodies, revealed the grotesque's potential to subvert ordinary forms and everyday references. Yet those invocations of the grotesque that broadcast imperial messages ultimately upheld an undeniably Western cultural dominance, asserting that only privileged players could control their environments, their nations. Announcing the "rightful" domination of foreign lands and peoples by Anglo plunderers, grotesque imperial spectacles import scenes from around world so as to assert what would become a common nineteenth-century narrative of civilization's triumph over "barbarism."[29]

This chapter has pointed to the particular moments when the grotesque arose in relation to emerging middle-class ideals in order to rebel against their completeness. With imperialist manifestations of the grotesque, however, it is important to recognize that the grotesque called attention to the racial and cultural boundaries of middle-class life, even as they allowed participants in parlor play to occupy the role of the "uncivilized" other. Tapping into an imperialist consciousness by combining representations of non-whites with portraits of social incompetence and deviance, genteel entertainments treated the cultural and racial "other" as ungoverned by an internalized social consciousness. Through the presentation of a "corporeal epistemology" of race, as Robyn Wiegman has termed it, and by calling for the enactment of racialized "oddities" and unsocialized barbarians, entertainment's activities reveal a profound fascination with appropriating the supposed physical and behavioral characteristics of foreign cultures, thus firmly establishing the idealized whiteness of middling America.[30]

By equating the grotesque with non-Anglo bodies and with what are presented as "uncivilized" cultures, entertainment forms locate grotesque bodies outside of genteel boundaries. In games of geography and exploration, where "foreigners" appear, Anglo explorers are frequently assigned qualities such as bravery, industry, and general good judgment, whereas black, Indian, Asian, and African characters appear as villains or as sources of comedy.[31] Under the auspices of a general interest in geography, history, or adventure, many entertainment books typically encourage players to equate rightful ownership with "superior" Western knowledge at a period, as Edward Said has suggested, when imperialist politics in England and America made it impossible to view any discussion of geographical interests as neutral.[32] Especially because the United States' relations with the globe were expanding notably throughout the latter half of the nineteenth century, with trade agreements emerging with Latin America and East Asia, particularly after 1820, contact with the outside world yielded a range of new references, including displays of exotic goods from the "mysterious" East, which were a source of pointed fascination in the 1850s and '60s.[33]

Allusions to remote and exotic places, then, appear inseparable from an emerging international politics. In the vernacular context, a passing knowledge of the international world produced broad stereotypes and widespread assertions of U.S. superiority for middling Americans. One of the more explicitly racialized debates that inflected home entertainment was the treatment of black citizens of the world, especially in regard to the Caribbean islands. After 1865, when the United States considered annexing Haiti amid excited debate about the racial makeup of the nation and Haiti's possible effect on race relations in the postwar United States, home entertainment forms produced spectacles closely related to minstrel shows, where, as Eric Lott contends, "Black practices" were "appropriated and regulated" as signs of middle-class white respectability.[34] As Lott contends, "In blackface acts and other forms of 'black' representation, racial imagery was typically used to soothe class fears through the derision of black people. . . . "[35] Here, as with other spectacles that were presented by entertainment books as socially or physically grotesque, controlling the representation of the other was of paramount importance in affirming the centrality of a white middle class to American civilization.

Parlor games based on the mastery of geography, which include representations of native peoples, implicitly suggest a parallel sense of mastery over material and intellectual forms of territory. Invoking and rewarding the psychology of conquest, geographical games make few attempts to humanize (or humanize sympathetically) the countries that they describe. Most dwell instead on the material resources of countries, cities, and continents, treating indigenous peoples as rightfully overtaken by practical invaders, portraying natives as squandering resources or as consumed by greed, stupidity, or native evil. The availability of foreign lands is mentioned in a number of games, particularly in a popular activity entitled "I sell you my city of Timbuctoo."[36] The game's narrative requires players to construct an expanding list of the city's material attributes; players are to speak of the riches of the city as their own possessions, selling "their" city of Timbuctoo. A model text for the game reads as follows:

> TOM: I sell you my city of Timbuctoo.
> GEORGE: I sell you my city of Timbuctoo; in the city there is a street.
> HARRY: I sell you my city of Timbuctoo; in the city there is a street; in the street there is a house.
> EDWARD: I sell you my city of Timbuctoo; in the city there is a street; in the street there is a house; in the house there is a room.
> FRANK: I sell you my city of Timbuctoo; in the city there is a street; in the street there is a house; in the house there is a room; in the room there is a cage.
> WALTER: I sell you my city of Timbuctoo; in the city there is a street; in the street there is a house; in the house there is a room; in the room there is a cage; in the cage there is a bird.[37]

Portraying a city devoid of inhabitants, the game calls for the repetition of the phrase "my city," creating the impression of a seemingly endless supply of concealed goods readily available for the taking.

Focusing on the Far East, Ireland, the Scottish Highlands, Egypt, Morocco, and Africa, parlor games consistently depict native peoples as unequal

Fig. 11. "The Cannibal," from *Parlor Amusements and Evening Party Entertainments* (London, 1885). Courtesy, The Winterthur Library: Printed Book and Periodical Collection.

to their country's resources. In this sense, invaders can be equated with the "nature" of the land in a way that countermands natives' rights. The natives' heavy dialects, perceived ignorance, and supposedly comical physical characteristics are emphasized, as evidenced by a number of "dialect" books devoted to mimicking the mannerisms and speech of indigenous peoples (fig. 11).[38] Here racial imagery allows for an emphasis on resource management by the Anglo forces, using the invocation of the "other" to help construct a notion of culturally dominant self-control among participants in play.

Although entertainment manuals existed in many different forms, abolitionist ones among them, a number of texts rely upon an American politics of race to guide participants to adopt imperialist stances. In *The Art of Amusing* (1866), for example, the figure of a Scotsman is positioned as a subject to be owned by the performer.[39] The entertainment manual contains directions for making a Scottish Highlander puppet for the amusement of young-sters; a paper cutout figure is to be attached to a glove, with the wearer's fingers providing the dancing legs. By way of explanation, the text openly compares the ownership of the Scottish puppet to the ownership of a slave, claiming, "When you reflect that a very moderate nigger used to fetch one thousand dollars, it will be exhilarating to know that you can have a High-lander, with all his natural characteristics, for nothing."[40] With the owner-ship of the human body considered an "exhilarating" bargain, the text re-flects on the amusement that a perpetually dancing Highlander provides. As in other grotesque forms of play, a defining characteristic (here, national ori-gin) is reduced to a single, exaggerated referent that severs the body from a broader social context. Variations in the activity call for a "dancing Spaniard" or a "Terpsichorean Matadore," positioning these figures as barbarically sim-plistic and, hence, as easily dominated as American blacks, projecting Ameri-can race relations (and notions of Anglo superiority) onto the larger globe.

Despite the prevalent tendency to invoke Anglo notions of race and "civi-lization" in relation to any distant land, an early and somewhat anomalous entertainment text, *The Juvenile Budget* (1802), attempts to defamiliarize Western culture so as to highlight the strategies of objectifying and sensa-tionalizing other nations.[41] "Travellers' Wonders" entertains through a read-ing lesson; here the short dialogue takes place between a storytelling father and his children. The father, "Captain Compass," a world explorer, is asked to tell "some stories about what you have seen in your voyages" for the fire-side amusement of the youngsters. The Captain complies, asserting that he has seen "a great variety of people, and their different manners and ways of living," going on to describe the inhabitants of a frigid land who cruelly skin animals for their hides, who live in homes of stone and clay, and who melt sand for the admission of light into their dwellings.[42] These strange natives also gather before hot stones for warmth, eat roots and animal flesh, drink a fiery liquid (even though it is poisonous to them), wear the webs of cater-pillars, and introduce tiny "tygers" into their dwellings. As one of the chil-dren finally realizes, the Captain has been describing his own country. He tells the children, ". . . I meant to show you, that a foreigner might easily rep-resent every thing as equally strange and wonderful among us, as we could do with respect to his country; and also to make you sensible that we daily call a great many things by their names, without ever enquiring into their nature and properties."[43] This cautionary note is markedly unusual among entertainment activities and responds to what was becoming a practice of creating lurid narratives about "exotic" lands and peoples, which, by the mid century, was dominating entertainment manuals.

More common are allusions to the "amusing" physicality of indigenous peoples, which appear, for example, in a popular play entitled "The Fejee Islanders at Home" which appeared in various texts throughout the 1870s. Containing all the titillation, adventure, and Anglocentricism of texts such as Melville's South Sea tales, the play stresses the exaggerated qualities of natives' physical characteristics.[44] The script describes the "woolly head," the "projecting nose, with a ring hanging from it," and the feathers in the hair of Kameha, "the king of the Cannibal Islands." Contrasting with Kameha is a Western missionary named Sleek. The show, which takes place in mime, and with the effects of wigs and burnt cork, involves the islanders' plots to cook and eat Sleek; there are additional subplots of violence among the islanders, who are depicted as devoid of all ethics. During the course of the intrigue, Sleek creates a dummy of himself and, because of natives' inability to distinguish him from the decoy, triumphs over them. In the play's conclusion, Sleek comes forward with a book that he holds "aloft as the triumph of civilization over barbarism" (222). Evoking fears of cannibalism, barbarism, and paganism, the play concludes with Anglo domination over the humorous and, ultimately, nonthreatening natives. The Westerners, by contrast, are presented as masters of both reality and representation. The play ends with the assertion that the Western conquerors' skills will be universally rewarded.

"The Crocodile of the Nile," another short play, relies upon a similar scenario of invasion.[45] This particular play is to be performed in a puppet-silhouette form reminiscent of "shadow box" play, which allows for the introduction of wild beasts as well as physical exaggerations among the cutout silhouette figures. The characters include an American couple, soldiers, a sailor, a black servant and his son, and a crocodile and its progeny, the parallel between the black and "beast" families suggesting one source of the play's intended humor. The servant, Sambo, who speaks in heavy, racialized dialect, is constructed so as to roll his eyes and wiggle his feet, echoing the exaggerated minstrel-show effects. Sambo begins the play by running to his mistress, Mrs. Smith, to announce the arrival of a crocodile. The alarmed Mrs. Smith bewails her life in "this dreadful country," calling her husband a "brute" for remaining in this "uncivilized" land (249). The crocodile soon abducts Sambo's son, Jim, then devours Mr. Smith, who, the narrative implies, deserves such a fate because of his general unfittedness for imperialist enterprises.

Salvation at last appears in the form of a sailor, one proud to be in "Uncle Sam's navy," who tracks the crocodile to its lair and kills its young, saving Sambo's son and winning the affections of the conveniently widowed Mrs. Smith. Together, Mrs. Smith and the sailor ride the crocodile off the stage, asserting their dominance over the land and its inhabitants. In the play's closing lines, which are accompanied by song, Sambo dances, reminiscing about "de ole times down in ole Virginny" (255). Sambo's enthusiasm culminates in his claim that he, too, can be an American sailor because of the Fifteenth Amendment. In response to Sambo's presumption, the sailor beats Sambo angrily. The message of conquest is clear. Sambo, a black American citizen, is to be treated as a threatening and foreign beast like the crocodile, uniting the text's racist and nationalist impulses. While using Sambo as the source of comic relief, the play depicts the Western conqueror as aloof, disdainful, and efficient. By contrast, the deceased Mr. Smith, the first casualty of the tropics, perishes because he fails to fulfill his racialized destiny as conqueror. Sailor Jack, in Western military clothing, kills one crocodile, tames another, disciplines Sambo, and wins Mrs. Smith in record time, demonstrating the rewards of invasion.

In addition to appropriating resources, various entertainments show an interest in appropriating the supposed mysteries of "Oriental" or "Eastern" characteristics in the fashion described by Said. The Middle and Far East, for middling Americans, represented a world governed by wisdom, stateliness, balance, but also a barely controlled passion. Such characterizations are especially reminiscent of the tales of *Arabian Nights,* which appear as a major source of inspiration for exotic tales and plays. *The Sociable,* perhaps the largest and most comprehensive entertainment manual of the period, was subtitled "1001 home amusements," suggesting its parallel to the thousand and one tales of *Arabian Nights* (with its suggestion of holding back barbarism with compelling and, in the end, civilizing storytelling). Many entertainment manuals mimic this formula, with their subtitles claiming the number of nights their entertainments will encompass.[46]

Celebrating the feminine exoticism associated with Oriental women was a popular enterprise among female Anglo players, from the numbers of Cleopatras, Rebeccas at the Well, Sultanas, Judiths, and Biblical queens represented in tableaux vivants. Even a mid-century text as seemingly demure as *Godey's* takes up the delights of "Eastern" beauty in an explanatory article on tableaux vivants, presented as a personal account of recent home entertainments. The article describes a company's evening of tableaux vivants, among them scenes of "the time of Cleopatra," "the quaint pageantry of the days of Elizabeth," "Puritan simplicity," and "Mary, Queen of Scots."[47] Yet among these sights, the writer notes, "the prettiest tableaux I ever saw or expect to see" was an "Eastern scene" of "Lalla Rookh." Drawing from Thomas Moore's 1817 poem, the scene depicts the famed princess, who is romantically influenced by her (disguised) future husband's passionate and romantic poems.

In the *Godey's* account, although the part of the Eastern beauty has been claimed by the young hostess, a self-absorbed Miss Lorimer, she appears ill suited for the role, given her "blue eyes and auburn ringlets," which render her "more like the pictures of the Grand Lama than the Princess of Cashmere," according to the author.[48] A young male participant, however, notices that a much younger, less assertive cousin of the hostess with dark curling hair and glowing eyes seems well suited to the Persian scene, but his observation is initially laughed off. When this young cousin, Florence, falls asleep on a velvet sofa before the tableaux vivants are to commence, interested viewers see a young girl with "an exquisitely moulded arm, around which her soft, dark tresses floated with the gentle evening air, was reposing, a crimson shawl lightly thrown over her on the velvet sofa, unconscious of the admiration she excited" (278). After adding the decadent accents of a "rich bracelet," "a string of pearls," and "a ruby necklace," Florence's admirers (including two young men) move the sofa onto a curtained stage, dress another woman as an attending Persian slave, and reveal the sleeping beauty to the audience (279). Florence's special admirer positions himself near the foot of the sofa, dressed as the poet/bethrothed, Feramorz.

While this scene is represented as unusually picturesque, the background of the story makes it clear that the young women who participate fetishize the Eastern beauty's role, squabbling over the luxurious fabrics, over the placement of successive tableaux, and over the notion of exotic beauty. The luxury and the strangeness of the scene hold great appeal for the women, despite their obvious suitedness to the English and Scotch roles also being presented. Further cementing the allure of a role indebted to exotic, romantic beauty is the action taken by the young men in the scene, who take advantage of demure young womanhood in order to transform Florence into an object of delight—sensual delight—for the scene's viewers. Hence the tale (one situated as a model event) culminates in the visual violation of the sleeper's inert body and in the illustration of the commanding nature of masculine admiration (and, along with it, feminine compliance to Eastern male authority, now assumed by the American men in attendance).

Along with the beauty of Eastern women, the supposed excesses and treachery of Eastern men held obvious fascination for the authors of entertainment texts. The power of a character such as Blue Beard is depicted as absolute, and serves as the subject of assorted tableaux vivants, charades, games, plays, and parlor operas.[49] Reveling in the character's mysterious and powerful attraction and simultaneously exposing the horror of his deeds, representations such as Sarah Annie Frost's "Blue Beard" (1868), situate the tale in contemporary England.[50] Blue Beard's difference from the Anglos appears immediately through his appearance, since he is dressed in elaborate Oriental clothing and, perhaps more significantly, appears slightly blue, which stands as a visual reminder of cultural and moral difference. Frost's play emphasizes this fact as his betrothed ("Lady Emmeline") admits, "At first, I own, I felt a prejudice against a beard of so strange a hue . . . ," but her fears are overcome by the man's good taste in music and food, evidence of his supposed adoption of Western traditions.[51] The play continues, focusing on the rumors surrounding the count (Blue Beard), the count's engagement to a young woman, his sumptuous home, his warning to his wife not to open the closet door, her temptation, gaining admittance, the gory closet, the bloodying of the bride's hands, her husband's return and consequent wrath, and the final rescue of the terrified wife, Emmeline, by her brothers. The young wife's horror and the gruesome spectacle of the murdered wives (seen by Emmeline and the tableaux audience) vividly attest to Blue Beard's power, which is heightened by his dispassion for his victims, his insistence on obedience, and his distaste for all conventional forms of order.

Despite the text's profound fascination with Blue Beard's power, he, like the "Fejee" Islanders, is conquered by the Anglo men who arrive at the end of the play, for they strike down Blue Beard as he attempts to execute his young wife. She has unlocked not only a door, but, with it, physical proof of Blue Beard's barbarism. With Blue Beard dead, his house and character are opened up for plundering. The play, however, ultimately attempts to mark a distinction between Western and Eastern forms of male power; the Western man, the play suggests, is violent only when the order of the world rests on his intervention, with predatory violence projected onto the machinations of the racial "other."

Although Blue Beard was soundly defeated in his appearances in the nineteenth-century parlor, it is impossible to dismiss his prevalence. As much as he offered participants in parlor play the opportunity to indulge in racialized fantasies of cruelty and conquest, he also represented a model of self-control as he managed to conceal his true evil with charming manners and good taste. His ubiquity in nineteenth-century representations, then, can be attributed to his dual intersections with genteel life. He is at once a genteel culture's exaggerated ideal and its worst nightmare, for while Blue Beard renders other bodies grotesque, his own deviance remains hidden, concealed under a skillful, polite facade. Yet his self-control has its limits, for he does kill, as the play suggests, with a violence that separates him from Western men.

As with other figures of the grotesque, Blue Beard offered parlor players the opportunity to invoke an exaggerated figure who overturned ideals of self-control by too nearly embodying the mechanisms on which a genteel social order was constructed. Acting out Blue Beard thus represented a means of both condemning and, at the same time, inhabiting a rebellion against an overtly "civilized" nineteenth-century culture.

The situation explored through invocations of Blue Beard as well as through other "foreign" figures was twofold in that it sought to excise non-Anglo individuals from the upwardly striving middling classes at the same time that these activities permitted participants in play a means of resisting the virulently "civilizing" effects of bourgeois life. A mid-nineteenth-century fascination with the racialized, imperial grotesque consequently appears as an ultimate exercise of imperialism, for it invited inhabitants of the parlor to consolidate genteel lifestyles and, simultaneously, to enrich the identity of a homogeneous group by appropriating (though condemning) other lifestyles. With the imperial version of the grotesque, the boundaries around genteel life become most apparent, for such activities reconfigure the complexities of genteel control over self-representations, thereby asserting the solidarity of genteel, white, middle-class traditions.

Conclusion: The Fate of the Grotesque

Grotesque transformations highlight the difficulty of altering customary behaviors to suit individual, idiosyncratic, or exaggerated interests as they point out the ways that grotesque forms depended upon the processes of gentility for their referential value even as they challenged the customs of genteel interactions. By purposefully fracturing genteel bodies and overturning social traditions, grotesque transformations disrupted the overwhelming completeness of the genteel enterprise, physically and behaviorally, even though the resulting alterations were momentary and any ensuing change was ultimately absorbed by the hegemonic imperatives represented by ideals of skill and cultural superiority. In this sense, the grotesque functioned as a spectacle of inversion, as a testing ground for individualized reinventions that represented the temporary rejection of everyday norms. As parlor play continued to evolve, the grotesque became a particularly recognizable tradition, its familiarity muting the promise of substituting individualized forms for established norms. Its claims to inversion and to oppositional stances, then, were absorbed into a tradition of the parlor and of middling social spectacles, becoming as much an axis of the middling experience as the captured, contained Blue Beard. Historically, then, the power of the grotesque was short lived, for grotesque spectacles, whether of severed heads, unsocial beings, or non-Western figures, could not function as disruptions once their mechanisms were widely known. Inasmuch as grotesque forms of play exposed the elaborate work behind socially produced bodies, including mannered facades, they also limited its long-term potential, for once Blue Beard's closet no longer held a mystery, the spectacle was robbed of its necessary shock value.

Gradually, too, more genteel forms of play replaced outrageous grotesque displays, judging from the trends visible in entertainment guide books. As middle-class lifestyles took a more definite shape in the postbellum decades, resisting gentility became less of an entertaining social event. While there is no single factor that led either to the grotesque's strange emergence in parlor life or its gradual disappearance, it is the complexity of the grotesque that remains most arresting. Its doubleness, or its paradoxically disruptive means of augmenting genteel constructions, highlights the complications embedded in exposing genteel expectations, complications born of operating from within gentility's boundaries.

4
Skills Rewarded
Women's Lives Transformed through Entertainment

While entertainment guide manuals provide evidence of clear patterns and changing trends in home entertainment, they are augmented by another type of narrative about entertainment—that appearing in nineteenth-century fiction. Fictional renderings of leisure enterprises, which often appear as lengthy and contextualized portrayals of games and theatricals, argue for the value of engaging in home entertainment. These narratives also assert that skilled participation in leisure enterprises could transform the lives of play's votaries. Contextualizing home entertainments within the lives of middling women, particularly those who seek a kind of domestic security that initially appears unlikely, fictions that detail lengthy scenarios of skilled play typically end with scenes of triumph. Their narrative is clear: skilled play showcases a heroine's self-command and displays her admirable abilities, allowing her an unprecedented, yet richly deserved social ascent.

Fictive scenarios of skilled play argue that for middling women (those persons most likely to promote and arrange home entertainment) leisure employments offered a specialized and fulfilling type of work that was at once congruent with the social life of a class, as well as personally transformative. According to novels of the 1840s through the 1860s, the triumphs of play could be translated into lasting security and would result in personal distinction, marriage, and affluence. These are the master plots, then, that portrayed middling women—or women without distinguished heritages, families, or protectors—as attracting admirers and infiltrating elite social tiers. These are women who gain or exhibit what Bourdieu terms "a feel for the game," who acquire a confidence in their facility and who recognize their potential for belonging in the social sphere where play has so significant a part.[1] Appearing at a time when middling women's work scarcely extended beyond paid companionship and children's instruction, suggestions that skilled social interaction could transform women's lives inscribed an unusual degree of personal agency; these tales also provided a value judgment that ranged well beyond morality and charity, the more usual axes for determining feminine worth.[2] In the two texts that I examine in detail here (two early renderings of entertainment's transformative potential for middling-to-marginal women), the heroines are both governesses, whose modestly remunerated and socially undistinguished professions contrast with what the fictions portray as their "real" abilities, their interpretive and acting skills.

I begin with Charlotte Brontë's *Jane Eyre* (1847) and its paradigm of unlikely social ascent, which serves as a prototype for later treatments of entertainment's skills. As a text voraciously consumed by Americans, *Jane Eyre* sets the tone for the American version of the entertainment scene, particularly in its merging of class and ability narratives. In its insistence that recognizable abilities challenge older class structures, *Jane Eyre* functions as a precursor of the later nineteenth-century narratives attached to entertainment scenes, introducing arguments that Louisa May Alcott's novella, "Behind a Mask" (1866), exaggerates and extends. Like Brontë's novel, "Behind a Mask" presents a disenfranchised governess who will triumph by exercising profound abilities during the events of home entertainment, for the dynamic power infusing Jean Muir's skills allows Alcott's protagonist to attack inherited privilege. Reflecting a greater comfort with the notion of social transformation and depicting an American disdain for aristocratic standing, Alcott's novella supports the idea that skills not only substitute for privilege, but also conquer elitism in combative scenarios.

Skilled characters such as Jane Eyre and Jean Muir are much more than working women who challenge the aristocrats around them. They are also domestic women whose interpretive skills afford them the unique opportunity to assert their abilities so as to reorganize an existing social landscape at a time when the power of an aristocratic class is visibly waning (although to different degrees, in Brontë's and Alcott's eyes). Part of the excitement surrounding these narratives centers on the cultural appropriation of entertainment by middling women, which (these texts suggest) offered them a way to assert their judgments and abilities. Especially when we consider the constraints governing unmarried women without family or fortune, the skilled behavior showcased during entertainment episodes offers a serious corrective to legacies of power that permitted male and aristocratic voices to set social agendas. Moreover, renderings of entertainment in fiction assert that women could appear feminine and self-determined, or conventionally social-ized at the same time that they could wield considerable power in determining their own fates and in countering class prejudices. Challenging portraits of feminine reticence, muted agency, and moral caretaking, entertainment scenes project successes for their focal characters, not just limited to the temporal encounters on the stage, but permeating their daily lives.

Granting permanence to home entertainment's promises was its link to another form of leisurely pursuit—the novel itself. As one of the primary sites of popular entertainment, the novel, as Cathy Davidson has suggested, mediated readers' political participation in the early republic.[3] By the mid-nineteenth century, popular entertainments, the novel included, continued to mediate individuals' relations to larger groups. Entertainment, in the broadest sense, continued to propel the politically constitutive act of claiming the right to leisure time that was so important in defining the middling classes. As readers engaged in their own form of entertainment encountered portraits of women who benefited so visibly from their own leisurely pursuits of charades, tableaux vivants, and acting, the act of reading was legitimated as transformative, rendering entertainment an important new arena for remaking personal identity. I am suggesting, then, that a significant by-product of novelistic entertainment stemmed from the textual presentation of the pleasures of watching, interpreting, and participating (the modes of engaging home entertainments), which in turn facilitated "a literal form of re-representation," as Said describes the mechanisms of affiliation.[4]

In addition, novelistic renderings of entertainment scenes focus on individual participation, highlighting the interplay of individual and collective interests, a dynamic that the whole enterprise of home entertainment had dramatized since its beginnings. Layering an individual subjectivity onto the field of play, fictional accounts of contest stress personal histories, romantic preferences, individual abilities, and the occasional social hostilities as a means of creating an individualized portrait of the middling experience. Most powerfully, here, the boundaries of class-inflected experience are figured in the observations, determinations, and spectacles of the individual player.

Reading for Entertainment

As renderings of entertainment's possibilities, fictional depictions of leisure practices argue for the potential of upward mobility as they chart the successes of able competitors possessed of keen interpretive skills. That such arguments were advanced through fiction lends them a narrative specificity and force that entertainment guide books, with their generic and succinct explanations, could not achieve. Entertainment guides, which saturated the Anglo-American textual market during and after the mid-nineteenth century, were printed at low cost and then pirated, excerpted, and circulated through popular magazines and weeklies. From the popularity of such publications, it is likely that many social-minded Americans of the mid-to-late century encountered entertainment texts in some form or another, despite the fact that many readers may never have seen *The Sociable* or subscribed to *Godey's Lady's Book.*

Despite the temptation to assume that fictional representations of entertainment functioned merely as didactic guides, there are numerous unanswered questions about how fictional portrayals of entertainment affected their readers. It is impossible, for example, to determine the degree to which interests in entertainment affected the purchase or reading of those tales with extended representations of entertainment. We can position fictions about entertainment as drawing from a notable cultural practice, but we cannot assume that readers approached novels such as *Jane Eyre* with this interest in mind. While someone who purchased a text such as *Home Pastimes* likely knew that she was buying a book about entertainment, probably anticipating advice, a reader who approached "Behind a Mask" could not know that she would be reading about entertainment. Additionally, it is impossible to assume that a novel reader, otherwise absorbed by the events of a plot, would begin to read solely for knowledge about entertainment practices at a particular juncture. And since, for example, Gwendolen Harleth's attempts at tableaux in *Daniel Deronda* are ludicrously, naively self-promoting, descriptions of her efforts may not have prompted imitators in the same way that a more generic set of directions may have. Such details remind us that while fictive entertainment episodes reveal the cultural currency of entertainment, they could not inscribe that currency in the same way that didactic books could.

The potential impact of novelistic representations of entertainment is also difficult to chart because of the immeasurable effect of fictions on their readers, particularly in light of the many possible relations between readers and the social practices represented by fiction. Novels and stories, which, in general, demanded a higher level of literacy than guide books, likely had fewer able readers; fictions, nonetheless, may have had more resonant effects than didactic guides, based on the texts' portrayal of rich, contexualized details. But it is also worth noting that fictions may deploy references to entertainment in order to critique middling ideologies or to expose the limited social insight or flawed morals of a particular character. Yet, a novel's critique may well have had little bearing on a reader's response to entertainment practices. It is possible to empathize with the heroine of *Jane Eyre* and yet admire the lovely Blanche Ingram's appearance as a "bride" in tableau. Within the nineteenth-century novel, levels of critique and character-oriented detail all had the potential to affect the reception of entertainment, but in highly individual ways and based on a reader's particular understanding of fiction's complexities.

One of the main argumentative trajectories infusing home entertainment scenes, across various mid-century texts, was an insistence that the middling classes should be defined through more than mercantile dominance, more than urban and suburban growth, and more than economic demographics, but primarily via cultural work. Among the portraits of fictional home entertainment are scenarios of the gaming at the Woodhouse residence (from *Emma*), Zenobia's "Veiled Lady" narrative tableaux (*The Blithedale Romance*), the March sisters' attic dramas (*Little Women*), a parlor social at Ma Smith's boardinghouse (*Contending Forces*), and Miriam Rooth's parlor acting exhibitions (*The Tragic Muse*), along with representations of tableaux vivants from Norris's *The Pit* and Wharton's *The House of Mirth* (discussed in chapter five). These are among the detailed fictional scenes of play that lavishly attest to the dynamism of entertainment.

Accounts of entertainment perform a specialized function, showing up as recognizable set pieces, or uniform structures in nineteenth-century fiction. These paradigmatic representations of entertainment typically appear in stand-alone chapters of novels and novellas, displaying interactions among multiple characters, dialogue interlaced with lengthy descriptions, references to literary or historical figures, and long sequences of action and interpretation. They are both complicated plot episodes and complex passages of reading. While arguing for the value of skilled play in characters' lives, they also demonstrate the need for a kind of interpretive finesse that parallels characters' abilities, making public the private practice of a character's cognition. Proving a character's ability to assert her fittedness for distinction, entertainment scenarios not only theatricalize skills, but they more importantly *individuate* the methods and practices of skilled, interpretive play, both modeling accomplishment and demanding that readers, like characters, organize the various clues before them.[5]

As such scenes recount the intricacies of play, they also decelerate narrative time with accounts of continuous action and interaction, invoking a technique of focused time-space narration that M. M. Bakhtin terms the "chronotope."[6] By focusing on the events taking place in a discrete, structurally contained arena (a stage, a drawing room, a picnic green), the spatial sense of the narrative is also, in effect, consolidated and intensified, so that a scene's focus narrows, like the modern technology of a close camera shot.[7] Because of their narrative consolidation and their performative nature, I term these episodes entertainment "scenes."

Most often, scenes of the entertainment chronotope appear in the first third of a novel or novella, focusing on a less privileged character who has been thrust into an elite environment and who initially feels (and is perceived to be) disenfranchised. At such moments, Jane Eyre will interpret the charades at Rochester's home, while Jean Muir will act out startling dramatic roles. Wielding vast powers, whether real or imagined, such socially marginalized figures trounce the surrounding aristocrats, who appear complacent and inept. The landed gentry, moreover, are identifiable in their reluctance to compete, along with their mistaken assurance that they cannot be challenged by individuals whom they fail to acknowledge as social equals. In such a context, Brontë's Jane Eyre appears as a daring and able infiltrator, whereas Alcott's Jean Muir is portrayed as the crafty, practiced aggressor. Inasmuch as such characters offer us an attractive portrait of social dynamism, they define social success as linked to unique abilities rather than traditional privileges.

Acting Charades and Social Challenge in *Jane Eyre*

While Jane Eyre is dispossessed socially, she is already a competent reader when she arrives at Thornfield Hall, and Brontë's 1847 novel charts her increasing assurance in wielding her interpretive abilities. As *Jane Eyre* champions the upward mobility of skilled individuals, the novel reflects on a moment when, for the larger population, success depended upon opportunities for personal distinction. Implicitly, then, the text links Jane's social acclivity to a widespread realignment of values stemming from the rise of a mercantile middle class.[8]

By treating its protagonist as a consummate interpreter, the novel foregrounds Jane's familiarity with dominant cultural conventions, here represented by the charades episode at Thornfield Hall. The text also details Jane's efforts to stand aloof from the values held by an elite, aristocratic milieu that is more interested in wealthy marriages than in either skills or uniqueness. Via an emphasis on Jane's interpretive prowess, Brontë's novel raises the possibility that the kind of skills that Jane possesses are both self-empowering and seriously disruptive to existing class alignments. For skilled individuals such as Jane, the processes of interpretation both bind them to existing hermeneutic conventions and permit them to claim their uniqueness, allowing them to express their skills within socially acceptable forms.

While presenting the reader with a haunted house, family secrets, and mysterious references to an indecipherable past, the novel stresses the necessity of flexible, adaptable abilities. Every hieroglyphic is of utmost importance to socially and economically disenfranchised characters, who depend on their interpretive powers for their sense of self-worth and who must use every possible means to gain personal advantages. Jane's interpretive skills thus appear as the logical means of an underrated individual's (as well as a marginalized class's) rise. Appearing during Jane's days at Thornfield Hall, the entertainment scene demonstrates Jane's interpretive prowess—both to Jane and to the novel's readers, constituting a sign of Jane's social daring, for at this historical juncture, charades would have been both new and somewhat controversial.

In their popular mid-century form, "acting charades" constituted a peculiar species of entertainment, contrasting with older modes of linguistic games simply known as "charades." Before the mid century, popular entertainments entailed the reading of rhymed, poetic lines, with participants trying to guess first the individual syllables, then the whole words. Depending on a limited array of literary and linguistic forms of play, early nineteenth-century home entertainment genres included puzzles, textual charades, and various other forms of nondemonstrative activity such as enigmas, transpositions, logogriphs, rebuses, acrostics, and queries, or activities that were rooted in word play, letter scrambling, and homophonic puns rewarding textual prowess.

Whereas later, mid-century guide books would challenge the parameters of gentility with boisterous play, unsocial bodies, and various impolite behaviors, earlier manuals present textual, linguistic play as a marker of status. Texts such as Samuel Tizzard's *The New Athenian Oracle, or Ladies' Companion* (1806) overtly emphasize the aristocratic associations of textual play, suggesting a consolidated audience for the book. Describing readers as discreet and learned, Tizzard presents his text as a faithful as well as exclusive companion, promising, "May you, dear Ladies, be blest with some gentle, wise, and faithful *friend*, pleasing and pleased with each other, pass through the busy and the amusing *scenes* of life; neither *captivated* by the one, nor *anxious* for the other."[9] Other examples of the text as an exclusive companion include *The Sphinx or Allegorical Lozenges* (1812):

In hopes my young Readers an hour to amuse,
I offer this Volume for them to peruse;
There's mirth for the wit, and work for the brains,
When they try to unravel the stores it contains.

If *Riddles* they like, a number they'll find.
To puzzle their senses whenever inclin'd;
If classical learning they've study'd with care,
The *Enigmas* will presently make it appear;
or if lighter *Charades* the fair Ladies require,
Turn over the leaves and they'll find their desire. . . . [10]

Focusing on ready wit, the similar activities outlined in *The Sphinx*—logogriphs, anagrams, questions, and transpositions—are for both the composition and interpretation of various literary genres. Such linguistically oriented activities bespeak a consolidated notion of what counts as entertainment; they also illustrate a focused understanding of an audience invested in aristocratic ease. By contrast, the physicality of mid-century forms of play would invite the middling orders into an expanded mode of gentility, where presumptions about grace, ease, and social prominence appear less frequently than allusions to prowess, dynamism, and competition.

Whereas linguistic modes of play held a prominent place in English guide books of the 1830s and '40s (and slightly later in the United States), subsequent and more daring versions of charades expanded so as to involve the gestures of pantomime, thus requiring bodily hieroglyphics. This shift in practice corresponds with a dramatic growth in entertainment manuals for middling adults, for whom physical activities came to substitute for classical wordplay. In the case of acting charades, a key word or phrase would be divided into syllables, which were pantomimed individually; these sequential scenes were usually followed by a "charade of the whole," or a physical representation of the "whole word" or answer. At times, homonyms complicated the clues. "Attenuate," for example, could be revealed as a scene showing the action, "at ten you ate." Combining linguistic and pantomime skills, acting charades demanded that viewers constantly translate between language and action, text and performance.

In the context of the mid century, the evolution of entertainment forms toward physicality reflects the middling classes' (and especially middle-class women's) encounters with new cultural avenues such as the public theater, which reinforced an interest in the physical interpretation of textual scripts. It was not until this historical juncture that attending the public theater came within the reach of a respectable middle-class audience. Theater scholars and cultural historians of both Britain and the United States have cited entrepreneurs' attempts to feminize their audiences with "middlebrow" events such as matinees, lyceums, and museum shows, pointing to theater owners' attempts to emphasize the emergent professionalism of acting.[11] As they flocked to commercial theaters, audience members began to take an interest in "theatrical" amusements in the home as well.[12] From the early years of the nineteenth century, home entertainment forms grew to include a broad repertory of acting charades, home theatricals, and tableaux vivants, all of which implicitly challenged the consolidated elitism of textual play.

Despite the professional theater's sanctioning of women's viewing as culturally legitimate and home entertainment texts' treatment of domestic acting as fashionable, acting charades were greeted with only qualified enthusiasm by the entertainment guides first representing them. Before detailing the rules for the new activity, the Mayhew Brothers' *Acting Charades or Deeds Not Words* (1850), presents a history of charades that highlights the activity's supposed "foreign" origin, revealing a pronounced ambivalence for the new entertainment genre, noting that "The French have made themselves singularly famous by their '*petits jeux*' as they call them. Their inability to sit still for more than half an hour has forced them to invent a long list of amusing exercises for locomotion. . . . "[13] Rhetorically transporting charades across cultures and geographical divisions, the text gradually dislodges acting games from a French context and incorporates them into the most "sainted" and historical of British traditions, contending:

> Lately, the game has been introduced into the drawing-room of a few mirth-loving Englishmen. Its success has been tremendous. Cards have been discarded; and a blind man's bluff, forfeits, and hunting the ring has been utterly abandoned. On Christmas day, it has been looked forward to and entered into with as much energy as the sainted plum-pudding itself. We have seen it played among literary circles with unbounded mirth. We have seen philosophers and poets either acting their parts with all the enthusiasm of school-boys, or puzzling their brains to find out how they could dress as Henry V, with only a great coat and a "gibus."[14]

Mid-century novels such as Thackeray's *Vanity Fair* (1847–48) just as carefully define the rules of play for acting charades, historicizing the new activity by noting, "At this time the amiable amusement of acting charades had come among us from France: and was considerably in vogue in this country, enabling the many ladies amongst us who had beauty to display their charms, and the fewer number who had cleverness, to exhibit their wit."[15] This introduction is followed by a narration that attempts to familiarize readers with the processes of the game, using separate paragraphs to correspond with subsequently pantomimed syllables. The text also records the characters' guesses at the appropriate moments. The most important clue, "AGAMEMNON," appears in all caps, allowing the reader to follow along with the processes of play, syllable by syllable. In *Jane Eyre*, too, acting charades are represented as a new and fairly alarming activity. And although the "foreign" origins of the game are not explicitly addressed (as they are in Thackeray's *Vanity Fair*), Brontë ascribes a French flair to charades, which accounts for their appeal to exotic participants such as Adele and Miss Ingram. Notably, like their French precedents, the charades at Thornfield Hall are associated with upper-class players and take place in an elite circle from which the Ingrams pointedly want to bar Jane because of what they see as her servile position.

Yet Jane will "read" events more carefully than the aristocratic players, thereby reorienting the issue of cultural authenticity to the use of skills rather than the cultural antecedents of play. In Jane's mastery of guessing the charades clues, Brontë suggests that charades were candidates not only for cultural appropriation by the British, but also by marginalized characters such as Jane, who base their notions of self-worth on skills rather than status. During the game, Jane will appear as a skilled viewer, although she will not participate by acting. Jane plays well, not in spite of, but *because of* her physical and ideological distance from the aristocratic players and "their" amusement, thereby reinvesting the vehicle of her ascendancy with a politically disruptive potential. Via Jane's interpretive successes, the novel posits that a seemingly disenfranchised viewer can assume prominence during the contests of play, investing a popular practice with the potential to reorganize an existing social hierarchy.

The narration of the charades in *Jane Eyre* particularly calls attention to Jane's abilities as a textually and culturally literate reader, even as Jane notes her inexperience with acting charades:

> I wondered what they were going to do the first evening a change of entertainment was proposed: they spoke of "playing charades," but in my ignorance I did not understand the term. The servants were called in, the dining-room tables wheeled away, the lights otherwise disposed, the chairs placed in a semicircle opposite the arch. While Mr Rochester and the other gentlemen directed these alternations, the ladies were running up and down stairs ringing for their maids. Mrs Fairfax was summoned to give information respecting the resources of the house in shawls, dresses, draperies of any kind.[16]

Although inexperienced with the game and emotionally unsettled by what will appear to be a bold assertion of Rochester's matrimonial intentions to-

ward Blanche Ingram, Jane nonetheless forces herself to interpret the events
of play. She also overhears Lady Ingram announce that "[Jane] looks too stu-
pid for any game of the sort," a comment that sets up a contest of analytical
abilities structured along class lines (160). Accordingly, the narration follows
Jane's facility as a literate interpreter who outshines the aristocrats.

As Jane interprets the successive charades, she also reveals the novel's vision of successful matrimony, a vision that ultimately supports Jane and Rochester's union. The first scene of the charade depicts the first syllable of the
word "Bridewell." In the charades that follow, "bride," "well," and finally,
"Bridewell" prison (a "charade of the whole") will appear. The sequence of
these scenes is especially significant, for the romantic felicity of a wedding is
undercut by scenarios that question individuals' motives for marriage. This
set of connections is all the more significant because of Rochester's participation in all three scenes, and his intended's (Blanche Ingram's) in the first
two. As the charade traces the possible fate of such a marriage, its underlying
commentary warns romantically attached women like Jane to beware the
consequences of hasty and uninformed alliances.

The initial charade scene, "bride," features Rochester as groom and Miss
Ingram as the "magnificent figure" of a bride, "clad in white, a long veil on
her head, and a wreath of roses round her brow" in the "dumb show" of the
marriage ceremony (160). Interspersed with the actual event is a narrative
attending to Jane's interpretation, for we are told that "A ceremony followed,
in dumb show, in which it was easy to recognize the pantomime of a marriage" (178). The pantomime causes Jane to focus on Rochester's reasons for
choosing Miss Ingram as a wife, culminating in Jane's assertion that Miss
Ingram is "too inferior to excite the feeling of jealousy," a claim reminiscent
of Jane's earlier attitude toward her similarly privileged and equally obtuse
Reed cousins (163). Jane goes on to detail the character defects of Rochester's
intended, noting that:

> She was very showy, but she was not genuine: she had a fine person,
> many brilliant attainments; but her mind was poor, her heart barren
> by nature; nothing bloomed spontaneously on that soil; no unforced
> natural fruit delighted by its freshness. She was not good; she was not
> original: she used to repeat sounding phrases from books: she never
> offered, nor had, an opinion of her own. (163)

After establishing the "magnificent" beauty's shallowness, Jane turns her attention to issues of skill, finding Miss Ingram lacking in the sorts of analytical interests and interpretive opinions in which she herself delights. In Jane's
eyes, Miss Ingram merely mimics what she reads. Flawed in one of the most

elementary levels of interpretation, Miss Ingram is also inept in the language of gestures, especially Rochester's. This inability, moreover, seems inextricably linked to Blanche's complacent, aristocratic hauteur. Because she has no need to be competitive (as do characters in less affluent positions), she lacks Jane's self-awareness.

When Jane observes that "*she could not charm him,*" she emphasizes Miss Ingram's inability to read Rochester. Miss Ingram remains, as Jane notes, "herself unconscious that [her actions] did fail; vainly fancying that each shaft launched hit the mark, and infatuatedly pluming herself on success, when her pride and self-complacency repelled further and further what she wished to allure—to witness *this*, was to be at once under ceaseless excitation and ruthless restraint" (164). Calling attention to her own superior abilities, by contrast, Jane contends that "when she failed, I saw how she might have succeeded" and that "without weapons, a silent conquest" of Rochester is indeed possible, if managed by an observant as well as literate lover (164). This suggestion leads to the conclusion that only a literate individual reads character well enough *to* love. Seeing the possibility for her own "silent conquest," Jane lays claim to the hieroglyphic world of interaction represented by the acting charades.

Jane's abilities mark her not only as a consummate interpreter, but also as Rochester's appropriate mate, a contention that Rochester later confirms as he tells Jane (after their disastrous and incomplete first wedding) that his interest had been piqued by her "keen," "daring," and "glowing" eyes, which disclosed a "penetration and power in each glance" (276). In short, he recognizes in Jane an interpreter much like himself.[17] The text confirms this idealized model of companionship, for both Rochester and Jane appear as surveillents, keenly interested in visual representation, as excellent readers who not only consume texts, but also actions, enthusiastically discussing and debating their impressions.[18]

With its predictions for the future thus tethered to an investigation of Jane's abilities, the novel details the ways that Jane interprets the pantomimes before her. Refocusing after a discussion of Miss Ingram's flaws, Jane decisively notes in the second scene, "It was Eliezer and Rebecca: the camels only were wanting," quoting a line from the Old Testament to prove her knowledge of the allusion (161). With a set of ready textual references, Jane is poised to expand upon her interpretive prowess. The narrative then turns to the scene of the second syllable, "well," where Jane observes an "Eastern" scene, with Rochester bedecked with a turban, "looking the very model of an Eastern emir," and Miss Ingram appearing in an "Oriental attire" that "suggested the idea of some Israelitish princess of the patriarchal days" (161). The scene, as Jane immediately recognizes, is that of Rebecca at the well; Abraham has sent a servant to his homeland to find a wife for his son Isaac. When Rebecca offers water, she is rewarded with gold bracelets and other treasures that serve as evidence of her future husband's social standing and as a sign of her betrothal. Rather than emphasizing the virgin's good temper in providing water, as does the biblical version of the story, Brontë's rendition of the scene turns its attention to the material offerings that seal the marriage promise, noting:

From the bosom of his robe he then produced a casket, opened it and showed magnificent bracelets and earrings; she acted astonishment and admiration; kneeling, he laid the treasure at her feet; incredulity and delight were expressed by her looks and gestures; the stranger fastened the bracelets on her arms, and the rings in her ears. (161)

While the first charade scene led to Jane's contemplation of Rochester's motives for marriage, the "well" pantomime is calculated to raise speculation as to Miss Ingram's. Based on Jane's careful interpretation, readers of the text see that Miss Ingram's charms are not as beneficent as those of the Biblical maid who serves the travelers. With Miss Ingram, however, the riches that secure the betrothal are much more in evidence. While Jane correctly estimates Blanche Ingram's character flaws (including the lady's lust for wealth, which is later borne out by her coolness when Rochester is rumored to be less wealthy than believed), she nonetheless misreads the purpose of the charade itself, believing that it bespeaks Rochester's interest in Blanche. What is not obvious to Jane is Rochester's plan to incite her jealousy.[19] It is here, then, that Jane's interpretive limitations become clear, for readers can ascertain only upon a second reading how prescient the charades are.

Having commented on the motives behind the presumed Rochester-Ingram match, the narration turns to the possible consequences of marriage, asserting a cautionary note about noncompanionable unions. Representing the "tableaux of the whole," or the word "Bridewell," the final charade reveals a "sordid scene" in which a begrimed, desperate, maimed, and scowling Rochester sits fettered in a prison cell. Desperate and friendless, the figure suggests that unhappy unions can make prisoners as well as criminals of spouses, an argument born of this scene's relationship to the two pantomimes on marriage and courtship. Providing a parallel to later portrayals of Rochester's incarcerated first bride, Bertha Mason, this scene depicts Rochester's emotional imprisonment as the counterpart to Bertha's physical bondage. The recognition that loveless marriages create prisons, however, is for the reader to acknowledge—not for Jane to assess.

While the novel points to Jane's interpretive success and while Jane is pleased with her viewing, her limits as an interpreter are nonetheless visible at such moments. Believing that she has inferred the motivations behind the "bride" charade, Jane confidently oversteps her actual knowledge in reading the charades. In light of Rochester's history, which is available only on a second reading, the figure of Rochester trapped and chained in his prison cell is more eloquent on the subject of marriage than even the observant Jane could imagine, for it foreshadows the maiming of Rochester in the Thornfield Hall fire. His appearance as a criminal additionally highlights his lawless tendency toward unsanctioned alliances, a circumstance soon proven by his attempted sham marriage to Jane.

Clearly, the interpretive possibilities hosted by such a scene challenge even the most able (and confident) of viewers. In pointing to the usefulness, indeed the necessity of careful, multifaceted interpretation to a woman of Jane's situation—whose cultural savviness allows her to feel that she participates fully in the activity of play—Brontë argues that a complex mode of interpretive prowess can be wielded as an important tool among liminal individuals. As a formidable skill, interpretive prowess highlights the merits of those who are culturally—if not socially—superior. By placing an extraordinary emphasis on skills, the entertainment scene sets up the expectation that Jane, as an able interpreter, will penetrate a closed system of privilege, that her skills are significant enough to decenter aristocratic claims to status.

There are, however, significant limits to the revolutionary edge of Brontë's vision. The potential associated with Jane's skill is overshadowed by Rochester's secret marriage, which is of such magnitude that Jane's skills cease to matter in an immediate way. A second and more important erasure of skills' potential occurs when Jane is recognized as an heiress in a plot development that supplants a narrative of personal ascendancy with a tale of familial restoration. Hence, once Jane is recognized as a moderately wealthy gentlewoman (as she is by her cousin, St. John Rivers), her abilities (once cast as unique) are recuperated as a sign of her aristocratic lineage. Jane's drive for acculturation, for example, once seemingly born of her individual love of learning, emerges as an emblem of a submerged upper-class heritage characterizing the entire Rivers family.

This recasting of Jane's interpretive prowess significantly blunts the edge of class-based competition in Brontë's depiction of skills. Thus in the end, *Jane Eyre* launches a narrative of hierarchical affirmation rather than a story of class inversion, for Brontë's approach to privilege is limited to those who can claim elevation by both behavior *and* birth. Neither interpretive abilities (which allow Jane to sense her self-worth) nor the higher social realms (which Jane will join) can be dismissed. While the novel highlights the fact that Jane has gained entrance to her rightful social plane via practices of attention and interpretation (that middling women, the book suggests, could adopt to improve their standing), it ultimately fails to fulfill its implied promise that skills lead to class-specific infiltration, for those once-restrictive class lines eventually dissolve for Jane, the restored gentlewoman.

The Socially Disruptive Potential of Skills

In Louisa May Alcott's 1866 "Behind a Mask," interpretive skills appear at the center of a plot that dramatizes class warfare rather than reinstatement as Alcott exaggerates the class-based tensions characterizing Brontë's depiction of entertainment practices. Thus the disruptive potential of interpretive prowess, which is retracted by the end of *Jane Eyre*, is fully and explosively realized in Alcott's later thriller. The novella pits an even more marginalized character (who is an actress and divorcee *masquerading* as a governess) against aristocrats who are much less astute than Rochester and who prove no match for the wily and talented Jean Muir. This governess's past is ultimately revealed no less dramatically than Brontë calls attention to Jane Eyre's inheritance. In Alcott's tale of class-based aggression, however, Jean is discovered to be an accomplished pretender—a skilled woman rather than an educated member of the gentry. This exaggerated portrait of class relations reflects Alcott's interest in reinventing a system of privilege as she makes use of an elite tier, not to imagine that change must be filtered through aristocratic preferences (as does Brontë), but to question the very merit of the elites. Setting her tale in England, Alcott imagines that even the most solidly entrenched class boundaries can be dramatically overturned by a skilled competitor who counters Old World privilege with a revolution of skills, replacing social rank with personal ability.

The nearly twenty years separating *Jane Eyre* and its vituperative American cousin shed light on Alcott's exaggerations, for Alcott writes as a populous American middle class is exercising its influence professionally, commercially, and socially. Like this dynamic rising class, her character reveals a profound level of activity that prompts an upward ascent. Whereas Jane Eyre responded to the entertainments that she witnessed, silently affirming her individual sense of worth, Jean Muir will actively participate in play, just as she will direct her life, intentionally deceiving her aristocratic viewers so as to infiltrate their ranks. Jean Muir controls the impressions that she creates as she deliberately plays to the prejudices of her employers, gradually ensnaring the affections of three eligible bachelors, and eventually choosing to marry the most elderly and the most wealthy. Alcott's text contains one additional exaggeration of *Jane Eyre*'s basic plot, which makes clear Alcott's championing of a set of fully mobilized interpretive skills. Whereas Jane's abilities will be subsumed under a mantle of aristocratic superiority, Jean Muir remains a powerfully subversive individual who is never fully gentrified. Compared to other nineteenth-century fictions containing entertainment scenes, Alcott's "Behind a Mask" more obviously champions a woman's choice to act on her aggressively vertical class aspirations, in part because of the novella's disregard for conventional morality. Focused almost solely on ability, "Behind a Mask" stridently indicts gentility, linking it with competitive failure.

Whereas Jane Eyre envisioned herself outside of a genteel milieu as she wielded her penetrating acumen, she nevertheless participated in the entertainment without visibly or immediately altering the structures of privilege on which the performance of Rochester's private charades depend. Yet even when Jane believed herself to be operating out of a liminal position, this is when she was most deeply entrenched in a notion of genteel propriety that encompasses deference, femininity, and caregiving, ideals that are deeply compatible with privilege. Through its somewhat conflicted portrait of skills, however, the novel forecasts how important a truly disruptive appropriation of entertainment forms will be.

Extending the potential for combative class relations that *Jane Eyre* predicts, Alcott's thriller argues that it is possible for a thoroughly marginalized figure to challenge traditional privileges. With her combative skills, Jean Muir exploits her abilities with full self-knowledge of her social transgressions, for the thriller insists that Jean's skills are not only admirable qualities, but that they are, in fact, Jean's *only* positive attributes, for she has no family, no money, and no sympathetic personal history. In addition, she is utterly devoid of any redeeming love for the aristocrats who surround her; she tolerates and exploits them only to gain access to their privileges. Solely on the basis of skills (rather than character), Alcott positions the sham governess as rightfully deserving the material and psychological rewards that she earns. Throughout, Alcott's text delights in Jean's deliberate unconventionality and encourages readers to appreciate Jean because she is a duplicitous, manipulative, and aggressively self-interested woman who transforms interpretive insights into what the novella's subtitle terms "a woman's power."

A Tradition of Genteel Inability

Domestic theatricals become a tool for Alcott's protagonist, in part because there are relatively few social resources available to Jean Muir, given the multiple disenfranchisements that plague the disreputable divorcée; Alcott contends that Jean's future hinges upon her ability to wield a set of dramatic skills as a powerful means of claiming material and social security. More typically, in nineteenth-century texts with entertainment scenes, both too much and too little skill are portrayed as problematic. Skilled heroines are rarely positioned as sympathetic, as Thackeray's *Vanity Fair* reveals. Like Jean Muir, Thackeray's Becky Sharp acts successfully off as well as on stage, and like Jean, Becky is motivated by an overpowering desire for a luxurious lifestyle. Thackeray, however, situates talent in relation to a moral barometer, representing Becky's skills as proof of her duplicity. In its confirmation that the heroine is innately flawed, the novel points to women's dramatic acting as proof of a ruthless mode of personal advancement equal to marrying and murdering for money.

George Eliot's 1876 *Daniel Deronda* is similarly critical of its genteel would-be actress, particularly as the issue of talent emerges. Here Eliot portrays a mode of genteel inability that indicts Gwendolen Harleth's self-flattering ambitions as an actress and, at the same time, highlights her perceptual failures. In satirizing Gwendolen's utter lack of ability, Eliot reveals how a powerful notion of skills allowed even the most marginally able women to imagine that they could reinvent themselves through artistic expression. In the novel, Gwendolen participates in tableaux vivants in order to satisfy her interests in beauty and culture, fantasizing about a supposed talent for acting, even though "She had never acted,—only made a figure in tableaux vivants at school; but she felt assured that she could act well."[20] Attitudinizing "before a domestic audience" at Christmas, Gwendolen is certain that her talents will be met with general approval.[21]

Acting the part of Hermione, Gwendolen attempts to rouse emotion by stepping down and having Leontes kiss the hem of her garment (a ludicrous proposition from the beginning, since the scene would situate agency and emotion in the figure of Leontes). Indeed, by taking up the role of the passive Hermione, the long-suffering heroine of *The Winter's Tale* who has been impregnated, wrongly accused of adultery, condemned by an enraged husband/ monarch, transfixed by grief, hidden in secret for sixteen years, and immobilized as a statue for effect before appearing alive, Gwendolen acts out a predilection for wronged women, for nobility and its self-imposed tragedies, and for the secure closure of happy, if improbable, endings. In addition to suggesting the difficulty of carving out a career based on a passive figure in tableau, Gwendolen's invocation of Hermione illustrates her regard for victimized women, invoking many of the qualities of womanhood that later entertainment scenes rewrite. In the end, Gwendolen's characterization is convincingly emotional only because of an accident that provokes "an unforeseen phase of emotion," as a hidden panel in the wall moves so as to reveal the picture of a "dead face"; as a result, the viewers witness Gwendolen's real and horrified reaction to the external stimulus, even as Gwendolen "cherishes the idea" that her viewers have been struck by her talent.[22]

In Jean Muir, Alcott gives us a character having sympathetic vulnerabilities (later visible in Eliot's Gwendolen) as well as razor-sharp skills (à la Becky Sharp), creating a domestic actress who deploys well-honed abilities and who simultaneously desires domestic security. Compared to Gwendolen Harleth's genteel inability, Jean Muir embodies a genuinely skilled command of interpretive and dramatic abilities. And unlike the greedy, cunning Becky, Jean Muir reacts to more obvious circumstances of oppression, intervening in the stark inequalities of social life, decentering traditional ideals of privilege, but without resorting to murder.

As Alcott dwells on the details of Jean Muir's clever and seemingly endless attempts to manipulate a family of British aristocrats, Jean's careful attention to the gestures and intonations of those around her predict her success. Jean's ability to interpret nuance first appears as she preys on the sympathies and interests of her employers, the Coventry family. When compared with the complacent and inept aristocrats who employ her, Jean shines as more intuitive, more observant, and more dynamic. Presenting herself as a young orphan who faints away at the piano, waking with a plea to her dead mother, spoken in a "pretty Scotch accent," Jean immediately attempts to counter her employers' class prejudices.[23] During her time in the Coventry household, Jean interjects herself into family life by carefully reading the interests of various household members, noting daughter Bella's fondness for flowers, Edward's painful position as the second son, cousin Lucia Beaufort's love for her deceased mother, the heir Gerald's appreciation for good music, and the elderly Sir John's devotion to the British peerage. When she notes in Sir John the "slight change" in his countenance as Jean identifies herself as the governess rather than the aristocratic guest for whom he mistakes her, the text announces that "few would have perceived" the alteration in the old gentleman's demeanor, but "Miss Muir felt it at once, and bit her lips with an angry feeling at her heart" (109). This type of detail insists that Jean is a sensitive reader of attitude; it also predicts her wielding of a formidable vocabulary of action and gesture. Jean will manipulate her employers, the Coventrys, because they are only minimally invested in the personality and prejudices of a replaceable servant. Here, as in *Jane Eyre*, the socially ambiguous governess possesses skills that the landed gentry think they can afford to neglect.

Jean's skills are most visible as she converts her interpretations into decisive actions. One of her ploys is to reveal a barely restrained emotional depth to the sympathizing men around her. When observed by the elderly Sir John, for example, Jean bursts into "a passion of tears, like one who could bear restraint no longer," in order to arouse his interest (119). Jean's show of barely constrained emotion also results in "a curious quiver in her voice, and the look of one who forcibly suppressed some strong emotion," when witnessed by Gerald (123). As characters mistake Jean's sentiments for signs of her aristocratic sensitivity (for Jean drops hints that she is a peer's daughter), and interpret her passion as directed toward themselves, the reader learns that Jean's motivations include her hatred of the aristocracy. The aristocratic men who take pleasure in Jean's complementary and dependent role thus appear myopically self-interested, particularly in their failure to note Jean's depth.

Because Jean is sensitively able to play to the deficiencies of untutored viewers, the class alignments of Jean's dramatic actions are fascinatingly complex. If Jean's machinations lack subtlety, Alcott suggests that it is because she is playing to viewers whose entrenched elitism has obliterated their interpretive skills, allowing them to perceive only overstatement and exaggeration. Hence, Jean's display of violent, barely contained emotionality, which could be construed as a crude exaggeration, instead marks her class-conscious sense that only overt emotion will be visible to viewers who are unaccustomed to nuanced behavior. As part of her argument about the transformative power of skills, Alcott emphasizes the irony of equating inability with privilege and, by extension, skills with disenfranchisement. With her interpretive skills and her acting abilities, her literary pursuits and musical accomplishments, Jean appears better suited than her employers for a life of accomplished leisure.

Jean Muir's Command of Action

Through her rendering of the tableaux vivants that constitute the most dramatic display of Jean Muir's skills, Alcott insists on the necessity of action among economically and socially marginalized women. In making this argument, Alcott endows Jean's tableaux vivants with an unusual degree of agency, compared to many renderings of tableaux.[24] Like acting charades, tableaux vivants formed a popular staple of home entertainment practices throughout the latter half of the nineteenth century, requiring viewers and participants to read the legible body, including frozen pantomimes. Because of the elaborate settings and costumes that characterized many tableaux, they were often described as the most "artistic" of home entertainment activities, especially during their first flush of textual popularity in the 1860s.[25]

Among tableaux vivants, inspirational scenes were common, as in a direction for tableaux in *Harper's Monthly* of 1863, which is presented as a record of a recent display. "Tableaux Vivans" records a narrative about efforts to raise money for the Northern army.[26] After rolling bandages and folding compresses, a benevolent society comprised of women decides to "get up an entertainment—tableaux vivans, charades, and what not" (699). In keeping with the charitable nature of the society, the tableaux are to be varied with music and with a "spirited colloquy" (defined as a "compromise between a dialogue and a drama"), which will be composed by a local hero (699). The poses are researched in old magazines and engravings, and scenes will include a Queen of Sheba, a "gipsy fortune-teller," and, in grand finale, a tableau (arranged to resemble a statue) of "Hope." Much of the text concerns itself with the difficulties of preparation, including behind-the-scenes descriptions of the final display. Met with "exclamations of delight," the grand finale statue of "Hope, serenely leaning on her anchor, her exquisite arms and shoulders bare, her upturned face beaming with a subdued 'joyousness,'" is inspirational (703). As profound as the statue appears, however, the text's narrator notes that the young girl under layers of powder and sheets is ready to break into laughter. Despite the insider's view of events, the narrative makes it clear that the tableaux are appropriately effective and that money has been raised for the cause. The tableaux are, then, uniquely suited to blending aesthetic and inspirational ideals.

Typically, mid-nineteenth-century tableaux vivants, like those associated with the war benefit, depicted women as allegorical figures and recognizable works of art, especially during the 1860s and '70s (fig. 12). In many spectacles, figures were powdered to resemble statues, posed looking downward, barely breathing. Compared to these frozen displays, the entertainments that Jean Muir will so successfully co-opt range far beyond a display of the inert form, for Jean is a dynamic figure. Instead of depicting Jean in a situation where she needs to situate herself "appropriately" (as in the war benefit society), Alcott has Jean act to fulfill her desires. By inflecting tableaux with more action, Alcott provides her first indication that Jean will achieve unprecedented results as she reinvents the spectacle of tableaux.

Tableaux vivants have raised critical questions about the agency that they afforded the women who were so often their idealized subjects. Yet Alcott's text describes the "living pictures" in which Jean Muir appears as an essential

Fig. 12. An allegorical woman in tableau. Frontispiece from *Home Pastimes, or Tableaux Vivants* (Boston, 1867).

part of an aggressive social and economic ascent. Although Jean appears as a still figure, Alcott insists that Jean is more than a frozen beauty; she is an emotive actress who becomes a volatile agent.[27] Moreover, Jean controls her own representation, selecting scenes that effectively reveal her skills, acting and creating carefully crafted effects as part of her daily work of masquerading as a demurely fascinating governess.

Women, Agency, and Private Theatricals

Understanding the larger context for women's wielding of agency during home entertainment means stepping outside of the tableaux tradition so as to ascertain a fuller portrait of women's participation in theatrical enterprises. To a greater extent than tableaux, parlor theatricals comment on the circumstances that incite women to act, outlining domestic crises as a means of justifying subterfuge and deceitful behavior—or acting, in short. Such scripts, which would have circulated in middling homes at roughly the time of Alcott's thriller, situate Jean's acting and her pursuit of domestic security as comparable to the motivations facing the beleaguered heroines of domestic dramas.

Within the scope of parlor plays, those women who act, who attempt to control their fates, are at once frightening and compelling, vengeful yet sympathetic. In many cases they are coerced into unusual and deceptive subterfuge because of their lack of control over their day-to-day lives. These women of the dramatic scripts, published in entertainment guide books, sympathetically represent the potential of dramatic skills as occasioned by moments of domestic crisis. As it celebrates skills, Alcott's tale also attempts to justify Jean Muir's dramatic ploys by pointing to the dilemmas that provoke her actions, providing readers with an invitation to view her motivations as understandable. In both Alcott's thriller and in home theatricals, acting by domestic women appears as a response to extreme threats against romantic love, marriage, and financial security. While Alcott's story builds outward from the premise that acting skills allow women to protect domestic values, it also expands the conditions under which women's domestic acting could be seen as sympathetic, for Alcott validates the machinations of a subversive social agitator whom she endows with considerable power.[28]

Positioning domestic acting by women as a means of asserting feminine desires in a patriarchal world, many home theatricals focus on women's limited control over their local environments.[29] In this context, acting is portrayed as a suitable vehicle for the uplift of a whole class of domestic women. Focal characters in parlor entertainment scripts of the 1860s through the 1880s are usually middling women who find it necessary to draw upon methods of dramatic representation during moments of crisis. In these scripts, the quandaries experienced by women include prohibited love matches, desperate financial burdens, grave marital misunderstandings, and leave-takings forever—situations prompting exaggerated responses.[30] The moments of dramatic crisis in these scripts suggest that a powerful command of spectacle was increasingly seen as within the legitimate reach of even the most "ordinary" of women, with subterfuge allowing otherwise marginalized women the opportunity to alter their immediate situations in appropriately feminized ways. Deploying an indirection that shrouds their ambitions, women could safely enter the province of economic manipulation and social self-protection, much the way that Alcott's Jean Muir will. At issue with such figures is women's skilled acting so as to improve their lives. As she uses her skills to marry and join the elite social ranks, Jean Muir acts in a more extreme manner than the characters in most parlor theatricals, but in accord with the same set of motivations.

One play for home production, entitled *Stratagem*, by Sarah Annie Frost (1866), depicts a female character who is coerced into acting.[31] The plot revolves around a deception that ultimately results in a marriage; initially, however, the young heroine, Fannie, acts without skill. Only gradually does she learn to disguise her real emotions so as to deceive her guardian, who plans to marry her for her fortune. Fannie, however, has chosen a lover (Frank) and plans to elope with him. In its insistence that Fannie's ability to dissemble is essential to her happiness, the play presents three scenarios that chart Fannie's evolving dramatic skills. In each scene, Frank enters the house in some disguise so as to gain a private interview with her. He first dresses himself as a prominent geologist, then as an Oriental peddler, and finally, as a doctor of mesmerism, summoned to cure Fannie's illness. These three episodes, the last of which results in a successful elopement, show that Fannie only gradually learns to conceal her abundant enthusiasm for Frank and her distaste for her guardian, for it is she who gives away the first two stratagems.

In suggesting that only dissembling will allow Fannie to escape sexual and economic tyranny from a lecherous guardian, Frost's play argues forcefully for the benefits of acting as a counter to gendered injustice, but the script nonetheless remains ambiguous about women's theatrical skills, for it situates Fannie as a reluctant actress for whom dissembling is a last resort. Indeed, it is Fannie's faithful, lower-class maid who develops the three schemes (and who in fact imagines them much more vividly than Fannie can). Here, women's acting skills, however useful, are nonetheless depicted as externally motivated rather than produced through interest or talent, even as the scripts encourage middling women to develop their dramatic skills, balancing notions of provocation and ability.

Mrs. Mark Peabody's parlor play *Poor Cousins*, printed by the dime novel publisher Beadle (1880), portrays similarly coerced acting.[32] The play attempts to draw a distinction between problematic and reasonable forms of dissembling. At the play's opening, Mrs. Millefleur urges her daughter, Maude, to attract the admiration of her long-absent cousin, Felix Hartley, "the sole heir to the great Hartley fortune."[33] Mrs. Millefleur also directs Maude to conceal their financial disaster, which has resulted in near poverty for mother and daughter. Resolving that her daughter's marital hopes will not be compromised by the family's financial collapse, Mrs. Millefleur despairs that "I am almost distracted to know how to keep up proper appearances during his visit."[34] Setting forth the supposed need to "keep up" genteel appearances, Mrs. Millefleur and the selfish Maude (who is groomed and sewn for by her dependent cousin, Marion) demand that Marion act as their maid while Mr. Hartley visits. Both Maude and her mother argue that Marion will be merely amplifying her true role in the household, for as Mrs. Millefleur puts it, "What are you better than a servant? Have you not always been dependent on my bounty, from a child up?"[35] Although indignant, Marion complies, making it clear that she will take on this distasteful role only out of a sense of duty.

Unknown to the inhabitants of the Millefleur household, their visitor is their penniless cousin, Frank Hartley, who pretends to be his wealthy kinsman, Felix. Via subterfuge of his own, Frank plans to marry into the Millefleur fortune, still apparently intact as a consequence of the Millefleurs' duplicity. "Maid" Marion discovers Frank's true identity and subsequently attempts to reveal the truth to her aunt. Yet she is treated as an impertinent servant rather than a faithful niece, a sign that Mrs. Millefleur has erased the line between performance and reality as well as that between social ambition and good sense. Meanwhile Felix, the true millionaire, appears and is mistaken for the penniless Frank. Marion, bursting into tears, tells Felix about Frank and Maude's respective duplicities, but is too late to remedy the situation, for Frank and Maude have married secretly. In the final scene, Felix praises Marion's sense of duty and proposes to her, claiming that she "deserves" to be a millionaire's wife. Although fraught with contradictory tensions about the uses of women's acting, the play sanctions women's acting by negotiating between acting for selfish reasons and acting as a response to duty. Despite the play's indictment of the duplicities practiced by Mrs. Millefleur, Maude, and Frank, the script views Marion's reluctant acting more leniently, since it is undertaken as a duty, then discarded when Marion finds her role too distasteful.

According to these mid-century scripts, domestic acting was viewed as a powerful means of recalibrating the mechanisms of justice for women who are marginalized by inheritance laws and dominated by tyrannical family members. Notably, however, those women who act in order to gain money rather than love often fail. According to these scripts, a heroine's actions should respond to specific scenarios of unfairness, with the scripts carefully balancing acting skills with a victim's need for a specific form of recourse. Even though these scripts suggest that acting may be a woman's only remedy for domestic distress, the plays obliquely hint that acting constitutes a peculiarly indirect assertion of individual will that is cast as more feminine than a blunt statement, a departure, or an elopement (all possible solutions in these plots).

Similarly focusing on the unfair treatment of its heroine, Alcott's thriller adopts the domestic woman's impetus for acting, extending it to a lower-class, socially aggressive character who disregards conventional morality.[36] Like the dramas above, Alcott's 1866 thriller sympathetically tells the story of a woman hoping to forge a marriage of her own choosing, a woman who seeks affirmation and appreciation while fighting the crises of "old age" (Jean is thirty), a sordid past, and potential poverty. Even with Alcott's exaggerations of class conflicts, Jean's goals are recognizably akin to those for the theatricals' heroines, for Jean longs for security and for domestic control, yet she is less sentimental and more combative, less love-striken and more of a ruthless strategist who acts aggressively for her own benefit.

A Success Narrative through Association

In addition to her likeness to domestic actresses, Jean Muir also wields unusual abilities. Jean is a consummate actress, and her mastery over interpretation and action culminates in a triptych of tableaux vivants scenes, or passages that set up her abilities as worthy of reward. In the first, Jean appears in her most aggressive stance, for she is Judith with Holofernes, waiting to behead her ravisher. Characterizing Jean through barbaric and Oriental nuances, the episode situates her against a decadent background arranged with various luxuries, among them splendid armory, gorgeous draperies, and "costly dishes." Reminiscent of the "Eastern" scene in *Jane Eyre*, the tableau reveals Jean's "dark" soul, here cast as foreign, for Jean, now with darkened skin and a wig, is revealed as "a woman robed in barbaric splendor," dressed in a white tunic, purple mantle, scarlet sandals, jewels, golden fillets in her hair. She holds a scimitar with a "steady yet stealthy look, so effective that for a moment the spectators held their breath, as if they also heard a passing footstep" (146).[37] Alcott's narrative particularly stresses Jean's vengeful passion, for Jean had

thrown some wild black locks over her fair hair, and thrown such an intensity of expression into her eyes that they darkened and dilated till they were as fierce as any southern eyes that ever flashed. Hatred, the deepest and bitterest, was written on her sternly beautiful face, courage glowed in her glance, power spoke in the nervous grip of the slender hand that held the weapon, and the indomitable will of the woman was

expressed—even in the firm pressure of the little foot half hidden in
the tiger skin. (147)

Revealing the full force of her will, Jean acts out a woman's outrage. The
narrator relates that "It was not all art: the intense detestation mingled with
a savage joy that the object of her hatred was in her power was too perfect
to be feigned" (147). By eliding the sexual indignities suffered by Judith with
Jean Muir's class-based hostilities, Alcott casts Jean's outrage as a response to
a type of gendered violence that nineteenth-century readers would have
been prepared to see as horrifically barbaric. But as Alcott's rendering of the
scene stresses the victim's desire for revenge, it also suggests that uncivilized
aggression creates an understandable response in a woman's counteragres-
sion, making it clear that Jean's anger, like Judith's, emerges from extreme
provocation. The tableau also stresses Jean's acting skills, for the successive
living pictures, the ones without Jean, lack "the charm which real talent lends
to the simplest part," according to the narrator (147). By suggesting that Jean
has harnessed her feelings of victimization and converted them into active
drama, Alcott points to the efficacy of talent, a point that the thriller's successive tableaux further emphasize.

The next set of tableaux depicts the fate of two Cavalier fugitives; as in
the Judith scene, Jean continues to play the role of the victim. Now a Roundhead damsel, Jean poses as a woman trying to conceal her lover "under her
little mantle, and presses his head to her bosom in an ecstasy of fear, as she
glances back at the approaching pursuers" (148). A subsequent pose portrays
the dying girl (who has been shot) with her lover, surrounded by captors,
during which Jean's eyes appear "eloquent with the love which even death
could not conquer" (149). Jean transforms the victim's sad fate into a scene
of her own triumph, for her Roundhead partner, Gerald, heir of Coventry,
feels for the first time "the indescribable spell of womanhood" during this
scene as "the power of those tender eyes thrilled Coventry with a strange
delight" (149).

Jean is asked to participate in a third tableau, one featuring "Queen Bess,"
but the narration fails to follow this staging, for the tableau is not of Jean's
design. Later, Jean presents a private and seemingly "unposed" tableau, don-
ning the costume of Queen Elizabeth, reclining alone in the drawing room
after the festivities. Here Jean adopts the role of a royal in repose. Assuming
privileges of wealth and rank, she awaits the newly infatuated Coventry.

She was leaning wearily back in the great chair which had served for a
throne. Her royal robes were still unchanged, though the crown was off

and all her fair hair hung about her shoulders. Excitement and exertion made her brilliant, the rich dress became her wonderfully, and an air of luxurious indolence changed the meek governess into a charming woman. She leaned on the velvet cushions as if she were used to such support; she played with the jewels which had crowned her as carelessly as if she were born to wear them; her attitude was full of negligent grace, and the expression of her face half proud, half pensive, as if her thoughts were bitter-sweet. (151)

By indulging in luxury and power, Jean cannily appeals to the prejudices of her viewer. She knows that the handsome young heir, Gerald, believes her to be the illegitimate daughter of an aristocrat (for she has planted such a lie); hence her portrayal of Queen Elizabeth is calculated to reveal her own "noble" tendencies and prove her kinship to other members of the British gentry. As she had calculated, Coventry responds sympathetically to the disparity between Jean's supposed caste and her present circumstances, assuming that her sensitivity is proof of her noble blood. "One would know she was wellborn to see her now," thinks Gerald. "Poor girl, what a burden a life of dependence must be to a spirit like hers!" (151). During their ensuing conversation, Jean skillfully evokes Gerald's pity by overtly pointing out her dependent position in his household, continuing to hint that her abilities are best suited to the aristocratic life that Gerald, as an unmarried male heir, can provide for her.

By this third scene, Jean has shed her victimization. Whereas she first claimed revenge, then right-mindedness, she now exhibits noble power. In this succession, the tableaux suggest that a woman's agency, in its earliest form, will be barbaric, uncontrolled, rebellious, and "foreign." Locating nascent power in aggression, these tableaux vivants also hint that Judith's thirst for revenge is the ancestor of the most civilized and regal versions of a more modern "woman's power." In a skilled but socially marginalized figure such as Jean Muir, barbarism and civilization meet. Her skills remind us of her cultivation, even as her motives remain vengeful.

Alcott's care in constructing Jean Muir's relation to unmitigated power serves as an important reminder of the dominant nineteenth-century ideal of the demure, sincere, domestic woman whose transparency would have made subterfuge unthinkable. Notably, Alcott does not attempt to engage the issue of sincerity (a sign of its danger to her tale), but instead suggests that a failure to claim agency over one's life results in the devastation of all that women hold dear, an argument echoed by parlor theatrical scripts, where borrowing empowered postures allowed women to exercise a measure of domestic authority. Through Jean Muir's example, Alcott offers readers the promise that by representing powerful women, domestic women could appropriate the ability to shape their lives according to their values.

Because Alcott's text extols Jean's acting talents during the tableaux, it is ironic that the Coventrys resist Jean by discrediting those skills. When, at the text's end, they apprehend and read the letters written by Jean to her confidante, they are able to discern Jean's "true" plans and "real" identity. Ascribing to Jean the most malicious of intentions, the letters reveal that she has trifled with Coventry in order to wound his proud lover, that she has appeased her hatred of the aristocracy by emotionally seducing Edward as well as Sir John, and that she has amused herself by belittling everyone in the family, at least in print. Read by the rapt Coventrys, who have long been inept at interpreting actions, the letters remind us of the aristocrats' preference for an unambiguous, written text as opposed to a more challenging dramatic one. Thus relegated to reading literal explanations, the aristocrats cling to a traditional and hierarchistic form of textual interpretation that has been threatened by a newer, more egalitarian arsenal of acting.

Conclusion: Exploiting the Possibilities of Skills

By detailing the vertical class ambitions of skilled protagonists, novels with entertainment scenes depend upon a reader's recognition that cultural labors count as legitimate forms of work, especially for women who have no other recourse to domestic security. Leisurely employments, then, are not only the markers of genteel status, but also qualifying mechanisms that indicate an individual's ability to belong, to participate, and to lay claim to a privileged social sphere. Published almost twenty years after Brontë's novel, Alcott's thriller not only represents an American exaggeration of class-based ability, but also reveals striking developments in the repertory of home entertainment practices, depicting a protagonist who makes use of the dynamism that more dramatic forms of play afforded their participants, ultimately resulting in a greater and more egalitarian redistribution of privilege. Alcott's text additionally portrays a permeability of class lines based on a strong and combative class that seeks to overturn, not just infiltrate, an existing social order.

In taking such a polemical stance, entertainment scenes also offered a reinterpretation of what counted as pleasure. The pleasing dimension of the novel, they suggested, arose from the real social possibilities exercised by characters. To be satisfying, then, the novel would both delight and empower through visions of skilled contestation and reward. By encouraging readers to take pleasure in characters' engagements with larger power structures, their exercise of personal ability, their risks of seeing themselves as agents of their own fates, these episodes asserted a politically engaged portrait of how (recrafting Alcott's subtitle to "Behind a Mask" slightly) to structure a woman's reading pleasure.

As powerfully as these fictive passages imagine the worlds of their protagonists, they also make implicit promises to their readers. Based on their hints of social empowerment in characters' lives, mid-century entertainment scenes invite readers to negotiate their own relationship to a skills-based culture, forging a connection between characters' and readers' abilities by weaving an overt discussion of interpretive skill into representations of social practice, thereby attaching implicit promises of uplift to women readers. As entertainment scenes provide character viewers with ways to reflect on (and hone) their interpretive abilities, they promise to unlock both the sealed doors of class privilege and the hermeneutic mysteries of texts. As successive fictions reimagine the entertainment scene, they continue to explore the disruptive potential of skills as a means of correcting social inequities. Such scenes also offer some hope that skilled readers, whose abilities are implicitly compared with those of the skilled characters in the text, could also triumph in their worlds.

5
Staging Disaster

Turn-of-the-Century Entertainment Scenes
and the Failure of Personal Transformation

By the century's turn, references to entertainment and to skilled play frequently appear in tales of defeat rather than triumph, thereby reversing earlier portraits of women enabled by culturally based forms of competition.
As part of this trend, entertainment episodes begin to treat characters' attempts to deploy their skills as occasions to question personal ambition as
well as the larger social efficacy of competitive skills. With this pessimistic
attitude toward entertainment and the transformations that it previously
showcased, fictional narratives provide cautionary responses to transformations rooted in cultural development. In contrast to mid-century scenes where
characters such as Jane Eyre and Jean Muir wield skills so as to achieve extraordinary social rewards, turn-of-the-century participants in entertainments fail utterly in their attempts to use skills to solidify their lives. For
them, confrontations with social hierarchies prove daunting, as established
privilege counters the skills that participants in home entertainments attempt to wield.

These are players whose awkwardness and lack of success allow for narratives where appearances of the "sense" of the activity and the "judicious
direction" of play are absent, leaving only those "questions about the meaning
of the world and existence which people never ask when they are caught up
in the game."[1] Not only are characters marginalized because of their performances, but ignorance, failure, and ostracism combine to render scenes of entertainment uncomfortably self-assertive, especially when these later narratives are compared to those scenes of performative successes in earlier fictions.

As these disaster narratives reveal, the broad cultural promise once attached to skills—and now so visibly retracted—reflects an entrenchment of

entertainment's practices. On a broader level, too, perceptions about the irrelevancy of cultural work cast doubt on the power of personal ability during a pronounced Gilded Age complacency, when rampant consumerism challenged exhibitions of individual ability. Famously exorcised by Thorstein Veblen, who condemned the "leisure class" and its modes of "conspicuous consumption," a prevalent, materialistic attitude toward "culture" at large filtered through characters' experience of home entertainments. A turn-of-the-century engagement with entertainment practices, as Veblen suggests, reveals a profound appreciation for material show congruent with an elite social register and its excesses.[2]

As home entertainments entered into a third phase of popularity, from roughly the 1880s through the century's turn, entertainment forms increasingly showcased material collections, particularly in tableaux and other presentational activities that dominated late-century leisure practices. In particular, a trend toward posed figures, or "living pictures" as they were colloquially called, conjoined a number of intersecting interests, including industrial advances in textile production, the development of photography, and the emergence of literary realism.[3] In addition, international commerce and imperialistic exploration allowed for the introduction of exotic imports into the home, producing a high Victorian aesthetic (now often satirized) that featured domestic details such as étagères, double draperies, and endless ornaments such as antimacassars, mantle scarves, and double rugs.[4] Such trends attest to the elaborate displays and stylized domestic arrangements now made possible by a global marketplace.

Whereas modes of home entertainment from earlier decades had pointed to dynamic skills, the domestic trends of the late century render less viable a narrative of social ascent via skills, in part because of a new pessimism surrounding ability. By this point, an older notion of skills intersects with, and often competes with, narratives of material self-definition, contributing to a skepticism about the transformative power of personal abilities voiced by later authors. The doubt embedded within these later tales points to an elitism that is economically, though not necessarily culturally, entrenched, especially in plots featuring upper-class figures who are increasingly aloof from skilled middling types. The lack of opportunity available to middling types is made particularly clear as late-century and turn-of-the-century fictions, like their predecessors, take up stories of domestic women who confront the elites, but without resounding success.

Associated with the most luxurious of resources, the late-century tableaux vivants appearing in Edith Wharton's *The House of Mirth* (1905) and Frank Norris's *The Pit* (1903) mark home entertainment's return to an elite milieu, reversing the mid-century trend toward a middle-class appropriation of entertainment's forms. In addition, during mid-century entertainment scenarios, middling women joined aristocrats, besting them at play in what earlier fictions present as scenes of pointed contest. But by the century's end, when middling women attempt to deploy their skills, they find that they cannot compete with the upper classes, which have reclaimed entertainment forms such as tableaux vivants, wresting leisure forms from situations where abilities leveled social hierarchies.

Despite the new narrative of class-specific entrenchment attached to home entertainment, the most prominent fictional depictions of the period continue to focus on domestic women who wish to be recognized. When ambitious figures such as Wharton's Lily Bart and Norris's Laura Dearborn Jadwin articulate their self-worth via tableaux vivants, we see that entertainment forms are less transformative in their potential, despite these characters' attempts to wield entertainment's skills as heroines before them did so successfully, playing out an older scenario. In addition to a new narrative of failed transformations, there are other signs that the social efficacy once associated with entertainment's skills is on the wane, at least according to fictional portrayals, resulting in scenarios where the participants come to question the value of their worlds. In addition to the fact that the women featured in texts by Wharton and Norris fail to refashion their lives, we also see that narratives about entertainment no longer promise to transform a new population of votaries. While African American novelists such as Pauline Hopkins and Charles W. Chesnutt, for example, portray the social worlds of their affluent, middle-class black characters, they uphold the value of genteel living—without pointing to the potential surrounding entertainment's skills. In their works, instead, allusions to and descriptions of domestic leisure activities serve as a testament that black American families have achieved a casual relation to domestic accomplishments.

Turn-of-the-century representations of middle-class leisure activities in black households, which are among the first fictional references of their kind, tend to be integrated into a purposefully broad portrait of acculturation. References to home entertainments in such texts encompass just a few characters, as in the description of Ma Smith's parlor reception in *Contending Forces*, where the entertainment, a "literary and musical programme," takes place. One character plays the piano while another sings. There are duets and a dramatic reading of the "Chariot Race" from "Ben Hur," rendered in "true dramatic style."[5] Depicted as enjoyable and successful, such events are nevertheless ancillary to the major plot developments about race, inheritance, and social reinstatement, or the types of concerns that determine characters' relations to the larger world. While Hopkins claims a cultured lifestyle for her characters, she does so without using a detailed description of home entertainment to reflect on individual self-worth. In addition, Hopkins does not measure her characters in relation to an elite, aristocratic class; instead, her cultured, successful mulatto figures *are* the elites of their race.

Hopkins's emphasis on a cultured, black middling class, like that of Charles W. Chesnutt, points to the characters' mastery of traditions that had long been linked to white privilege, but it is equally clear that individual skills (as featured in Alcott's plot) are neither a stepping-stone to society nor a substitute for social and economic equity.[6] Hence, when Mr. Ryder in "The Wife of His Youth" (1899) prepares to recite British Romantic poetry or Rena and John Walden in *The House Behind the Cedars* (1900) participate in a reenactment of the Scottish Highlanders' tournament, the texts celebrate their cultural knowledge rather than hint at transformative abilities. These experiences, then, while making important claims to occupying an affluent, respectable class position, are not presented as revolutionary.

Although comprising a relatively small part of the textual market, Hopkins's and Chesnutt's fictions suggest that the new infusion of diversity into the marketplace affected the types of narratives associated with entertainment's forms. Significantly, Hopkins and Chesnutt, like other late-century authors, sever entertainment's practices from the possibilities of social transformation. Most importantly for the treatment of home entertainments, however, there was no new group of readers, no new group of participants—white or black—for whom entertainment's practices were positioned as transformative, revolutionary, or dynamic vehicles for a dawning century.

The Lost Efficacy of Skills

Among mainstream fictions, too, entertainment's forms ceased to be portrayed as transformative, in part because of the prevalence of entertainment forms such as tableaux vivants, which deemphasize interactive work and instead point to material selection as a new axis of interest. More object-oriented than competitive and more aesthetic than inspirational, they differ from both mid-century games and from the tableaux of earlier decades. In this new era of display, too much effort, too much bodily labor could appear markedly out of sync with aesthetic trends, particularly if an individual's labors appear to be calculated to achieve personal transformations. Reflecting on a movement toward less active popular entertainment forms, fictions by Wharton and Norris suggest that when cultural work appears too laborious, it loses its value, dooming upward strivers to a secondary social tier, thereby ensuring that the middle classes cannot compete effectively with the elites. In their assessment of a solidification of boundaries between the middle and upper classes, Wharton and Norris were not alone.

Henry James's *The Tragic Muse* (1900) also draws a clear distinction between entrenched elitism and cultural striving as it examines the ways in which laboriousness marks a young actress as a social oddity rather than a potential peer of the elites. In its focus on the ambitious Miriam Rooth, an aspiring actress, the novel begins by detailing the young woman's blatant ambition, which separates her from the elegant, ambivalent upper-class women in the text. Having recently met the young aesthete, Peter Sherringham, and having been invited to perform at a ladies' tea, which he hosts for his aristocratic family and friends, Miriam performs various roles. The guests' vast social difference from Miriam, who is treated as a lower-middle-class eccentric, predicts something of the strangeness to come. In this setting, the society women envision entertainment as a remedy for social monotony; Peter's aunt, for example, "had inherited the fine old superstition that art's pardonable only as long as it's bad—so long as it's done at odd hours for a little distraction like a game of tennis or whist."[7] Peter accordingly decides that he will ask Miriam to recite for his guests because he "had only to see them all together to perceive that she couldn't pass for having come to 'meet' them— even her mother's insinuating gentility failed to put the occasion on that footing—and that she must therefore be assumed to have been brought to show them something" (I, 141). In this context, Miriam can be accepted only as an entertainer, for "She was not subdued, not colourless enough to sit there for nothing, or even conversation—the sort of conversation that was likely to come off—so that it was inevitable to treat her position as connected with the principal place on the carpet, with silence and attention and the pulling together of chairs" (I, 141). Miriam's presence makes sense if she is seen as a worker (of a sort); only then is she visible to the aristocratic women.

With great theatrical vigor, Miriam performs "Juliet taking the potion," poems by Victor Hugo, Longfellow, Lowell, Whittier, Holmes, and "two or three poetesses" (I, 143). Punctuated by shrieks, gasps, contortions, and above all, naked ambition, Miriam's laborious recitations firmly position her outside Peter's milieu.

> The space was too small, the cries, the convulsions and rustle of the disheveled girl were too near. Lady Agnes wore much of the time the countenance she might have shown at the theatre during a play in which pistols were fired; and indeed the manner of the young reciter had become more spasmodic and more explosive. (I, 143)

Ultimately, James situates Miriam's future in the professional realm of acting, where Miriam will find her niche and will be severed from all but casual
contact with this aristocratic circle. But in the opening domestic scene, it is
clear that Miriam is working far too hard for the context of an afternoon
social, revealing how skilled (or at least, seriously ambitious) activities have
become negligible in society at large.

Like James's novel, other turn-of-the-century fictions depicting home entertainments point to the ways that characters tend to prioritize material articulation, framed as aestheticism, over individual skills. In 1899, Veblen
described the leisure class as increasingly oriented toward "honorific" expenditures rather than physical realities, or expenditures based on status rather
than necessity, a discussion that sheds light on the marginal value of skills
among the elites, for whom consumption, display, and status were united in
a "canon of reputability."[8] Veblen goes on to explain the role of work in relation to status, noting that

> the fact that members of the leisure class, both men and women, are
> to some extent exempt from the necessity of finding a livelihood in a
> competitive struggle with their fellows, makes it possible for mem-
> bers of this class not only to survive, but even, within bounds, to fol-
> low their bent in case they are not gifted with the aptitudes which make
> for success in the competitive struggle. That is to say, in the latest and
> fullest development of the institution, the livelihood of members of
> this class does not depend on the possession and the unremitting ex-
> ercise of those aptitudes which characterise [sic] the successful preda-
> tory man.[9]

In separating members of the leisure class from those of a competitive or
"predatory" class, Veblen allows us to understand the significant ways that
vestiges of work in the turn-of-the-century United States have been excised
from the more affluent social tiers, which seek to distinguish themselves as
discerning purchasers instead.

Historicizing this argument in relation to trends of home entertainment
practices, we see a period when the competitive skills that were once so valuable to a rising middle class have become serious liabilities. As Norris and
Wharton, like James, reveal, it is not that characters disregard skills, but
that they are gravely mistaken about what skills can accomplish. Characters' insistence on their own abilities, then, often appears capricious or self-
indulgent rather than the product of a well-honed sensibility. The consequences of this shift have enormous ramifications for the entertainment

chronotope, once the predictor of a character's social ascent. In Alcott and Brontë, scenes of entertainment allowed readers to anticipate success, for heroines could be trusted to conquer their less able adversaries. But with personal skills coming into question by the late century, the entertainment chronotope offers very little promise for the votaries of home entertainment, no matter how talented.

Realism, High Society, and Tableaux Vivants

Unlike charades of the mid century, tableaux, one of the most significant late-century entertainments, hosted little opportunity for competition, since they were not part of an actual game. Hence, the dynamic of triumph and loss, once so congruent with the story of personal ascendancy, disappears from depictions of home entertainment. Moreover, the skills involved in tableaux are significantly more difficult to define than the skills of acting or gaming.

Part of the challenge in applying the concept of skills to tableaux vivants lies in the genre's emphasis on aesthetic concerns such as "taste." Late nineteenth-century guide texts insist that good tableaux require elaborate materials, or excellent properties and accoutrements, along with fine lighting, stages, and various other types of presentational machinery. Because directions for tableaux may call attention to the "artful" grouping of materials, they make it all but impossible to separate the construct of "taste" from manifestations of material privilege. In fact, most tableaux descriptions from the century's turn equate the most effective presentations with the best props; in so doing, they deemphasize skill, dislodging the concept from its traditional centrality in narratives of home entertainment. Moreover, as references to "taste" intersect with notions of material accumulation, the primary activity signaled by tableaux vivants becomes commodification. According to Jean-Christophe Agnew, this interest stems from a period characterized by the "power of purchase," which "held sway over the older authority of personal mementos and personal craft alike."[10] Such beliefs helped advice book authors to credit tableaux vivants as aesthetic triumphs when they were, essentially, the results of good shopping and discerning collecting. The confluence of home entertainment forms and consumerism echoes other turn-of-the-century trends. William Leach, for example, has written of the ways that department stores sought to position shopping as entertainment, or a form of "individual fulfillment." Also blurring the line between pleasure and consumption were women's magazines, which now included copious advertisements.[11] In such a context, tableaux vivants reflected a profound level of material participation in the larger economic sphere.

In guide books about creating effective tableaux, costly, difficult, and time-consuming preparations for entertainment are presented to readers with alacrity. Mary Elizabeth Wilson Sherwood's *Home Amusements* (1884) matter-of-factly presents the following directions in its section on tableaux vivants, contending that "A tableau can be given in parlors separated by folding-doors; but they are not by any means as good as those for which a stage, vista, and footlights, flies and side-lights, are arranged"; Sherwood insists on a gauze or black tarlatan curtain (with no seams) and an outside drop curtain, pure white "lime light," and additional colorations provided by such chemicals as "nitrate of strontia, chlorate of potash, sulphuret of antimony, sulphur, oxymuriate of potassa, metallic arsenic, and pulverized charcoal," among others.[12] In another advice text, Sherwood provides directions for creating an elaborate stage, calling for professional builders, noting that "Any carpenter will lay a few stout boards on end pieces, which are simply squared joists, and for very little money will take away the boards and joists afterwards, so that a satisfactory stage can be built for a few dollars." Sherwood also contends that the difficulties of curtains can be solved "with the help of an upholsterer" and continues to insist on realistic costumes, makeup, wigs, and stage furnishings.[13] As an author of various decoration guide books and entertainment manuals, Sherwood combines multiple domestic interests, uniting them in a way that would have been impossible several decades earlier, when home entertainment guide books had little intersection with interior decor.

As depicted in period articles and reviews, tableaux vivants were realized through elaborate productions, often performed in semipublic settings such as charity or benefit societies, with society leaders taking prominent roles. In these exhibitions, neither the beauty of the female form nor aesthetic ambitions were as significant as the "appropriateness" of the overall effect.[14] The careful display of material markers is noted in an 1893 notice from *The Critic*, detailing a display at the Madison Square Garden Assembly Rooms for the Society of Decorative Art. Coordinated by affluent matrons (one of whom was Edith Wharton's sister-in-law, Mrs. F. Rhinelander Jones), the society women are described as "ably assisted by Messrs. Leon and Percy Moran, who suggested most of the pictures and posed them all."[15] The subjects for tableaux included "The Countess Potocka," "Louise of Prussia," "Mme. Adelaide," and a "Madonna." A similar exhibition of tableaux vivants is described (and pictured) in an article entitled "Some Society Tableaux" by Sherwood in *Cosmopolitan* of 1898. Both reviews hint at a notable level of material sumptuousness in these spectacles, a luxuriousness rhetorically encoded as "appropriate." The *Cosmopolitan* article, for example, notes that tableaux have replaced theatricals and have emerged as pleasant diversions for social figures such as Mrs. Belmont and Mrs. John Jacob Astor.[16] Here, too, the tableaux vivants have been arranged by a professional overseer, in this case a Mr. Daniel Huntington. The topics displayed, according to Sherwood, are "wholly fresh and original," the committee having decided that there should be no "Sleeping Beauty" or "Rebecca at the Well," instead electing to "illustrate the history of the hundred years from 1775 to 1875, preceded by scenes from Puritan and Knickerbocker life" as well as "all the nations to honor America," among them the scenes "Egypt," "Cuba," "France," "Greece," "Spain," "Ireland," and "Japan."[17] According to the photos accompanying the article, both the historical and international poses required a liberal use of properties and underlying references to global conquest.

As these scenes suggest, references to exotic locations and to international trade frequently appeared in tableaux. Like grotesque and physical forms of entertainment from earlier decades, elaborate tableaux vivants treated foreign lands as a source of attractive exports, severing objects from their original contexts and positioning them as available to an exclusively wealthy class. Particularly in the "Egypt" tableau, imperialist themes are prominent as an Anglo woman dons Egyptian plunder, while attended by a dark-skinned servant (fig. 13). Similarly, the fanciful arctic scene incorporates a stuffed polar bear, an object representing geographical, if not cultural conquest (fig. 14). What is not fanciful, however, is the suggestion that the participants of tableaux reap the rewards of a uniquely privileged type of consumerism. Sherwood's article also reveals that references to historical effects serve as a shorthand for conquest. Society leaders who represent Puritan and Knickerbocker America hark back to centuries of Anglo ownership and a notably consolidated, northeastern form of cultural dominance.

Sherwood's account of the tableaux vivants also stresses the "realistic," "historical," and even "archaeological" accurateness of the living pictures, noting that the "splendid costumes" were "made of the finest stuffs" and fashioned after a "choice collection of prints." A group of stuffed wild animals, among them a tiger, bear, swan, leopard, goat, eagle, and horse (lent to the committee for the tableaux), create "the law of effective and harmonious contrast" when coupled with the women's figures. Pursuing an argument for a pointedly material mode of realism, Sherwood goes so far as to contend that "sham and tinsel do not wholly deceive; the picture is far finer if the brocade stiff, the velvet three-ply, and the diamonds are real."[18] Under the canopy of "historical" accuracy, Sherwood suggests that only the most lavish,

Fig. 13. "Egypt," from "Some Society Tableaux" (*Cosmopolitan*, 1898). Hillman Library, University of Pittsburgh.

expensive accoutrements are convincing, with her judgments reflecting the expectations of a high society audience trained in viewing luxurious commodities. Sherwood thus positions the elite participants at such events as consummate consumers who recognize the finest materials, consequently situating successful tableaux vivants as out of the reach of all but the most extravagantly rich.

Sherwood's logic, encompassing concerns with tasteful interiors and fashionable amusements, illustrates how the elites gradually appropriated the practices of home entertainment, selecting those forms that most obviously connoted privilege. By contrast, at the mid century, entertainment had been thoroughly associated with the competitive middling classes. But by the century's turn, pointed hierarchies of entertainment emerge as class lines be-

Fig. 14. Tableau with stuffed polar bear, from "Some Society Tableaux" (*Cosmopolitan*, 1898). Hillman Library, University of Pittsburgh.

came rigidly defined by stock market expansions and by the growth of innovative technologies. Although printed in *Cosmopolitan* in 1898, the tableaux pictured in Sherwood's article actually took place in 1875, a fact with compelling suggestiveness regarding class lines. The lag time between the event and the public, textual circulation of the tableaux, (a fact that is never directly addressed by the article) reiterates its extreme exclusivity. Not only do class lines separate readers from participants, but so do twenty years, which shroud participants in privacy. Moreover, the time difference effectively prevents readers from mimicking upper society's most current activities, suggesting that trends fashionable among the elites circulate among common readers only after the upper classes choose to relinquish them.

Tableaux Vivants and an Older Tradition of Social Commentary

The tableaux vivants in vogue at the century's turn built upon a long tradition of living pictures, but indicate a radical shift in tableaux vivants' cultural cachet. Whereas late-century tableaux were directed toward wealthy and privileged participants, earlier versions of the activity had been less hierarchical, their displays implying sympathy for individuals beneath the middle-class border. As early as the 1860s, tableaux vivants guide books assigned aesthetic value to the display of scenes deemed both inspirational and artistic.

Highlighting the aesthetic skills involved in tableaux, William F. Gill wrote in 1866, "*Tableaux* have, for several years, been a favorite entertainment with persons of taste."[19] They also idealized figures of an allegorical nature, which appeared as simply garbed female forms, as in the display of the "Hope" statue discussed in chapter four.[20] Frequently, too, tableaux vivants focused on economic discrepancies and abrupt reversals of fortune, merging social commentary with aesthetic poses.

According to didactic texts of the 1860s and '70s, tableaux vivants were deeply indebted to striking contrasts via pathetic, sentimental commentaries. Eschewing elaborately material as well as photographically realistic scenes, these living pictures advanced narratives that inclined toward social commentary of the type represented in earlier nineteenth-century literary works such as Melville's "The Paradise of Bachelors and the Tartarus of Maids" (1854). In such texts, the dissonances between scenes of wealth and poverty, privilege and want are put into deliberate focus, encouraging readers to respond sentimentally and reminding them of the ways that the relatively affluent can so easily dismiss experiences unlike their own, even while benefiting enormously from the exploitation of unknown, unnamed figures like those in Melville's "Tartarus."

Highlighting the contrast between labor and gentility, Melville's "The Paradise of Bachelors and the Tartarus of Maids" is composed in two separate sides of a diptych, united by a single narrator. In the first section, genteel British bachelors engage in a social evening of revelry, wine, and food; by stark contrast, the next scene depicts laboring maids, who have no existence outside of the paper factory that is literally consuming them, for as the particles of paper and the humid working conditions affect them, the women die of consumption. One of the ironies of the diptych is that the worlds of isolating labor (production) and companionable leisure (consumption) never confront one another. They remain as distinct as the bachelors' residence in London and the maids' life in rural Massachusetts. Only the narrator traverses these two worlds, but he is so deeply affected by the stark extremes that he lapses into incoherence. At the end of his travels, he can find no syntactic resolution, wanly exclaiming, "Oh! Paradise of Bachelors! And oh! Tartarus of Maids!"[21] For this narrator, the two worlds that he witnesses never converge, and no explanation adequately links the two experiences. The work of meditating on the extremes is left to the reader.

A pictorial rendering of a similarly contrastive diptych, one also calculated to elicit readerly sympathy, appears in an illustration entitled "Pin money/Needle money," from *Godey's* magazine of 1853. It depicts the contrast between a comfortable, middle-class woman (who sews in a well-appointed

Fig. 15. "Pin money/Needle money," from *Godey's Lady's Book* (Philadelphia, 1853),
Courtesy, The Winterthur Library: Printed Book and Periodical Collection.

boudoir with the help of a servant) and a seamstress (who appears wrapped
for warmth in a rude dwelling), calling attention to the difference between
a working woman's hard labor for mere sustenance and a young woman's
leisurely pleasure in sewing or ornamenting what appear to be her fashionable garments (fig. 15). Part of what marks these scenes as reliant on an earlier sentimental tradition of contrastive tableaux vivants is the suggestion
that the viewer pierces the private life of the individuals represented. By
gaining access to private moments, viewers are invited to reflect on characters' daily realities, particularly the solitary and pathetic neediness of the
inarticulate. Hence, the presence of an unseen viewer (or the diptych's audience) is linked to a kind of social commentary that those being portrayed
cannot voice.

Gill's *Parlor Tableaux and Amateur Theatricals* (1867), one of many texts
guiding productions of sentimental, contrasting tableaux vivants, contains
comparable scenes illustrating the extremes of need and affluence, among
them scenes entitled "Light and Shadow" and "Charity and Poverty." Other
tableaux narrate the consequences of various actions in "before and after"
effects, as in "The Reprimand" and "The Reward of Merit" (which outline
the rewards gained by both good and bad behavior in school) and another
set of scenes, "The Pardon Refused" and "The Reconciliation" (which visually narrate a lovers' quarrel and its subsequent resolution). The scene for
"New Year's Eve," for example, features characters who represent age and

youth, as does the setting for "Past and Future." These paired representations depict vast changes in fortune and affection, urging readers to imagine a narrative that links the scenes. Emphasizing fluctuations of wealth and poverty, hope and despair, fortune and misfortune, these scenes depict the possible fate of an individual seemingly entrenched in a comfortable situation, a commentary that continually reminded readers and viewers of the possibilities that lay just beyond the comfortable boundaries of moderate affluence. These tableaux additionally announce the possibility, one gilded with pathos, that even beauty, comfort, and pleasant surroundings offer little protection in an unstable world.

Like "Pin money/Needle money," directions for contrastive living pictures attempt to inculcate a social consciousness by focusing on women's particular vulnerability to fluctuating fortunes, featuring once-comfortable women as impoverished victims. In so doing, these scenes articulate a very real problem among those middle- and upper-class women who found themselves alone after years of economic dependence on fathers, husbands, and brothers. Sarah Annie Frost's "Neglected Flowers" from the 1869 *Book of Tableaux and Shadow Pantomimes,* for example, calls for the depiction of two little girls, dressed as flower sellers in a market. They are meagerly garbed, described as looking cold, sorrowful, and "imploring." In the foreground of the scene are a lady and gentleman, wearing "winter walking clothes." The man wears an "overcoat, fur collar, and thick gloves," while the lady appears in "a handsome silk dress, velvet cloak, furs, and velvet bonnet."[22] Through the pointed contrasts here, the working girls are implicitly compared to the more acceptable posies that surround them. The tableau's second scene contrasts the comfortable, complacent couple with the needy, miserable children, highlighting the wealthy's callous self-absorption.

Compared to these socially conscious tableaux rooted in emotional affect, the glamorous, high society tableaux vivants popular near the century's turn appear markedly self-indulgent. Whereas earlier scenes of contrast attempted to elicit viewers' sympathies, later tableaux, such as those described by Sherwood, align subject and accoutrements in deliberately "effective" scenes, but scenes that reveal no sense of the viewers' social obligations. In upholding notions of social "appropriateness," to borrow a term from Sherwood, late-century tableaux were arranged so as to convince viewers of a social Darwinist logic, which suggested that the subjects of such scenes were destined to be surrounded by beauty and luxury.

The distinctions between these two traditions of tableaux vivants become most visible when they operate in different ways within a single narrative. Wharton's *The House of Mirth,* for example, makes reference to both modes of tableaux. In addition to Lily Bart's much-discussed tableau vivant at the Wellington Brys' party, Wharton creates another visually inspired scene of contrast, harkening back to an older, less hierarchized tableaux vivants tradition, one that predates the economic stratification characteristic of the century's end.[23] These scenes evoke a distinct narrative permeated with sympathetic pathos for misfortune, interjecting a sentimental moment into the narrative.[24] In making this point, Wharton pairs Lily's society tableau with a later, private moment when Lily, now fired from her work as a milliner's assistant and consequently impoverished, picks up her tableaux vivants costume from an evening of glamorous entertainment so long ago. Setting luxury, affluence, and social acceptance in contrast to poverty, loneliness, and social liminality, these scenes echo a tableaux sequence similar to the one described in Charles Harrison's 1882 *Theatricals and Tableaux Vivants for Amateurs*. Entitled "The Silk Dress," the first scene of Harrison's paired tableaux features a lady and gentleman in evening dress situated against a background made up of an array of foliage that should give the "appearance of a conservatory" (fig. 16).[25] Reminiscent of Lily's post-tableau romantic interlude with Selden in the Wellington Bry conservatory, the first tableau conjures a setting of hothouse romance. In Wharton's novel, the conservatory episode, during which Lily is dressed in her tableaux vivants costume, positions Lily and Selden alone together in the "fragrant hush of the garden," with Lily's diaphanous garments standing out against the "emerald caverns in the depths of foliage" (137).

The second illustration in Harrison's text depicts another setting of "The Silk Dress" and its wearer. Taking place in a "poverty-stricken room" furnished only with a table and a trunk, the scene features a lady, now a "shabbily dressed woman," who holds the silk dress of the previous scene. To be accompanied by blue lights and "somber" music, the scene situates the impoverished beauty as the object of pathos. A strikingly similar "living picture" takes place near the end of Wharton's novel as Lily, nearly penniless in her dingy boardinghouse room, unpacks her few remaining "handsome" dresses, each with "the long unerring lines, the sweep and amplitude of the great artist's stroke" (317). Evoking Lily's memory of the past (as Harrison's tableaux scenes similarly imply), the costume harkens back to "each fall of lace and gleam of embroidery . . . like a letter in the record of her past" (317). As Lily draws the shapeless drapery of her Reynolds costume from her trunk, the narrative notes that the dress still retains the odors of the conservatory, now cast as the place "where she had stood with Lawrence Selden and disowned her fate" (317). Occurring on the night of Lily's drug overdose and after her good-bye to the coolly critical Selden, this silent interlude, posed

Fig. 16. Parts one and two of "The Silk Dress" from
Theatricals and Tableaux Vivants for Amateurs (London, 1882).

only for the reader, vividly portrays the contrast between Lily's apparent so-cial triumph and her undeniable current impoverishment.

Not only does the pairing of these two moments call attention to a wom-an's defenselessness in a competitive economic world, but the juxtaposi-tion of such contrasting scenes invokes an older style of paired tableaux. Emphasizing the magnitude of Lily's fall from privileged circles, these scenes chronicle the tragedy of the heroine's life in a sympathetic pictorial tradition. Because Wharton's novel depicts Lily's fall through narratively suggestive visual images, it obliquely reinscribes the value of an older tradition of rep-resentation, thereby hinting at the deficits of the more modern renderings of tableaux vivants in which Lily participates. Moreover, by sharing a silent tab-leaux sequence with the reader, Wharton points to the *reader's* alignment with older, sentimental styles of representation. Although Lily's "official" tableau of Reynolds's *Mrs. Lloyd* is stunningly and experimentally artistic, it accomplishes very little in terms of social commentary, appearing ideologi-cally impoverished, for all its investment in physical beauty.

Cultural Initiation and the Search for Skill in *The Pit*

As with Wharton's rendering of Lily Bart's famous tableau vivant (which I will go on to discuss) other late-century authors represent the conventions of home entertainment so as to raise—and discard—the possibility of trans-formative skills, even authors whose relation to the "genteel tradition" has long been overlooked.[26] Norris's "wheat" novel, *The Pit*, for example, con-tains multiple descriptions of entertainment, all of which problematize char-acters' relation to skilled cultural participation, leaving only what the novel casts as problematic avenues of self-advancement. The opening of the novel begins auspiciously, given the expectations of cultural transformation infus-ing the depiction of the entertainment chronotope, for the novel begins with a trip to the theater, where the young Laura Dearborn attends a grand opera for the first time. The placement of such an explanation predicts that this will be the first of Laura's profound cultural experiences and the nascence of her ability to hone and exercise her own skills. The opera is, we learn, "a thing desired and anticipated with all the eagerness of a girl who had lived for twenty-two years in a second-class town of central Massachusetts."[27] The novel's first chapter anticipates a transformation, detailing Laura's "spell-bound" attention to the show, which, to her, is a "revelation," but is described by the narrative voice as "not a very high order of music" (20). Having thus cast Laura's judgments into doubt, the chapter goes on to detail Laura's su-perficial focus on the benefits of wealth and of "this world of perfume, of flowers, of exquisite costumes, of beautiful women, of fine, brave men" (30). Given the myopic nature of Laura's response to the opera's spectacle (rather than its artistry), Laura is poised to learn little about wielding her own skills.

As she continues to soak in the opera, her desire for escapist pleasure becomes preeminent.

> Laura shut her eyes. Never had she felt so soothed, so cradled and lolled and languid. Ah, to love like that! To love and be loved. There was no such love as that to-day. She wished that she could loose her clasp upon the morbid, material modern life that, perforce, she must hold to, she knew not why, and drift, drift off into the past, far away, through rose-coloured mists and diaphanous veils, or resign herself, reclining in a silver skiff drawn by swans, to the gentle current of some smooth-flowing river that ran on forever and forever. (22)

More problematically, the opera becomes a transactional pleasure for Laura, and she begins to treat cultural events as status symbols rather than moments for personal development. She is essentially a consumer who seeks transformation via purchases, and, as such, projects her desires for change onto objects, evoking a kind of purchase-driven self-definition, or a "commodity aesthetic."[28] In a novel that will trace a country girl's marriage to a man of enormous wealth and power, Laura's experiences with cultural achievements appear troubling when compared to the narrative infusing earlier settings of the entertainment chronotope. Instead of an active participant who challenges social designations by her wielding of unexpected abilities, Laura is merely a mass-culture consumer.

Laura's desire for culture, for worldly exposure, then, ranges far from the approach to leisure enacted by Alcott's Jean Muir, who possessed considerable skills, having honed them as part of her pursuit of material security. Whereas Jean was ever ready to use her talents to improve her status, Laura waits to be transformed by external forces. Just as the novel's central wheat speculator (Laura's husband), Curtis Jadwin, will emerge as a desperate, self-absorbed gambler, Laura will appear as a vain, society spendthrift, seeking a purchased affirmation that substitutes for true ability.

Charting the misuse of purchased culture, *The Pit* describes Laura's unaccomplished and unfulfilling interludes with home theatricals, a musical, and tableaux vivants. In all these areas, Laura fails to wield cultural power because she comprehends so little of it. As a consequence, disastrous engagements with the arts plague Laura, beginning with an amateur theatrical for a church benefit. Punctuated by personal embarrassment, missed cues, and an inopportune nosebleed, the theatrical is a miserable affair. During one forlorn rehearsal, Curtis Jadwin proposes to Laura, but in so doing, inverts the expectations raised by a long history of fictional entertainment scenes. As far back as *Mansfield Park,* private theatricals in fictions have been associated with flirtations, but rarely *before* the heroine performed. More usual is an emphasis on the heroine's imaginative acting, which prompts an emotional response from a male participant (or two). Here, however, Norris inverts this order of events, for Jadwin's proposal occurs before Laura takes her part in the rehearsal and is prefaced by his observations about her lovely hair rather than his acknowledgment of her talent, passion, or intelligence. With this protestation of love preceding any demonstration of the heroine's skill (a demonstration which, indeed, never occurs), the scene suggests that Jadwin's admiration is more indebted to Laura's coiffure than to her abilities. Moreover, upon receiving the proposal, Laura proceeds to take part in the rehearsal, a turn of events that hints at an astonishing lack of depth in the two lovers.

When Laura later poses in a series of tableaux vivants in her home's art gallery, she attempts to transform her lonely marriage, but even here, her display is less focused on ability than on highly commodified ideals of beauty. Beginning with a "Theodora," then an "Athalia," and finally a "Carmen," Laura appears as an "incarnate flame, capricious and riotous, elusive and dazzling" (311). Taking on wildly disparate feminine roles, Laura invokes the figure of Theodora, a Byzantine empress and the powerful, diplomatic, and egalitarian wife of Justinian I.[29] Next, Laura appears as Athalia, another figure of royalty, but also a power-hungry woman who attempts to usurp the throne of her deceased son, arranging the murder of possible successors.[30] Finally, as Carmen, Laura appropriates the role of another forceful woman, here a rowdy, self-actualized, and overtly sexual gypsy.[31] Part of the problem in the scene lies in Laura's attempt to locate a suitably ambitious feminine role model. As she drifts through life as an estranged, bored wife, she continually reconsiders her marital and social role, so much so that a just empress, a murderous usurper, and a seductive gypsy appear to her as equally attractive figures of feminine power. These three theatrical figures also represent Laura's inability to make sense of the models available to her, as with the opera she attended early in the novel. Ultimately, she can achieve little with her representations because they mean so little to her.

As she explains to the bemused Jadwin, her only viewer, she could have been a great actress had she not married. Demanding admiration, Laura interrogates her husband, still dressed as Theodora.

"Isn't it gorgeous?" She turned about before him, her arms raised. "Isn't it superb? Do you remember Bernhardt—and that scene in the Emperor Justinian's box at the amphitheatre? Say now that your wife isn't beautiful. I am, am I not?" she exclaimed defiantly, her head raised. "Say it, say it."

"Well, what for a girl!" gasped Jadwin, "to get herself up—"

"Say that I am beautiful," commanded Laura.

"Well, I just about guess you are," he cried.

"The most beautiful woman you have ever known?" (309)

As in renderings of many high society tableaux vivants of the period, Laura's self-display is oriented toward personal gratification. Confronting her husband, Laura insists that her beauty be admired (without regard to role), even while prefacing her remarks with the oddly consumeristic comment, "Isn't it gorgeous?" Laura's unusual use of the pronoun, "it" highlights her attempt to create a copy of another rendering of Theodora, specifically a replica of Bernhardt performing the part. Paradoxically then, Laura simultaneously insists on the beauty of "it" (or the original, as represented by Bernhardt) along with her beauty, linking her own identity to purchasable experiences at the theater (while ignoring other aspects of the Theodora character and plot). This conflation of easily appropriated identities bespeaks Laura's preference for exact representations, or a devotion to realistic copies, fervently pursued in many late-century "historical" tableaux.

The problem articulated by such a scene extends beyond consumerism and into its consequences for individual agency. Turn-of-the-century consumers like Laura, Norris suggests, have lost the ability to examine and express their life choices, so invested are they in common, mass culture ideals. For this reason, Laura's attempts at personal transformation fail, for she alters herself wildly, without discrimination. Yet her husband's response denies her any potential for lasting change, as he responds that her display is "sort of overwrought—a little, and unnatural," contending, "I like you best when you are your old self, quiet, and calm, and dignified. It's when you are quiet that you are at your best" (312). Despite this apparent pragmatism, the novel treats Jadwin's lack of imagination as equally stultifying as Laura's inabilities, for his obsession with cornering the market in wheat parallels his wife's efforts to purchase beauty as a self-defining act. This substitution of the material world for the personally engaged one highlights a disastrous combination, which is made manifest in Laura's invocation of elaborate costumes and unlimited resources of time and money, which render her little more than a self-adorned society queen and dramatize her discontents.

What is most damning about this scene of self-display is its contrast with earlier fictional renderings of entertainment. As Laura strains wildly from one pose to another, she does so with very little strategy and even less ability. Attuned to singular and myopic desires for beauty and devotion, her tableaux appear the ultimate self-indulgence. For this reason, her display, in the end, is devoid of any confirmation of her ability or any potential to alter her life. Instead, the tableaux scenes predict the failures of both Laura and Jadwin, who become increasingly estranged, leading to Jadwin's obsession with the wheat market and Laura's dalliance with an old lover. Despite the text's references to an established tradition of potentially transformative entertainment, there is no triumph in their future and, notably, no self-empowerment for Laura.

Formal Predictions in Wharton's *The House of Mirth*

When Wharton's heroine, Lily Bart, performs a visually stunning, physically revealing tableau vivant during the rising action of *The House of Mirth*, she seems poised to claim the kind of success that the entertainment chronotope formally predicts, for here, as in earlier nineteenth-century texts, a heroine asserts her notion of skills in an elite social context. By exhibiting her talents for producing striking visual effects and graceful poses, Lily attempts to use the medium of home entertainment to gain recognition and, ultimately, social power. While Wharton allows us to believe that Lily's tableau is, in itself, an artistic success, it is equally clear that the exhibition is in some way foreboding, for it signals Lily's grave misreading of her associates and predicts her fall from high society. The tableau vivant episode, however, has long prompted readers to ponder the reasons why Lily's display of her lissome, pliant form could have failed, especially in a patriarchal society where women's bodies were subjected to the powerful male gaze under the auspices of wealth and taste. In this context, Lily's tableau, as Wharton scholars have long noted, would seem to portray her as an ideal prize. Such interpretations, however, posit that Lily is an object rather than an agent in her tableau. Emphasizing Lily's participation in a skills-based culture reveals that the central problem facing Lily lies in the receding value of skills, and with them, opportunities for rapid social ascent. Using the methods of distinction so long associated with nineteenth-century heroines, Lily Bart mistakenly depends upon an outdated paradigm of personal advancement.

Like Laura Jadwin, Lily Bart experiences failure rather than success; these two turn-of-the-century inheritors of an older entertainment tradition, then, fail to convert leisure enterprises into social power. In Wharton's novel, Lily is threatened by her age and reputation as a fortune hunter in high society New York, where she is valued primarily for her good looks and youth, both of which are about to fade as she nears thirty. While Lily will fancy herself a skilled aesthete, a careful crafter of elaborate impressions, she can do very little to alter her position, aside from becoming more accommodating to powerful men. Yet, at this moment of impending crisis, instead of reaffirming the value of skilled participation, the tableaux vivants in which Lily participates vividly remind us that cultural abilities are now problematic for any woman attempting a lasting social transformation.[32]

Although living in a privileged circle, Lily Bart struggles to preserve her status, which is already eroding; to maintain her position among the elites who surround and assess her, Lily attempts to highlight her aesthetic skills as proof of her superiority. Deploying the now-familiar device of the entertainment chronotope, but by severing the chronotope's customary reference to skilled success, *The House of Mirth* marks the end of an era when marginal women use culture as a means of highlighting their worth. In the context of high society, the value of individual skills has been eroded by the showy and materialistic entertainment forms popular among a newly wealthy class of turn-of-the-century consumers. In entertainments such as high society tableaux vivants, we see the consequences of a more exclusive version of middle-class cultural practices, where an emergent nouveau riche society threatens the most basic tenants of upward mobility. While acculturation was an important aspect of nineteenth-century development and while relative "highs" and "lows" existed before the century's turn, historian Lawrence W. Levine suggests that near the turn of the century these categories were widely recognized as social and economic barriers.[33] In Lily Bart's situation, such a change in attitude effectively erases the equalizing potential of a skills-based culture that had operated so powerfully during the mid century (at least according to fiction). Within the vertical stratifications of the century's turn, for example, a personally expressive tableau rather than an "accurate" or "historical" one could be seen as troublingly out of touch with current trends and, hence, devoid of the potential to yield success for tableaux participants.

On the periphery of her elite milieu, Lily competes for a more stable position, but without discerning that an uplift through culture no longer affords its votaries any appreciable power. As Wharton's novel reveals, Lily's "leisure class" milieu excludes cultural strivers, reserving its praise for highbrow artists and their wealthy patrons. Instead of able competitors, famous designers abound in Lily's set, as evidenced by Gwen Van Osborgh's Paquin wedding dress and Bertha Dorset's "new man in Paris, who won't take an order till his client has spent a day with him at his villa at Nevilly," a designer who flatters his patrons by claiming that "he must study his subject's home life."[34] Particularly among the nouveau riches, who hesitate to display their personal taste, recognizable works of art stud the houses of the Wellington Brys and the picture gallery of Simon Rosedale's new home.

Notably, these exhibitions display the power of purchase rather than a command of individual aesthetics, for patrons supply the money and professional designers shepherd "culture." Lily's milieu then, effectively counters any implied potential that readers might be tempted to attach to Lily's display of her aesthetic inclinations. With tableaux pointing to a self-definition through material display, they suggest how disastrous tableaux will be when deployed by an ambitious but impoverished individual. Devoid of resources, Lily Bart will opt for an "unornamented" pose, and one that is in many ways the inverse of Laura Jadwin's consumerist self-adornment, which might, one imagines, have been more successful in high society New York than the tactics that Lily will advance.

Lily's Exercise of Skills

Lily Bart participates in a tableaux vivants production characterized by elaborate, artistic poses and arranged by painter Paul Morpeth. These representations typically depend on splendid props and rich settings, like the scene featuring Miss Smedden of Brooklyn, who carries a golden tray and wears a "rich" brocade; such sumptuous displays are characterized by the "sheeny textures, pearl-woven heads and marble architecture" of the Veronese scene and the running fountain and "sunlit glade" of the Watteau tableau (134). By contrast, elaborate, expensive props and costumes are not necessary for Lily's rendition of Reynolds's experimental portrait of Mrs. Lloyd, which requires only a small knife, a tree trunk, and filmy garments (and few of them). In Reynolds's portrait there are no jewels, no periodized finery, no gorgeous props—indeed no "historical" effects bespeaking privileged possession.

Among the successive scenes featuring society women, Lily's is the only tableau where the subject has chosen her own pose, with Lily throwing off the mantle of protective professional guidance that serves as a visible status symbol. She thus leaves her "scene" too exposed as an exercise in personal taste. As Wharton's narrator claims, Lily did originally consider a display similar to the sumptuous scenes surrounding her own, experiencing an "impulse to show herself in a splendid setting," but that "she had thought for a moment of representing Tiepolo's Cleopatra." Yet by selecting an obscure and experimental Reynolds painting, Lily chooses a model with a less easily defined value, portraying a woman in a pastoral scene wearing very simple garb.[35] Through these deviations from the expectations facing her, Lily "had yielded to the truer instinct of trusting to her unassisted beauty, and she had purposely chosen a picture without distracting accessories of dress or surroundings" (134). Both in its rejection of material "distractions" and her choice of Reynolds's *Mrs. Lloyd*, Lily's presentation fails to connote the fame associated with Carry Fisher's representation of a "typical Goya" or with the other Veronese, Watteau, Kauffman, and Vandyke living pictures (133).

Invoking a minimalist aesthetic, Lily's tableau produces what the narrative terms a "thrill of contrast" to the others. Her scene is not "brilliant" with diamonds and jewels, but as Wharton projects a language of emotive effect onto the narrating Selden, "soaring" and "poetic" rather than sumptuous, "noble" rather than "historically" accurate (134–35). Lily's viewers see "pale draperies, and the background of foliage against which she stood, [which] served only to relieve the long dryad-like curves that swept upward from her poised foot to her lifted arm" (134). This pose highlights the fact that (again from Selden's point of view) revealed here is "the real Lily Bart, divested of the trivialities of her little world, and catching for a moment a note of that eternal harmony of which her beauty was a part" (135).[36] Notably, the characters who most completely approve of Lily's pose and who appreciate her skill in directing it are those such as Lawrence Selden, Gerty Farish, and Simon Rosedale, all of whom stand aloof from rigid high society standards. They are also the characters of the least social consequence.

By evoking a little-known portrait, Lily appropriates the painting, becoming "a picture which was simply and undisguisedly the portrait of Miss Bart," as the narration comments that "She had shown her artistic intelligence in selecting a type so like her own that she could embody the person represented without ceasing to be herself" (134). Stressing the personal, nonimitative nature of Lily's appearance, Wharton hints at Lily's agency in directing her display, which is problematic in the context of her high society viewers, for it is utterly impossible that the painting could be seen as hosting the "historical" possibilities noted in Sherwood's treatment of society tableaux.

One of Wharton's central points in this entertainment scene is that a rapidly shifting social landscape results in a stylistic conservatism as the newly wealthy increasingly rely on famous clothiers, interior decorators, and professional architects, purchasing codified taste as a qualifying mechanism. Like the Wellington Brys, other newly wealthy families compensate for their cultural deficits by engaging the most esteemed tastemakers of the period, along with social coordinators and other professional advisors. Simon Rosedale, a recent millionaire, serves as the novel's primary example of a wealthy businessman determined to purchase the best (and most elaborately arranged) taste. Having prospered on Wall Street, Rosedale purchases a home, equipped with a "picture-gallery with old masters" where the previous homeowner had entertained "all of New York," although, the narrative notes, the "guests explained to each other that they had dined with him only because they wanted to see the pictures" (121).[37] Rosedale, like other nouveau riches, depends on experienced aesthetes rather than make independent choices, espousing a belief similar to the one that prevents him from selecting Lily for a wife once her value declines in the public eye.

Lily's tableau is characterized by blended nuances that, in the most positive light, render her exhibition a complex artistic effort of the sort that might be treated as accomplished in an earlier context. But these same nuances host the possibilities of multiple misinterpretations. Judith Fryer has shown that tableaux vivants, as a popular entertainment form, were associated with both high and low art forms by the late nineteenth century. Most notably, tableaux were notorious in certain areas of New York as nude shows, some for men only.[38] Thus while living pictures could have a high-culture context, there were also well-known associations between tableaux and sexualized bodies. Period advertisements such as the one for Velvet Skin Soap and Powder (*McClure's Magazine*, 1895) illustrate the complex nuances surrounding the tableaux form (fig. 17).[39] In the advertisement's illustration, a naked female figure (partially turned away from the viewer) appears against a dark, natural setting, decorously draped with a filmy swath of fabric. This scene is "framed" by a scrolling calligraphic flourish resembling a three-dimensional picture frame. Thus positioning the picture as a higher brow "portrait," the copy describes the artwork as a "specimen illustration from 'The Source of the Living Pictures or Ideal Forms and Faces.'" After ordering the soap, consumers are to receive an "elegant souvenir" of sixteen color plates featuring the "sources" for living pictures. Technically, the pictures are not for sale, but they are nevertheless distributed along with the soap, encouraging consumers to purchase the product so as to attain a supposed proximity to "real" models.

Even within this single cultural artifact, the complexities of women's tableaux are apparent. An undeniably naked body (one titillatingly cast as a "real" model rather than just a "portrait") is encased within a frame and treated as an artwork, even as the ad hawks soap by promising consumers souvenirs of naked women, "artistically" posed. At the same time, the advertisement assures consumers that they will become beautiful enough to be the inspiration (or "sources") for great art, if only they purchase Velvet Skin

Fig. 17. Advertisement for Velvet Skin Soap (*McClure's*, 1895). Hillman Library, University of Pittsburgh.

Soap. By repeatedly eliding real bodies with artistic representations and strategically encasing nude "souvenirs" in a language of aesthetic value, the ad attempts to obscure a fine line between "artistic" nudity and titillating exhibitions for combined private pleasure and commercial gain.

As it harkens to high art (via Reynolds), but also suggests the lower brow, titillating nuances associated with peep show tableaux and with consumeristic advertisements like the one for Velvet Skin Soap, Lily's tableau is layered with contradictory valences. And like the Reynolds portrait on which the tableau is based, Lily's pose reveals filmy garments, bared limbs and feet, and the clear outline of bust and thighs.[40] Although the evening of tableaux in which Lily participates is most obviously meant to point to famous works of art and elaborately realistic costumes, there remains the possibility that *any* tableau could be considered improper (particularly Lily's nearly naked revelation) and thus associated with another category of entertainment altogether. This opportunity for cultural slippage highlights the problem of invoking and showcasing skills at the century's turn, for the multiple nuances surrounding tableaux and the display of a lovely female form problematize Lily's attempt to assert her social value. Like the soap advertisement, where there is considerable confusion over what is being sold—soap or nude pictures—Lily's tableau obscures its purpose, harkening both to artistic effort and a nudity that hints at a compromised sexual purity. Read sympathetically, Lily's tableau calls attention to her skills as an aesthete with a unique personal vision; at the same time, there is in her tableau the suggestion that it is a body, not a skill, on display, complicating Lily's claim to an authentic, personal culture in the context of a consumeristic world.

In her description of Lily Bart's misunderstood tableau, Wharton depicts what is perhaps the last fully realized, extended setting of the entertainment chronotope, yet one that fails to fulfill a narrative of triumph because of entertainment's placement in a world riddled with mixed messages about ability, agency, and status. Wharton's pointed revision of the entertainment chronotope thus illustrates the considerable and widening fissures between a status linked to skills and possibilities of upward mobility in a society inclined to what Veblen termed "pecuniary leisure."

In an earlier rendering of the entertainment chronotope, perhaps, Lily's talent for creating vast impressions with little money would have predicted her triumph, but in pursuing her aesthetic choices, Lily has overlooked one of the skills that nineteenth-century fictions such as *Jane Eyre* and "Behind a Mask" position as essential to the success of a marginalized, beleaguered heroine—the ability to read others. While Wharton would have us believe that Lily has long possessed the ability to interpret those around her, this capability fades over the course of the novel, for as Lily's artistic interests become clearer, they coincide with her growing disregard for society's rigid standards, leading Lily to a peculiar predicament that combines artistic success with social failure. Given Lily's social precariousness, any perceived disruption or unconventionality has the potential to end her ambitions. Until the tableau episode, however, Lily has possessed a "passion for the appropriate," continually appearing "keenly sensitive" to the scenes around her, just as she is "unfailingly adaptable" to the interests of others (64, 56). Despite these protective gestures, Lily gradually forfeits the self-awareness that should accompany the strategic deployment of skills, ultimately helping to negate her own value, unlike earlier (and more successful) nineteenth-century heroines of the entertainment chronotope.

Yet by sympathetically presenting the tale of Lily's demise, Wharton asserts that Lily may in fact be skilled, but that her abilities fail to translate into lasting value, in part because of the uncontrollable nuances surrounding her self-representation. As Lily loses the ability to control her public image and, in turn, the ability to note a growing misreading of her, she loses an essential, mobilizing self-awareness. Lily's artistic efforts, *The House of Mirth* suggests, may be misapprehended or discredited because of changing social structures that are no longer oriented toward the abilities of tasteful strivers. Unlike Jane Eyre and Jean Muir, who powerfully deciphered their worlds, Lily Bart mistakenly clings to outdated promises associated with the power of a skills-based valuation system, which has a residual value (in the novel), but no immediate application (in her life).

In writing her version of the entertainment scene, then, Wharton inverts the kind of event so important to "Behind a Mask," where the heroine triumphs because of dual abilities to satisfy herself (by asserting her talents) and to simultaneously read others in order to gauge her social potential. Curiously, while Wharton narrates the demise of transformative skills in the early years of the twentieth century and in high society, she also invokes the meaningful tradition of the entertainment chronotope, creating a pronounced dissonance between the plot's events and the novel's structure. In this odd conjunction of a still-functioning narrative trope that traditionally champions skills within a plot where skills are defunct, Wharton points to the absurdity of Lily's situation, where skills are displaced by a lifestyle rewarding purchasers rather than inventors. Despite Wharton's sympathy for the personalized, skills-based mode of culture that Lily attempts to invoke, we can see Lily's social marginalization as a sign of a massive reorientation of values. The novel thus stresses the value of easy money, the increasing commercialism of art, and the displacement of older modes of cultural expression, launching both a critique of an exhibition-oriented society and a formal elegy for the past efficacy of skills.

Conclusion: The Waning Value of Skills

Ending a narrative pattern of portraying detailed descriptions of successful and transformative home entertainments, *The Pit* and *The House of Mirth* point to the century's turn as a moment of transitional cultural values, or the apex of an uncertain future for skills, both in the novels' treatment of entertainment and in the larger social efficacy attached to transformative abilities. In part, as home entertainment forms ceased to circulate as vital forms of cultural expression, they were less visible as narrative touchstones, less valuable to authors who portrayed popular interests. In addition, as the middling classes became increasingly associated with cultural complacency and moralistic piety, their claims to cultural dynamism declined, resulting in portraits of contest that, rather than upholding the potential of an individual's performance in both the entertainment and the larger field of play, stress the weight of communal restriction, the sublimation of individualism to communal judgments.

By highlighting cultural hierarchies that enforced defined class tiers (and disallowed older narratives of class warfare, rooted in skills), fictions that described upward mobility suggested how old-fashioned this narrative had become—particularly in regard to the story of triumphant ascent by domestic women. In light of the new century's skepticism about personal transformation, the entertainment chronotope serves as a remnant of a waning ideal of middling ascent—one as dead as the imported, preserved, stuffed polar bear displayed in late-century, high society tableaux vivants—now arranged for incidental effect.

6
Old Games, New Narratives, and the Specter of a Generational Divide

There are, of course, many fortunate girls and boys who do not require any help whatever—who always know what to do and how do it. For them some sections of this book may have little value. It is for the less resourceful children that the book was prepared, and also for such of our elders as those who, when they give a party, can never think of what game to play next.
Three Hundred Games and Pastimes, or What Shall We Do Now? (1903)

By the early twentieth century, guide books on home entertainments repeatedly refer to a generational crisis, one supposedly threatening the social organization of U.S. culture. By suggesting that young people were socially inept, and, more troublingly, that their leisure employments differed broadly from those of their parents and grandparents, authors of entertainment guides suggested that a troubling ideological divide was in the making. After all, changing notions of leisure bespoke different values and interests, advice authors suggested, pointing to a vast chasm between generations of Americans. Almost uniformly, they offered one alternative to a severed value system: repairing a generational divide through cohesive, intergenerational leisure employments, thereby creating a new argument for participating in amateur entertainments.

Helen Hollister's introduction to *Parlor Games for the Wise and Otherwise* (1896), an entertainment manual that relies heavily on competitive and boisterous parlor games, details what youngsters can learn from their elders and imposes a generational narrative on readers. Hollister presents a dialogue between an older aunt (who is the narrator of the book's introduction) and her youthful niece and friends, who are incapable of amusing themselves on a rainy day.[1] Throughout, the young people appear as products of institutional learning and, as a consequence, have little experience with organized forms of recreation, particularly two college boys, referred to as "Harvard" and "Yale" by the narrator. As Hollister stresses the importance of handing down an established set of cultural practices to the young, she also points to the potentially divisive notions of both work and play separating generations. By presenting a figure such as "Auntie," Hollister outlines the kind of overt so-cial guidance needed to bring adolescents in line with adult values.

Hollister, like other turn-of-the-century guide book authors, paints a por-trait of modern youth as uninspired and as requiring corrective intervention through guided recreation. She sees little spontaneity in the young people of her acquaintance, positioning older forms of physical and competitive play as the most useful social stimulants for youngsters devoid of any visible dy-namism. In addition, she suggests that social play can forge lucrative (and professional) friendships as she casually alludes to the prominent citizens (a judge among them) with whom she herself spends leisure time. Hollister thus situates parlor play as a means of qualifying oneself to participate in an adult social world—ironically, by returning to a state of perpetual child-hood, judging from the repertoire of nonintellectual, physical games ("Fly Feather" and "Jack's Alive") cited. As Hollister's notably successful entertain-ment book (which remained in print for multiple decades) suggests, youthful consumers promised to revitalize a dying market for home entertainment books, if only they could be convinced of entertainment's benefits.[2]

Somewhat paradoxically, in an age when parlors began to disappear from houses, publishers made a concerted effort to revive the game-playing trends of the past decades, essentially remarketing parlor games to a new genera-tion. In apparent anticipation that a renewed success in the guide book indus-try could be fueled by a new generation of consumers/participants, enter-tainment publishers sought to extend what had been a diverse and lucrative entertainment enterprise, despite the various obstacles that awaited them: the parlor's fall from fashion and competing forms of entertainment out-side the home. These two trends challenged an older fascination with home games and encouraged publishers to focus on larger, institutional spaces out-side the home. In a decade or so, many "home" entertainments would make their way into educational scenarios and public spaces.

The essential link in this marketing enterprise was a generational divide. By claiming that modern youth lacked the ability to amuse themselves, that a generational malaise threatened the cultural inheritances of past genera-tions, entertainment guide books both recast the games of the past and in-troduced new "amusements" such as the memorizing of scripted recitation pieces. They claimed that entertainments permitted the generations to com-municate with one another in playful, yet significant ways. With notably less fanfare, such texts also suggested that coercing participation from young people assured their elders that common values could be instilled in the young. Thus entertainments were to serve the social goals of youth as well as their parents, teachers, and counselors, uniting play with useful instruction.

In an era when middle-class and upward-striving young people attended clubs such as the Boy Scouts and the Campfire Girls, they were encouraged to participate in social rituals such as community pageants and in the edifyingly corrective performances of Creative Dramatics. Like the games in Hollister's book, Creative Dramatics focused on heavily guided social interaction for youth. As a drama-based form of recreation, the activity required direction by adults and enlisted child actors in roles that would correct youth by countering their perceived personal defects and helping to develop character and confidence. Additionally, dramatic play was described as creating stronger communal ties among children, particularly in cities with large immigrant populations. A nostalgic portrayal of the Creative Dramatics pioneers, Emma Sheridan Fry and Alice Minnie Herts, written by one of Fry's assistants, claims that

> . . . Mrs. Fry's work not only resulted in fine theatre for children, young people, and their parents, but reached into the lives of the players, raising their ethical, moral, and social standards, developing personalities, improving speech and appearance, stimulating imaginations, broadening horizons. The work reached back into the homes, drawing the generations together, uniting them in a common pride in achievement, introducing them to new literature, new ways. It reached into the community, lifting morale.[3]

Much of Fry's work took place in the Lower East Side of New York, a section populated by Russian, Polish, and Jewish immigrants. According to the above account, "New York has known many waves of immigrants and often, it is said, it has been a melting pot without a fire under it," hence the task of the Educational Alliance (where Creative Dramatics began), was to act as "a showcase for educational dramatics," and to "Americanize" immigrant children, or metaphorically, to provide the fire under the melting pot.[4] Frequent allusions to "improving speech," "broadening horizons," and introducing participants to "new literature, new ways" stand in as methods of encouraging immigrant children toward assimilation under the auspices of educative entertainment.

Alice Minnie Herts, Fry's primary assistant, similarly emphasizes the communal nature of the project.[5] Speaking of a production of Frances H. Burnett's *The Little Princess,* Herts remarks, "When Mrs. Burnett saw her play performed by these children of immigrant parents, she marveled, as have so many neighborhood teachers since, at the clean, flexible delivery of English."[6] In addition, Herts contends, the children develop a profound social consciousness (albeit one permeated with white, middle-class values) through role playing, arguing that "herein lies the great opportunity for using the drama as a means of moral instruction for the forming mind . . . [for] it shows that fate is largely determined by character."[7] Typically, Fry and Herts cast children so as to develop an ideal of well-roundedness, often placing them in roles that required them to play against their perceived "type."[8] The "broadening" of horizons also meant counteracting perceived individual, familial, or ethnic peculiarities by encouraging alternative forms of identity seen as more compatible with the goal of a unified, nationalistic community.

As the prescriptive nature of such activities suggests, communal, club-oriented, and developmental activities often failed to meet an older generation's understanding of recreational "fun," as these entertainments were coached, scripted, and noncompetitive. Such entertainment forms also tended to separate performers from overseers, suggesting that children and youth operated best in peer groups, save with an insistence that they required adult supervisors, counselors, and sponsors. Yet because many of these new, communal forms of leisure activity so little resembled the parlor games and other home activities of the past, they often drew pointed criticism.

The justification for heavily guided entertainment, however, stemmed from a common portrait of inept youth. As the epigraph to this chapter suggests, many guide books position "modern youth" as alarmingly unaccustomed to play, their development hampered by a dependence on external stimuli. *Stunt Night Tonight!* (1928) similarly castigated young people, claiming that "modern youth" "have pitifully few opportunities for their imagination to flame into plans for real recreation. Many of them do not know how to have fun. They must depend, many of them, on the moving picture or musical comedy comedians to make them laugh, and their ideas of humor are culled largely from the joke papers."[9] According to such texts, modern youth are unable to have an authentic experience of fun, for they rely on the ingenuity of others. This trend in depicting lackluster, inept young people allowed guide book authors to insist that adolescents and young adults differed from their elders in potentially troublesome ways and required social instruction. When compared to older-styled games, popular entertainments in the forms of recitations, pageants, and other group spectacles were particularly didactic and, hence, seen as ideally suited to bereft youth.

Ironically, there appears to be a significant relationship between activities that were heavily guided and critiques of lackluster youth, yet this was an overlap accompanied by little discussion of the ways in which children's recreations granted them few opportunities for individual direction. We might posit that scripted plays and guided theatricals may have looked stifling to a generation of adult critics, many of whom likely experienced much more individualistic and competitive modes of play in their own youths. Indeed, anxieties about a loss of personal agency were also attached to newer, more technological forms of entertainment that attracted youth viewers, such as nickelodeons and films, which were criticized as lacking personal investment and as negatively influencing youth, despite their novelty.[10]

As the inheritors of old-fashioned, competitive parlor games, the activities outlined by entertainment manuals still faced residual expectations surrounding ability, success, and playful competition. In part, nineteenth-century forms of parlor play had been so successful because they intersected suggestively with the tensions attending the middle class's mid-century rise, particularly in regard to the competitive scenarios infusing economic success. Yet by the century's turn, home entertainments focused their attention away from competition and personal skills. As Harvey Green has noted, the rapid growth of sports around the century's turn encapsulated ideals of competition and teamwork.[11] Ideals of fitness and team sports, then, absorbed some of the competitive behaviors and success-oriented ideals previously associated with the home leisure activities, leaving entertainment's spectacles to define other avenues of the participants' lives, namely familial and communal interests.

Among the most critical portraits emerging from entertainment forms is the representation of perceived deficiencies in modern youth, often portrayed as inauthentic in their modernity. As both Lears and Bledstein have argued, middle-class professionalism resulted in an increased emphasis on success, compartmentalization, and the measurement of progress.[12] Lears has argued extensively that progress itself posed a dilemma for a generation of what he has termed "antimodernists," who criticized the methods of mass production in industrial America and searched for more authentic experiences. Like Lears's antimodernists, parlor entertainment guide books also looked backward, seeking to situate the past as more authentically homespun, and, most of all, more appealingly personal than the anonymous, impersonal present inhabited by modern youth. By the early 1900s, neither borrowed nor European precedents, once so troubling to nineteenth-century Americans, are overtly called into question by prevalent leisure forms. Instead a notion of how to honor the past, a topic inflected with generational implications, is most prominent.

The Fate of Games in a Communal Age

Despite publishers' campaigns to reintroduce parlor games to a new generation, only a few entertainments from the nineteenth-century parlor would survive the century's turn, and many of those would be phased out of entertainment guide texts within a decade, particularly games. Forms of entertainment such as recitations, which became the most pervasive type of "amusement" chronicled by entertainment guide books, were inherently more presentational, and much more formal than games. No longer were popular forms of amusement characterized by skilled, physical, grotesque, or even materially elaborate forms of play; instead, recreations increasingly addressed a disjunction between "modern" youth and the values attributed to the "old-time" past, hinting at the unity they could provide—at least during performances.

Although communal and institutional forms of recreation dominated turn-of-the-century entertainment texts, games continued to appear in various entertainment guide books from the century's turn. These were not the physical, ungenteel activities of the mid-nineteenth century, which had defined middle-class participants as active agents of their fates and as individuals resisting the totalizing mechanisms of etiquette. By the late nineteenth century, game playing served as a cultural cliché of middle-class life, so well known were its associations. At this point, parlor games no longer stood for nascent dynamism, but suggested predictable entrenchment as well as complacent mediocrity. In short, game playing became a sign of middle-class conventionality, especially in an age when controversies were focused on conflicts that had to do with national as well as social equity.[13]

Faced with group affiliations that were increasingly specific—by activity, church, school, neighborhood, and less explicitly, by gender (as in suffrage groups), race (the black women's club movement, for example), and ethnicity (such as the heritage foundations)—participants in recreations were encouraged to emphasize communal identities. Offering a burgeoning set of affiliations, clubs and other groups broadened notions of peers, while claiming to develop the body, the standard of living, the mind, and most importantly, the community. The older activities of the nineteenth-century parlor could appear, by contrast, as apolitical, insular, and, most of all, as relics of a bygone era.[14]

Visible signs of attempts to recycle older forms of entertainment appeared as the same games previously oriented to adults were situated once again as children's fare. Games such as "Blind Man's Buff" and other active, physical recreations that had overturned the rules of ordinary social interaction were recast as "pretty" or "amusing" in congruence with a younger audience. In this context, their titillating sexual nuances were erased and their complex relations to adulthood streamlined. Clearly, associating these older entertainment forms with children had the effect of erasing their complexity. This erasure, moreover, could take on broad consequences, reflecting not just on current social practices, but also on the past. There is here little recognition in home entertainment guide texts that entertainment's games, with their long and complicated histories, had ever been anything but quaint, making their infantilization appear somewhat matter-of-fact. Through their new associations, the games of the parlor were severed from an argument about dynamic class ascendancy via skills and were instead transformed into social niceties for children's parties, club socials, and bridal showers. The actual games that appear in guide books of the turn-of-the-century period, however, are the same activities that had been popular in 1850, but are inflected quite differently in much the same way that reading *Uncle Tom's Cabin* in 1852 would have marked one as a very different reader from the one taking up the book in 1870.

The waning dynamism of games is particularly apparent as they became associated with the effeminate middlebrow. In the *Book of Entertainments and Frolics* (1911), for example, games help to commemorate "festive" occasions such as New Year's, Halloween, and May Day; many also appear in relation to bridal showers and other parties exclusively for women.[15] Activities such as the "Bride's Klondike," a bridal shower game, call for gifts to be wrapped in gold foil and buried in boxes of sawdust for the bride to "excavate." A "Linen Shower" calls for gifts to be hung on a clothesline for the bride to retrieve, and a "Book Shower" requires guests to dress as the titles of their books (in rebus form). Across such activities, there is little connection between ability and the right to receive gifts, with the games setting up elaborate scenarios of material reward. It is understood that only the bride will receive substantive rewards. Hence, the context of play erases the competition of older play forms, for here the "winner" is predetermined. As Wharton's *The House of Mirth* illustrated, tableaux vivants experienced a period of revitalization near the end of the century, a resurgence propelled by the newly wealthy class's love of display (not its desire for transformation). In the upper echelons of society, cultural amusements allowed the *nouveau riche* to argue that they improved upon existing social practices. Old-time parlor games, charades, and dramas for home performance, by contrast, offered an elite audience very little in terms of self- definition. Once removed from their original context in mid-century American middle-class life, games were assigned a value based largely on nostalgia.

Indeed, publishers and advertisers for entertainment guides claimed a nostalgia for games as a marketing tool. An obvious redundancy appears in the games market at around 1900, despite many texts' assertions that their activities were "new" and "improved." Notably, however, even those enter-

tainment books claiming that their games are updated have difficulty arguing "parlor" games into the lives of a new generation. Texts such as George B.
Bartlett's *New Games for Parlor and Lawn* (1882) claim to be presenting "a
few old friends in a new dress," but very few activities appear updated.[16]
Other guide books on games of the last two decades of the nineteenth century reveal similarly vague accounts of their supposed "newness."

Claiming innovation for parlor games posed a difficulty. Some entertainment texts describe the transhistorical, ancient qualities of play, pointedly
disregarding both the nineteenth-century past and any suggestion of present innovation. Jessie H. Bancroft's entertainment manual, *Games* (1937),
for example, describes "Blind Man's Buff" as "one of the oldest recorded
games and is found in practically all countries."[17] The text goes on to position the game in ancient Greece (where it was supposedly called "Brazen
Fly") and in "old" Japan. To support this unexpected genealogy, the manual
includes an illustration of an ancient Japanese scene of play, severing the
activity from the recent American past. In a similar strategy of ignoring
the games of the past, Catherine Miller Balm's *Stunt Night Tonight!* (1928)
contends that "no one . . . remembers how the idea of a Stunt Night began, but countless leaders of youth—teachers, camp directors, directors of
recreation in local churches, and club advisors—have been thankful that it
had a beginning."[18] By obfuscating the origins of the common leisure practices inherited from the nineteenth-century parlor, such texts erase the suggestion that their games were outdated and present them as timeless diversions.

One striking example of vexed attitudes toward parlor play appears in
Sinclair Lewis's *Main Street* (1920). Any arguments for the contemporane-
ousness of games must have been made more difficult by satirical texts
such as Lewis's, which thoroughly indicts such activities as pretentious, self-
interested, and hopelessly insular, even in a situation where a politically cog-
nizant protagonist attempts to unsettle the nationalism, patriarchalism, and
isolationism of a prairie town. As the novel charts the social life of Carol
Kennicott, Lewis's protagonist, the text voices a skeptical response to the continued presence of games in a modern world, where they appear impossibly
retrograde.[19] Moreover, in Gopher Prairie, Minnesota, where Carol attempts
her reforms, all political activism, all attempts at intellectual or social disruption are doomed to be absorbed into a powerful, complacent, and politically conservative mainstream. Seemingly, the old-time games that Carol attempts to introduce would suit the town's inhabitants wonderfully, yet even
these traditional activities are too challenging. As Carol, a newlywed and
newcomer, naively attempts to launch social reinvention (or at the least, the

type of reinvention that she can imagine), the rest of Gopher Prairie obdurately clings to its conservative propriety.

Irritated by the social gatherings that have been as exciting as "comas" and have included a somber "circle of mourners," Carol attempts to remake society through physical, ungenteel games of the type characterizing the mid-nineteenth-century parlor. Customarily, in Gopher Prairie, entertainment has been provided by "stunts," or individual, noninteractive, repetitive tricks, including standing on one's hands, making strange whistles, and presenting short, humorous skits. "Stunts" manuals from the early twentieth century, for example, stress the possibility of discovering unexpected skills among participants, who create a circus-like panorama of "talents." The narration notes that "during the winter, Carol was to hear Dave Dyer's hen-catching impersonation seven times, 'An Old sweetheart of Mine' nine times, the Jewish story and the funeral oration twice."[20] Carol's goal, however, is to have a lively party that unsettles both the quiet circle of ordinary conversation and the usual "stunts."

As the guests, "a shy avalanche" of the "entire aristocracy of Gopher Prairie" arrive, that is, "persons engaged in a profession, or earning more than twenty-five hundred dollars a year, or possessed of grandparents born in America," Carol watches them "form in dress parade, a long uneasy circle round the living room" (83). Resolving to make her guests "hectic" at the very least, Carol calls for a square dance, some singing, and a rowdy game of "Sheep and Wolves," which involves fighting for shoes in total darkness. The disorder of the game delights Carol when the lights come on.[21]

> . . . In the middle of the floor Kennicott was wrestling with Harry Haydock—their collars torn off, their hair in their eyes; and the owlish Mr. Julius Flickerbaugh was retreating from Jaunita Haydock, and gulping with unaccustomed laughter. Guy Pullock's discreet brown scarf hung down his back. Young Rita Simon's net blouse had lost two buttons, and betrayed more of her delicious plump shoulder than was regarded as pure in Gopher Prairie. Whether by shock, disgust, joy of combat, or physical activity, all the party were freed from their years of social decorum. . . .
>
> Carol was certain that she was a great reformer. (86–87)

Despite Carol's certainty that she will reinvigorate Gopher Prairie, she has made few forward strides by working through the outmoded genre of parlor games—a sign of her own inability to imagine the scope of true reform. Rather than challenging the ideals of Gopher Prairie's citizens, Carol provides activities that appear childish rather than reformist, regressive rather than revolutionary. During the ensuing chapters, it is clear that Carol overturns nothing in Gopher Prairie—not in her own home, not in the local literary club, not in the Little Theater, and not in regard to the poor, to newcomers, or to unpopular political dissenters. No reform known to Carol can shake the small-town complacency, for as the narrator steps in to note, the accumulating inertia of Main Street's collective philosophies have made the town representative of a middlebrow country, where the "conception of a community ideal is not the grand manner, the noble aspiration, the fine aristocratic pride, but cheap labor for the kitchen and rapid increase in the price of land"—a place where commonsense leaders "[keep] themselves men of the cash-register and the comic film, who make the town a sterile oligarchy" (310–11).

Lewis's concern, of course, encompasses far more than the lost efficacy of parlor entertainment. The perceived loss of dynamism in Gopher Prairie and, indeed, Lewis suggests, in mainstream American culture, reflects on the ways that entrenched cultural practices cease, in Lewis's eyes, to challenge traditional structures, if they ever did. And as Lewis further hints, small-town cultural life has lost its dynamic potential, for Carol's parlor games fail her, just as her efforts to transform the literary club are met with resistance and as her theatrical ventures are doomed by self-centered thespians. Carol's world is a mind-numbingly silly, self-absorbed modern world, where "stunts" form the basis of adult social interaction. The lost efficacy of parlor games is but one sign of the alarming fact that there are no viable substitutes for the dynamic activities of the past, no avenues through which to disrupt a dominant culture so comfortably ensconced in mainstream America.

The Entertainment Publishing Market in Transition

Turn-of-the-century publishing history reveals concerted efforts to try to reinvent entertainment trends in a modern context. Trends toward narrative and historical forms of entertainment are visible in many publishing companies of the century's turn, among them Philadelphia's Penn Publishing Company. Penn, a relatively small, regional company, reached a national distribution through the Sears, Roebuck and Company catalogue.[22] Its highly traceable late-nineteenth- and turn-of-the-century products reveal successive stages in the process through which "parlor" games and entertainment books gradually ceded dominance to texts such as recitation guide books, dialogue manuals, and performed reading collections, constituting a significant shift in what publishers defined as popular entertainment. Operating from the 1880s into the 1930s, Penn Publishing Company was one of a number of firms specializing in entertainment guide books, along with companies such as New York's Dick and Fitzgerald (mass entertainment publishers), New York's Beadle and Adams (dime novel publishers), and lesser known companies such as Chicago's T. S. Denison, and Paine Publishing of Dayton, Ohio.[23] Penn's offerings are largely composed of guide books. Like decorating guides and etiquette books, these manuals were often grouped in series. Invoking a cult of inexperience among readers, advice manuals encouraged consumers to view themselves as requiring specific guidance. Entertainments produced for Thanksgiving, for example, did not prepare consumers for Christmas events or May Day activities. Each new category of text indicated that there was a specific knowledge for sale. Publishers and distributors sought to convince nineteenth-century readers that they required new advice to operate in a new century; in addition, they sought to translate modern interests into an existing market niche, deploying the category of "parlor" entertainment as a descriptor for texts that no longer mention either "parlors" or games.

During the 1890s, when leisure activities became more presentational and less interactive, Penn published numerous kinds of texts, including parlor games, speakers, dialogue books, readings, dramas, marches and drills, recitations, comedies and "novelties," monologues, "entertainments," temperance pieces, humorous dialogues, and Delsarte pantomimes, with this extreme diversity suggesting a transitional moment.[24] "Parlor" games, although still visible during this decade, no longer appear to be a central textual category, for during the first decade of the twentieth century the company would issue "speakers" and "dialogue" books in the place of games manuals, with only an occasional dramatic or "entertainment" text, a trend continued in the company's 1910 to 1919 offerings.

As such trends suggest, after 1890 or so, publishing companies such as Penn gradually replaced "parlor" offerings with texts to be used in schools and club settings. Sears, too, gradually substituted its game-playing books (still called "parlor" books in the 1890s) with "recitation" guides and "dialogue" books. Sears, however, used the heading "parlor" books to refer to an array of entertainment books, making a legacy of entertainment visible to consumers. The 1897 Sears, Roebuck and Company catalogue indicates several ways that the entertainment advice market attempted to reinvent its products.[25] The catalogue relied on descriptive categories such as "Dialogues and Recitations," grouping a broad array of texts under this heading, a sign that publishers expected this label to assert a widely varying use. Sold at prices ranging from twelve cents, as with *The Child's Own Speaker* (in paper bindings) to forty cents for *Parlor Games* (bound in cloth) to $1.40

for the *Peerless Reciter, or Popular Program* (in full morocco and gilt-edged pages), the selections shown in the "Dialogues and Recitations" section include games and recitation manuals.

During the two decades that bracketed the turn of the century, Penn's entertainment and "dialogue" books were distributed through Sears, which allows us to read Penn's offerings as an indicator of a larger national market.[26] Penn's growth, certainly a consequence of its connection with Sears, was also fueled by its acquisition of other companies' holdings.[27] Penn characteristically acquired titles from smaller companies when their copyrights ran out, expanding its own holdings with proven sellers.[28] Penn also issued the work of writers who had been successful at other companies, often printing their texts in several formats, from multiple-authored selections to single-authored selections, frequently publishing collections of short plays by groups of authors before offering a single-author text by a new writer. Of the sixty-odd turn-of-the-century entertainment texts sold by Penn during the twenty-year period, only four make any reference to the parlor in their titles and subtitles.[29] While it appears that "parlor" texts were no longer widely produced, it is nonetheless important that the category of "parlor" entertainment books was still visible through the turn of the century; largely out of date by 1890, but simultaneously comfortingly familiar, the term "parlor" was invoked as synonymous with "entertainment." Penn's holdings confirm the multiple and interdependent trends away from home entertainment: (1) texts citing multiple arenas of use were reprinted frequently[30]; (2) frequently reprinted entertainment texts allude to their appropriateness for institutional use, particularly in schools[31]; (3) those texts most frequently reprinted (at least six and seven times) were school-based texts, which contained many entertainment forms deemed suitable for children[32]; (4) dialogue and recitation books for public commemorative and festive occasions boasted long printing runs, generally of thirty years or more[33]; (5) the market oriented to children's recreations overtook an adult entertainment market.[34]

From 1895 to 1905, the Sears catalogue, which sold other entertainment texts in addition to Penn's, confirms the trends at Penn and speaks to the tendencies of a national market in transition. During this time, Sears promoted traditional entertainment forms, a strategy likely related to its dependence on a rural market that lagged behind cosmopolitan trends.[35] In 1896, the first year for which an extant catalogue survives, the "Big Book" (as the comprehensive catalogue was called) offered an ample, if somewhat unorganized, "Book Department" containing debating manuals, letter-writing guides, etiquette books, fortune-telling and card-playing manuals, speech-making guides, dialogue books, minstrel books, joke books, and parlor entertainment books as well as popular fiction and household references. The entertainment text offerings at this time were primarily for adults, particularly the speech, minstrel, dialect, and joke books.

Across the broad spectrum of entertainment books advertised in the catalogue from 1896 to 1898, several adult-oriented "parlor" game books appear, "Professor Hoffmann's" *Parlor Amusements and Evening Entertainments* and Helen Hollister's *Parlor Games for the Wise and Otherwise*. A growing interest in speaker's books, dialect books as well as dialogue, drama, and recitation manuals is also obvious, as is an increasing number of children's books. In catalogue number 104 (1897), a section of the book department is labeled "Dialogues and Recitations," a category that would endure through catalogue number 107 (the fall of 1898) and which would gradually incorporate more books for young people. In addition, the catalogue also offered a section of "Plays and Entertainments" that contain scripted dramas. By now, "entertainment," "amusement," "jolliness," "mirth," "wit," and "droll humor," key words of earlier nineteenth-century parlor entertainment guide books, are absent from descriptions of the dialogue and recitation books; instead, texts are described according to the age of performers or the particular holiday festivities included.

In catalogue 109 (1900) the book section contained numerous offerings in the field of entertainment, including sections on "Books on Magic, Puzzles, and Parlor Amusements," "Dialogues, Readings, and Recitations for General Purposes," "Dialogues, Speeches, and Recitations for Children," and "Books on Conversation, Addresses, Speeches, Debates, Etc." These categories would remain relatively stable.[36] By catalogue 113 (1904), the category of "Books on Magic, Puzzles, and Parlor Amusements" disappears entirely. Instead, a single group of entertainment texts appears, now labeled "Entertainments, Amateur Theatricals, Readings, Etc.," which is dominated by interests in recitations, dialects, and children's books. By now, the terms "parlor" and "entertainment" are recognizable as separate categories.

In a coda to this story, as entertainment guide books waned, late nineteenth-century and turn-of-the-century etiquette books attempted to fill the publishing void by incorporating brief chapters on a wide variety of "entertaining" parties. Ending a long-held separation of etiquette and entertainment, etiquette books begin to include directions for amusing company in some detail, stressing elegant and presentational activities such as Shakespeare readings, private dramas, charades, and tableaux vivants.[37] Mrs. John Sherwood's *The Art of Entertaining* (1893), for example, offers advice on how to produce private theatricals, how to entertain children, and how to follow the rules for games, far exceeding the general hints on hostessing typical of books on social behavior.[38] Like Sherwood's text, other etiquette books such as *Decorum: a practical treatise on etiquette and dress* (1882), Richard A. Wells's *Manners, Culture and Dress of the Best American Society* (1890), and *Social Culture* (1902) provide specialized information about game-playing parties. Maud C. Cooke's *Twentieth-Century Hand-Book of Etiquette* (1899), *Correct Social Usage* (no author cited; 1909), and Frances Stevens and Frances M. Smith's *Health, Etiquette and Beauty* (1899) each contain chapters on philosophies of entertainment, including information on musicales, Delsarte therapy, masquerades, and other typically adult offerings.[39]

Unlike the etiquette books of fifty or even twenty-five years earlier, which merely address methods of sending invitations and receiving guests and detail what refreshments to serve, turn-of-the-century texts treat home entertainments as aesthetic, amusing, and conducive to admirable hostessing, integrating entertainment practices into those of general hostessing. This unprecedented alignment between entertainment and etiquette indicates the thoroughly entrenched position of entertainments in cultural life and suggests something of the difficulties facing entertainment guides, whose market niche was rapidly disappearing. The shifting alignment of entertainment and etiquette is in part attributable to the fact that the more active and physical games typical of mid-century adult amusement were now mainly relegated to children. Adults, after all, now had sports and athletic trends as avenues for physical play; these pastimes included pursuits such as Delsarte movement therapy, table tennis, marching drills, and an array of activities such as bicycling, rowing, and calisthenics.[40] With the old-style, competitive games now aligned with children, a new athleticism as well as a new communalism emerged as appropriate for social-minded adults.

In part, a pervasive late-nineteenth-century shift from interaction to presentation and, more generally, from play to display, suggests that home entertainment became understood as a cultural relic, and was viewed as equally stifling as the parlor's staid accoutrements. At such a juncture, the home ceased to house the vital conversations and competitions of early twentieth-century culture. In turn, amusements still associated with the home suggested a similar loss of vitality. As recitation pieces and other elaborately prepared, dutifully scripted forms of leisure amusement suggest, such forms were visible as a community-based, public-minded descendant of nineteenth-century domestic life.

Public Spaces and the Group Ethic

With the century's turn and with changes in the genres of popular entertainment forms, there are corresponding signs of a shift in what defined a public.

In part, the disappearance of the old-time parlor contributed to a changing sense of social parameters, a shift that entertainment forms register in their migration out of domestic settings. Scholars have noted the striking turn-of-the-century interest in breaking with the past and embracing an emergent modern consciousness. There is, perhaps, no single location that more dramatically reveals a technological society's discontent with the past than the parlor, which in many houses was replaced by a less ostentatious living room.[41] Modernists voiced typically critical views of nineteenth-century relics as they focused on the parlor; Gertrude Stein wrote in 1931, "A parlor is a place. Who knows why they feel that they had rather not gather there."[42] As the parlor's horsehair settees and intricate étagères were relegated to basements and attics, living rooms and spatial informality grew in popularity.

In contrast to more public social lives, the home no longer connoted the secluded, ritualized privacy that it had at the mid century, when layers of physical ornaments projected a sense of defensive isolationism, as if more layers of decorative ornamentation could shield the family from the bustling world. With Americans affiliating via groups and clubs, and with more civic organizations meeting outside the home, the nineteenth-century notion of a deep chasm between public and private spaces faded amid signs that many entertainment forms were slowly adapting to larger, more public arenas.

Through shifts in their spatial enactments, home entertainments bring up issues of public representability. For Jürgen Habermas, theorist of public space, the parlor, like the eighteenth-century salon, allowed for the circulation of discourses, thereby constituting a dimension of public culture, or a public sphere of discourse—despite the actual confines of the room. Referring to the parlor as a "public sphere constituted by private people," Habermas describes the room's "public character," especially during "social evenings," when it "became a reception room in which private people gather to form a public."[43] Linking public and textual modes of representation with public and private and bodily ones, the activities of home entertainment had forced readers to embody representations that bespoke participants' knowledge of the outside world.

By the century's turn, domestic management guides, etiquette books, and entertainment manuals alike voice a discomfort with the "old-timey" parlor, now a symbol of gilded excess and "best-room" provincialism. These texts ascribe to the parlor a stuffy, private nature, invested as they are in modern notions of openness and informality. Reflecting these new understandings of space, narratives that satirize the traditional parlor became a marker of an emergent modern consciousness as authors such as Edith Wharton and Ogden Codman, Jr., wrote that the old-fashioned drawing room "too often fails to fulfill its purpose as a family apartment" and that this overly decorated room is one "from which the inmates of the house instinctively flee as soon as their social duties are discharged."[44] Arguing for less formal spaces became a standard feature of turn-of-the-century advice books, among them Emma Whitcomb Babcock's *Household Hints,* a domestic management guide from Appleton Home Books (1881).[45] Babcock claims that "It is true that this modern room is not kept hermetically sealed, as is alleged of the older one," with the "openness" of new living spaces suggesting their appeal.[46]

In championing a comparative openness of domestic spaces, such texts set up a model of extradomestic spaces, where clubs met, civic leaders gathered, and where communities engaged in commemorative programs. Compared to an old-fashioned nineteenth-century parlor caricatured as stuffy and imprisoning, the community meeting hall, the club, and the social settlement must have appeared thoroughly modern. We can, of course, see that even events held in such spaces can hardly be described as egalitarian, especially in the days of racial segregation (legalized by *Plessy v. Ferguson* in 1896). Confronting debates about publicness thus means situating these arguments against earlier definitions of the public sphere—a difference of degree, certainly. Yet this was a difference that turn-of-the-century Americans took up with vigor, insisting on the radical nature of a new spatial and conceptual "openness" in leisure life.

The Performance Dynamics of Recitations

Recitation pieces, as inheritors of a long tradition of leisurely enterprise, promised to revitalize an entertainment market, for they were flexible forms, as appropriate in homes as they were in schools and club meetings, and as such, allowed for institutional presentations and communal representations of shared values. Just as turn-of-the-century tableaux vivants charted a movement from play to display, recitations too, were presentational spectacles, notably more didactic than playful. Changes in home entertainment forms—from participation to presentation, from amusing to enact to amusing to behold, and from strictly domestic to institutional—suggest that the individual's power to display personal agency through late-nineteenth-century play had been declining steadily. Of all the era's entertainment forms, recitations are most difficult to view as individual or amusing. Indeed, the pleasures of recitations seem to have been claimed by audience members rather than those who participated, a situation that robbed performers of the kind of playful release previously associated with active, competitive entertainments.

As part of their prescriptive nature, recitations combined youthful speakers and a scripted respect for the collective American past, uniting in the peculiar spectacle of recitations by children about the past. One of the most beloved children's books of the early twentieth century, Carol Rye Brink's *Caddie Woodlawn* (1935), suggests how prescriptive these entertainments were. Set in 1860s and '70s, the novel depicts Caddie and her brothers, who are assigned roles in a school commencement exercise for parents and community members. Filtering through this tale is the story of how adults supervise the children's involvement in the recitations. First, the pieces are assigned by a teacher, then coached by parents. We learn, for example, that Caddie's "speaking day" presentation is prepared "under Mother's coaching," and that "Caddie had practiced it with gestures and a fine Boston accent."[47] This level of preparation is notable for its extreme performative quality, for the Woodlawn family, originally from Boston, now lives in Wisconsin, making the Boston accent remarkably out of place in the rural Midwest.

The drama infusing the tale centers on Caddie's brother Warren, who, despite his memorization difficulty, is assigned a short proverb, "If at first you don't succeed, Try, try again!" Confusing his assigned recitation with the silly version invented by his brother, Warren mistakenly recites, "If at first you don't fricassee, Fry, fry a hen!" at the crucial moment.[48] At Warren's gaffe, there are titters, but also reprimands. The school mistress, a "poor, outraged" Miss Parker, "grimly" raps on her desk and orders Warren to stay after school, where she drills him to recite the correct version. Flustered and humiliated, Warren can only recite the "Fry a hen" version. In the end, Miss Parker relinquishes Warren with the parting remark, " . . . You're nice children, all of you, even if Warren did disgrace me."[49] This offhand comment draws attention to the ways that adults could claim the successes of recitations, even though the children were the actual speakers. This anecdote, though cast as comic relief, suggests the ways that prevalent entertainments become more presentational than playful. They were now serious obligations involving reluctant, nervous participants. Because entertainments circulated in and, increasingly, out of the home, it is hardly possible to overstate the degree to which nonprofessional entertainment—at one point the primary form of middle-class amusement—had metamorphosed since 1850. Along with changes in entertainment genres and performance spaces, we see here a notably limited, prescribed role for young participants.

Throughout home entertainment trends, the separation between participants and viewers had been notoriously difficult to chart with certainty. The slippage between players and viewers, for example, was essential in activities such as charades and games, where performers and interpreters took turns so as to compete. But with more presentational forms of entertainment, viewers were divided from actors, and the more amorphous concept of "participation" began to break down into specific and limited tasks. By the century's turn, such exchanges were no longer possible, particularly with elaborately prepared tableaux and with equally rehearsed recitations.

Recitations' Idealized Unity

As an entertainment form, recitations required rote memorization, privileging textual fidelity and allowing for little spontaneity or personalization. The object of the entertainment was to bring a text "to life," although there were limited permissible effects, which included discreet gestures, Delsarte poses, and expressive intonations, all effects that would not detract from the primacy of the text. As a means of emphasizing the importance of presenting texts, recitation guide books and speakers' collections illustrate ways to use "subtle" and "graceful" *gestures* (not *actions*), complete with charts and illustrations indicating how to create nuances eloquent with meaning—a small hand gesture, a lifted finger, a tilted eyebrow. Such subtlety suggested that overt physicality was not necessary, for recitation pieces and dialogues relied on only the gestures of ordinary social life, situating entertainment forms as once again refined rather than carnivalesque or melodramatic. In addition, by inscribing subtlety, entertainment guides insisted on the "natural" quality of recitations, invoking the terms that had long applied to the acquisition of mannered behavior. Despite these claims, recitations were, in fact, among the most performance-oriented entertainment practices. In this respect, as well as with suggestions of facilitating intergenerational harmony, recitations were often fantastically prescriptive, especially in their invocations of idealized communities.

As entertainment guides sought to repair a chasm between generations, they situated the child as capable of repairing perceived generation-specific dislocations in ideology. Recitations, which were essentially scripted narratives composed by adults and memorized and performed by youth, became popular as elocutionary displays and group pageants rose to prominence; because of these trends, the adults who had once participated in forms of parlor play became relegated to the audience as children took focal roles, vocalizing inspirational or nostalgic narratives about the past, that is, projecting adult values and experiences.

Entertainment books repeatedly suggested that recitations connected youth with the values of their elders. While such claims catered to entertainment's elder audience members, they also intersected with the other hints of an idealized unity promoted by recitations. Embedded in entertainment's evocation of a generational divide was the implied promise that stories of the past encouraged youth to exhibit (if not embody) a likeness to their elders. By involving youth, recitation scripts sought to narrate a return to the happy days of a mythically formative, nostalgic past. This effort, however, was mitigated by the very manner by which a return to the past was set in motion, for recitations themselves, in all likelihood, offered their participants no more "fun" than a vigorous grammar drill. They left a youthful generation little to do but admire a history rooted in an affectionate nostalgia. Like previous forms of home entertainment, recitations assigned value to the major tenets of middle-class life, frequently contrasting the modern, technological present with a simpler past. Moreover, as recitations assigned value to their subjects, they honored the middle class's formative period with narratives that included mercantile and material successes as unifying elements.

As part of their mythologizing of the nineteenth-century past, recitations presented earlier periods as "simple" or "plain," and, often, as honest and dull, erasing the dynamism of the past while lauding its successes. At the same time, recitations paradoxically suggested that the foundational, middle-class cultural work had been accomplished by ancestors, grandparents, and settlers. While depicting these ancestors as successful, recitations also present predictably triumphant stories, detailing a few struggles leading to seemingly inevitable successes.

In the face of splintering allegiances—to increasingly differentiated schools and clubs—and acknowledgment of diverse heritage, this invocation of a common struggle to inhabit the nascent middling classes presented a seductively consolidated tale of a shared past, even if that experience had not been lived by the speakers or, perhaps, by their listeners either. In part, the fantasy of imaginary unity could remain intact only if projected back onto an inaccessible past. In a sense, presenting a unifying narrative had long been the central task of home entertainment. By the century's turn, however, recitations' invocations of a collective (and often, pioneer), middling experience circumvented the more divisive issues characterizing the early twentieth century: conflicts over labor relations, stratified class tiers, and the challenges of acknowledging identities based on race, religion, ethnicity, and gender. As if in response to contentious events such as the Homestead and Pullman strikes of the 1890s, the anti-lynching debate (which laid bare racial disparities), and fears of anarchy, recitations' reference to an ideal, unified past sidestepped the divisiveness of the current political arena. An imagined unity was also significant because of events such as the Spanish-American War of 1898, which, combined with an increasingly interventionist foreign policy, propelled an idealized nationalistic homogeneity. In addition, efforts to limit numbers of immigrants, especially those from what were considered less desirable regions such as Eastern Europe and China, gave way to proposed exclusion acts and immigration caps. In this new climate of contentious diversity, recitations countered with evocations of a collective national past, providing a master narrative of unity, one yoking different generations and national ideals. At this point, too, entertainments that emphasized class narratives faded from view, in part because the efficacy of the middling tiers was no longer a point of contention now that it ceased to be a radical concept that the middling classes could appropriate and remake the practices of the elites or could compete effectively with those who were more traditionally privileged.

Ventriloquized Nostalgia and the Child Reciter

Recitations about the past were narratives about specific events and places, usually from the past, narrated from an adult perspective, but presented by children, with the discrepancy in age creating the illusion that the narrator's younger self presents a particular memory. In a phenomenon with striking implications, the turn-of-the-century child was used to articulate what could only have been an adult relation to the past, grafted onto him or her by recitation's conventions. Supplanting an interest in identification via class with the evocation of a shared, imaginary history, recitations positioned child performers as essential in the creation of nostalgic histories as they fondly related stories of a past that they never experienced. They performed before teachers, parents, older relatives, and family friends, essentially ventriloquizing adults' histories for adults to appreciate. A speaker's youth, moreover, was an essential part of a spectacle. Many stories presented the experiences of parents or grandparents, creating the illusion of personal sentiment.

The effects accompanying such recitations were, in fact, carefully created illusions. Carolyn Steedman has described a similarly produced nostalgia in her study of the child in late Victorian England, where "the child-figure becomes a central vehicle for expressing ideas about the self and its history."[50] Focusing on late nineteenth-century child performers on the stage and street, Steedman describes performances where "the meanings attached to childhood were . . . recognized by adults watching them," a process, according to Steedman, that left children out of the hermeneutics of their own significance.[51] As Steedman's study suggests, child figures could be used to fill problematic lapses in meaning. By presenting "simple" stories of the past, recitations attempted to supply a common story of heritage, despite children's removal from the essential struggle.

Recitation pieces about the "old-time" past are especially effective in their attempts to create totalizing representations—ones personal as well as "historical." This they accomplished by engaging both memory and history. As Pierre Nora contends, memory and history yield vastly different vantage points on the past, vantage points that recitation pieces purposefully intertwined so as to create nostalgically authoritative comments. Memory, Nora claims, is the product of lived experience, a "perpetually actual phenomenon, a bond tying us to the eternal present."[52] History, by contrast, offers an official, representative narrative and results in the reinvention of tradition. Even though many recitation pieces can be considered institutional via their context, they also attempted to present history as more like memory than an official narrative. By conflating the stylized effects of history with the deeply individualized nuances of memory, historical recitations deflated individual identity, treating speakers as representative of their time (most obviously), but also of their region, class, and nation. Hence these figures become stand-ins for archetypes surrounding "old-time" days and "Grandma's time."

Based on the incongruities of youthful performers appearing to possess transgenerational "memories," or coherent recollections of times when they were not yet born, it is possible to apply Nora's observation that textual history, because of its unchangeable nature, dominates and replaces fleeting and intangible memory.[53] Instead of locating memory and history as the products of an individual thought process, it is useful to consider the effects of memory and history as generationally specific. For adults, personal memory could withstand the challenges of a written and authoritative historical text. Among children, the only memory of the past comparable to historical versions of the "old-time" past would have been memories of recitations themselves. The varying functions of memory and history across generational lines suggest that the ultimate outcome of historical recitations was the recognition among youth that the "old-time" nineteenth-century past was accessible only through a carefully controlled textual invocation, a message that positioned recitation pieces about the past as indispensable in capturing and communicating the history of an era.

Despite obvious disparities between "old-time" subjects and youthful speakers, children's recitations attempted to equate the nostalgic past with "innocent" child speakers, thereby amplifying nuances of innocence and simplicity in the text. In many recitation and oration guide books, performance pieces are divided according to subject matter, including the "Solemn," the "Grave," the "Humorous," the "Sincere," the "Sublime," the "Startling," the ever-popular "Miscellaneous," and the "Pathetic," a category containing most selections about the past. "Pathetic" selections address the past in several ways. Some are about ancient customs or cities, others about older people, immigrants, the unspoiled land, the "quaint" ways of the past, and the death of a simple and obedient child as recalled by the speaker. As a general effect, "Pathetic" pieces yield a composite portrait of a simple and fondly recalled past, one that is simultaneously outdated and infantilized, as suggested by the child speakers who paid homage to it.[54]

For a piece such as Alice Cary's "Pictures of Memory" from *Choice Readings for Public and Private Entertainments* (in print from 1878 to 1920), the performer would recite a poem about a forest where an adult speaker's dead brother lies buried.[55] "Among the beautiful pictures / That hang on Memory's wall, / Is one of a dim old forest / That seemeth best of all," the poem contends, conjuring the past in an approximation of an antiquated idiom.[56] Mentioning ancient and gnarled trees and quaint habits, the recitation produces a history of a "long ago" moment. The "memory" evoked by the poem, however, seems doubly removed from its performer, once by the lack of experience with the antiquated past (a fact enhanced by the poem's adult narrative voice) and, second, by the production of someone else's memory. What results from such a performance is the transformation of a "simple," personal memory into a careful manipulation of someone else's past.

The features of the past, furthermore, are deeply entangled in the characteristics of the speakers who were to present it. In "Pictures of Memory," the narrative builds on the speaker's presumed innocence and reverence as a means of inflecting the subject as pathetic. But in addition to *voicing* an adult nostalgia for the past, the child speaker also *represents* the object of nostalgia, here standing in for the grown narrator, who recalls the death of his younger brother, which occurred when the narrator was a child, thereby positioning the speaker as both impetus and incarnation of memory. A similar recitation entitled "Grandma's Wedding-Day," from *The Young People's Speaker* (1895), positions the performer in a supposed historical lineage.[57] In the narrative, children recall the tale of their grandparents' simple wedding (as remembered from the grandparents' descriptions to the children), a ceremony with no bridal gifts, no jewels, and only homespun clothes, and a wedding of "sweet simplicity" that led to a life in a large forest, with the newlyweds combating Indians. Encased in a premodern frontier individualism and illustrative of deeply racialized notions of civilization, the past here is meant to contrast with the harried and troubled present, the world of the reciters, who can access the past only through a grandchild's recollection of a grandmother's memory. Such a poem serves as an example of the way that adults with authentic memories were privileged over child reciters, even though recitations were predicated upon the transferal of memories and, along with them, a continuation of older attitudes toward materialism, race, and the landscape.

Another recitation piece directly addressing the need to smooth out relations between the past and the present also deploys an intergenerational interlocutor. The widely anthologized "The Boy Orator of Zapata City," originally an 1892 *Harper's* story by Richard Harding Davis, like many nostalgic pieces, dramatizes a generational conflict.[58] The courtroom story begins with the announcement that a young local man, once called the "boy" orator of Zapata City, now a lawyer, is to appear in his first trial, his nickname calling attention to the way in which the story will infantilize him and position him as a representative of a younger generation. Harvey, the young professional, is, of course, expected to win the case, having been "one of the most promising young men in the whole great unwieldy State of Texas," a confident and "clever" young man.[59] As a "Serious" presentation (as labeled by the anthology), the piece attempts to show that appearances of confidence and modernity, along with institutional affiliations, do not always represent inherent value. "Pleasant" and unfailingly "polite," the "Boy Orator" personifies the polished, institutional present, where oration substitutes for experience. By situating the story's focal character as a "boy" orator, the narrator invites viewers to question youth, even a youth who is so obviously accomplished.

Beyond this framing narrative, "The Boy Orator" relates the story of the trial and records the young lawyer's prosecution of a murderer, a man described by young Harvey as "a relic of the past," who lived during the rough old days of Zapata City, when there was no operable law. Harvey contends that the prisoner is unfit for the civilized and progressive present. The prisoner responds directly to the lawyer's accusations, telling a sentimental story filled with the desire for redemption, a happy home, and restoration to his loving wife. During a lengthy and detailed self-defense, the prisoner relates his history in a simple language, admitting to his crimes, but asking for one last chance to prove to his wife how much he loves her and how deeply he regrets his wild actions. He pleads for the chance to reward his wife for her faithfulness to him, despite his imprisonment and shame (which have gone on for ten years). The man's speech spellbinds his courtroom audience, and the judge resolves that his case should be appealed to the governor in order to facilitate the man's release. The story ends as the judge asks Harvey to "go to Austin and repeat the speech that man has just made."[60] Laughing, Harvey replies that he'd "like d—d well to try," alluding to the almost impossible task of reproducing a personal, simple, and pathetic story, a reaction that reflects on a kind of impossibility stemming from the dynamics of recitation.[61]

As the story involves the grafting of a personal memory onto an individual who did not experience it, and as it transforms a critical, youthful listener into a sympathetic vehicle who will continue the tale, the piece promises to promote past values by looking to a new generation. The disciplinary overtones of such a plot are resolved only as the "boy" orator agrees to represent the prisoner's argument as well as his sentiments. Here the mending of generational fissures can only occur through what appear to be common sympathies indicative of shared ideologies of past and present. But taking on the tale also means an obliteration of the young speaker's identity, for the young lawyer must forego his professional role as prosecutor in order to appropriate the personal story of a criminal, thereby becoming the organ of a personal tale rather than the representative of a larger, anonymous system of institutional values. His identity, like that of other youthful reciters, has been subsumed by the narrative itself and by his new role as a respectful performer ventriloquizing sentiment from the past.

Conclusion

Because of the deliberate use of youth as an ideological link between generations, it is of more than marginal historical interest that the generation performing such recitation pieces went on to claim for itself radical separation from its elders. The children of the century's turn, or those who had been, we might posit, the reluctant reciters of the era, would make obvious breaks with the past, becoming the leaders of the Progressive era, the fighters of World War I, female suffragettes, and the first recognizable Modernists, who vociferously rejected the nostalgia that they associated with the nineteenth-century past. In addition, this group of youth would furnish material for the young and "lost" generations of the early twentieth century, continually castigated for their distance from their elders' values. According to Marc Dolan, a critique of young people was widespread among the moderns (extending into self-critical portraits furnished by the young), varying from fears of personal dislocation to confessionals by youth themselves.[62]

The perceived generational divide characterizing early modernity makes for a speculative reinterpretation of modern youthful rebellion, long understood as a reaction to Victorian notions of propriety and fueled by the experience of new technologies: the automobile, access to electricity, air travel, films, and exposure to wide-reaching mass media. An equal, if not more plausible motivation for rebellious breaks with the past, however, stems from leisure hours, where youth were steeped in narratives meant to evoke respectful allegiance to simplified visions of the relations between self and society. The effects of youthful cultural participation appear to have been equally strong, particularly when the youthful reciter appeared as a curiously docile signifier of collective values. Indeed, the many developmental dramas characterizing a modern version of young adulthood are visible in the enlisting of the young reciter, a conscripted speaker whose narrative sympathies were constructed through carefully staged performances that ventriloquized a deep appreciation for ancestors and their accomplishments. Despite—or one might posit, because of—the respectful, nostalgic impulses obvious in the leisure practices of the century's turn, these youth, who broke with their elders' traditions more obviously than most, focused their eyes upon the future, even though they were encouraged to look backward.

7
Imagined Unity

Entertainment's Communal Spectacles and Shared Histories

> To see one of their great annual festivals, with the massed and marching stateliness of those great mothers; the young children, taking part as naturally as ours would frolic round a Christmas tree—it was overpowering in the impression of a joyous, triumphant life.
>
> Charlotte Perkins Gilman, *Herland*

Charlotte Perkins Gilman's 1915 utopian novel, *Herland,* details the adventures of three male explorers who encounter a society entirely inhabited and governed by women.[1] Confronted with a peaceful, orderly nation where social problems such as ignorance, poverty, child care, and socioeconomic competition no longer exist, the three explorers find themselves less than content, curiously enough. Because the women have learned to reproduce at will and, as a consequence, because there are no social practices that surround and ceremonialize a sex drive, daily life is focused solely on the intertwined values of motherhood and community. "Herland," as the explorers fatuously term the state, appears to them childish, prescriptive, and boring. As Terry, the egoist and domineering male of the group, attempts to pinpoint his frustration with the society, he describes the nation "an everlasting parlor and nursery," bemoaning the absence of personal and "adult" interests (98).

Arguing that there is no real excitement in what the story's narrator, Vandyke Jennings, describes as a "perfectly run country," the explorers call attention to aesthetic products that lack complexity born of conflict. Van concedes, "The drama of the country was—to our taste—rather flat. You see, they lacked the sex motive, and with it, jealousy. They had no interplay of warring nations, no aristocracy and its ambitions, no wealth and poverty opposition." Rather than base their arts on the contentious conflict that is common within more masculine nations, the occupants of Herland take part in elaborate pageants, or "a sort of grand ritual, with the arts and their religion broadly blended." Uniting "the drama, the dance, music, religion, and education," national pageants result in "great annual spectacles, with the massed and marching stateliness" of young and old alike (99).

Viewing the nationalistic drama of Herland, Gilman's visitors respond with a profound sense of discontent, even as the pageants celebrate such seemingly uncontestable principles as "Peace, Beauty, Order, Safety, Love, Wisdom, Justice, Patience, and Plenty" (100). For them, the nation's pageantry compares unfavorably with the memory of the play that children "naturally" have around a Christmas tree, or domestic entertainment that seems (to Van and the others) more natural than pageants, where stately nobility overshadows spontaneous interaction. Inextricably bound up with the pageants is a profound sense of a loss of "real," competitive play.

Opposing personal goals and interests to communal ones, the explorers in Gilman's text bemoan entertainment's departure from more vigorous spectacles of personal agency and clear accomplishment. The shift that they witness, from individualized entertainment to communal display, commonly appeared throughout early twentieth-century leisure life in the United States, where similar pageants were in vogue. As Gilman's text suggests, the larger trend in amateur entertainments involved a stark contrast between self-indulgent pursuits and socially conscious group platforms. Locating individualism in the nineteenth-century past, new entertainment forms sought to mute and problematize personal achievement by casting past accomplishments as culturally formative, yet arising from a simpler world, where individualism was uniquely possible in a more homogeneous, less developed society. A comparable strain of individualism is difficult to locate in the early twentieth-century communal spectacles. By the century's turn, the exercise of personal accomplishments was unsuited to public display, entertainment forms suggested, gesturing toward the complexities of a globally conscious, internally divided nation, where spectacles of collective values performed the vital work of defining broad, uncontestable goals.

As William Gleason has argued of Gilman's novel, *Herland* envisions what Progressive Era leisure guides and playground reformers alike would have been prepared to see as a "very utopia" of the "recreational, educational, and social changes play reformers sought to make in a modernizing American society."[2] As Gilman's novel champions the finely developed values of an egalitarian society invested in noncompetitive, communal spectacles and, simultaneously, allows characters to critique them as lacking the so-called "natural" qualities of less scripted leisure activities, it enters a fraught debate about the receding value of personal investments in entertainment's goals and methods. In early twentieth-century America, where pageants and group festivals had become popular forms of entertainment, group entertainments frequently dramatized a sublimation of selfhood to identifiable, public group identities. Among early twentieth-century Americans, leisure

hours were frequently devoted to reforms of various types, whether via suffrage, dress reform, race reparations, social settlements, or heritage societies.
Emphasizing community values and group affiliations, the entertainments
connected to clubs and reform groups (like the pageants of Herland) promoted strong religious, civic, and national bonds, creating spectacles of solidarity. Yet Gilman's text, which champions many other aspects of the utopian state, portrays communal entertainments as strangely unsatisfying, a
reflection on the flawed, hypermasculine explorers who view the country, but
also a rendering of common critiques of the rigidly institutional recreations
that formed the inheritors of the parlor entertainment tradition.[3]

Upon reading entertainment forms historically, it is indeed difficult to
point to obvious forms of agency exercised during communal recreational
pursuits. To locate the agency infusing modern entertainment forms that de-
scended from the parlor, however, we must look to the deliberate, ideological
narratives that these leisure practices promoted. With dramatic vehemence,
they crafted a narrative of past accomplishments, treating the past respect-
fully, while simultaneously highlighting its limitations. They situate the personal agency they locate in decades past as endearing, yet deeply suspect
manifestations of an individualism they link to a simpler era, an insular, homogeneous, and infinitely more naïve world.

Institutional Entertainments

Institutional forms of entertainment dominated recreational life after the
century's turn, offering a striking contrast to the more individualistic activities of nineteenth-century leisure time. As Paul Boyer argues, "In the Progressive years, efforts to exploit the social-control possibilities of civic idealism
reached unprecedented levels of intensity."[4] Stressing the values of "intense"
uplift, many turn-of-the-century entertainment guides were published by
groups with specific affiliations, among them the religious publishers such as
the Cokesbury Press and the Christian Herald.[5] Displaying a zeal for social
reform, these entertainment guides promote forms of play that emphasize
character development and Christian values. Additionally, in their extended
arguments, such texts situate individual development as merely one step toward the more important goal of community (or church or club) solidarity.

The social bonds forged through entertainment, ideally, were to create
tightly consolidated, if not homogeneous, communities. Amos R. Wells's *Social
—To Save* (1895) asks, "What is it to be social?" and answers, "It is to appreciate the meaning of life."[6] According to the text, creating a secure social
sphere promotes Christian values. Published so as to rejuvenate Christian so-

cieties, the text argues that properly "social" qualities such as "the charm of winsomeness" can be used to "win souls for the Master"—while producing an attractive social arena for worshippers.[7] Despite its "new" interest in recreation, the text is composed of the same parlor games that characterized mid-nineteenth-century guide books. Clearly, what counted as fairly outrageous amusement at the mid century was now tempered enough for introduction into conservative sites such as churches. Texts such as Wells's also indicate that the activities that had made up parlor entertainment had become important enough to be included in and controlled by the church (or school or club) in direct ways. Significantly, this inclusion occurred only after the perceived disruptive potential of home entertainment forms had waned considerably.[8]

As Wells contends in his 1894 *Social Evenings,* the importance of recreation in the church should be widely accepted, for "This is no place to argue with those who do not believe in the value of the social element in church work. I believe that recreation is a Christian duty, and that all Christian duties fall within the province of the Church." The goal of social activities, Wells argues, "is not so much *sociability,* as sociability *diffused.*"[9] Wells urges his readers to consider an emphasis on individualism by inviting individuals to form a "committee of Columbuses," or a united group of cultural explorers. In the interest of what Wells terms "Christian socials," he advocates efforts to "diffuse" individual differences between the wealthy and the poor as well as the social and the bashful, with the ultimate goal of bridging social divides.

Like church-affiliated clubs, various other organizations sought to create a broader sense of community by invoking older forms of entertainment. Jane Addams's 1910 retrospective on Chicago's social settlement, *Twenty Years at Hull House,* positions entertainment-based clubs as vital to the life of such community centers. Debating, reading, and theatrical clubs appear throughout her account of the Chicago settlement as Addams describes their effects on community members, especially the "great desire for self-improvement, for study and debate" as well as the development of "standards of tastes and codes of manners."[10] Throughout, Addams makes it clear that club members' individual accomplishments are a significant part of her comprehensive project of community development.

Even books seemingly championing individualism, such as *Character Building Through Recreation* (1929) by Kenneth L. Heaton emphasize the unifying, communal goals of play. The text, which is presented as a teachers' guide to recreational leadership, begins with a utopian vision of children playing as Heaton claims that "developing strong bodies, alert minds, a spirit of fair play, of co-operation of bravery, of loyalty, of unselfishness" leads to a "consecration of purpose" and a desire to follow Jesus' way of life."[11] Unselfishness, cooperation, and community building form the heart of Heaton's argument for entertainment. Here, "social" play transforms personal interests into institutional and communal projects.

Other entertainment texts overtly urge individuals to subdue personal interests and adopt roles based on local history, highlighting an allegiance to broad, communal ideals. *Producing Amateur Entertainments* (1921), for example, directs young people to perform tableaux vivants of such typically "American" scenes as "Democracy's Children" and "The Texas Rangers." Such displays host incongruous "histories" that span varying generations, religious beliefs, and cultural heritages, erasing diversity with a broad rhetoric of unified sociability. One example provided by the text features a group of armed Pilgrims ready for a siege; the additional detail provided by the text appears in the picture's subcaption, "Young Jewish Folk in a Pilgrim Father Production" (fig. 18).[12] Substituting Puritanism for Judaism, the text encourages events that spectacularize an imagined past uniting groups of Americans in the same beliefs and experiences. Moreover, as the text makes clear, part of the entertainment's project is to harness an identifiable subgroup ("Jewish Folk") and supply it with images or experiences that harness its members to an inclusive, homogeneous society. Similarly, the communal performances in J. C. Elsom and Blanche M. Trilling's *Social Games and Group Dances* (1919) are calculated to produce a spectacle of mass social cooperation. The authors argue, "In plays that are natural, unrestricted, and enjoyable we throw off all artificialities and abandon our pretense. A spirit of comradeship immediately takes possession of us in our games, and some of the most valuable social characteristics are developed."[13] Relying heavily on militaristic marching drills, the text highlights stunning visual effects possible through mass spectacles. In such cases, participation could not appear individualized, so numerous are the participants (fig. 19). According to such texts, the grander the effects of play, the more valuable the entertainment.

From educational dramatics to community pageants to militaristic drills, participants in group events were described as contributing to a complete ensemble. In some pageants thousands of men, women, and children, many of whom would have been immigrants, were grouped in scenes representing national history.[14] Deprived of movement, speech, and heritage in the creation of unified public spectacles, individuality was all but obliterated.[15] As in recitations, where child performers were conscripted in representing adult memories, participation in dramatic spectacles such as pageants and drills meant that overseers, directors, and authors organized participants into spectacles of mythologized unity.

Fig. 18. "Ready for the Indians: Young Jewish Folk in a Pilgrim Father Production, Community Service," as pictured in *Producing Amateur Entertainments: Varied Stunts, and Other Numbers with Program Plans and Directions* (New York, 1921).

In light of this distinctly modern ideology of communal, unified entertainment, the parlor play of the past, on which modern games relied heavily, must have appeared devoid of direction. Older entertainment guide texts, it is important to recall, never stated a goal of class consolidation, for they hinted only vaguely at recreation's "undeniable" social and educational benefits. Compared to the more directive, ideological prefaces of early twentieth-century guide books (many authored by medical doctors, doctors of philosophy, school presidents, and clergy), the individualism characterizing past forms of entertainment lacked a communal spirit.[16] Indeed, the practice of promoting widespread homogeneity in the name of communal or national unity pervaded many early twentieth-century entertainments. They characteristically demanded that participants work toward the greater project of honoring a communal past—if not a community of their own, then a community that a dominant culture's ancestors could claim.

The Decadent Indulgences of Individualism

In their support of communal affiliations, many texts about entertainment practices inscribe individual pursuits as troublingly self-indulgent. Whereas

Fig. 19. A group marching drill, as viewed from afar, in *Social Games and Group Dances: a collection of games and dances suitable for community and social use.* (Philadelphia, 1919).

at the mid century, leisure pursuits suggested serious cultural work (reading experience, broad cultural knowledge, and finely tuned interpretive abilities), by the century's turn, entertainment forms that deviate from the communal model appear decadent and pretentious. As much as the institutional forms of entertainment from the century's turn and into the twentieth century aroused some dissatisfaction with a perceived loss of individual liberty, it is equally true that forms of individualized leisure were commonly portrayed as indulgent to the point of selfishness.

By 1900, older notions of the talent and acumen exercised during leisure hours—once seen as signs of an individual's effort to improve herself through steady labor—were now recast as narcissistic. Devoid of the ethos of self-improvement, individual skills could take on radical new meanings. Because of the vociferousness with which even ambitious and talented individuals were treated as suspect, honing one's abilities (the work once associated with class building) appeared problematic. The era's literary characters who pursue their talents, for example, commit an ultimate betrayal of the community, forsaking their potential for leadership in order to pursue individual desires. In both Emma Dunham Kelley's *Megda* (1889) and Harold Frederic's *The Damnation of Theron Ware* (1896), individuality and community are at odds; according to these novels, there are no compromises between the advancement of the individual and the development of a unified, centralized social sphere.

Kelley's novel contains multiple allusions to entertainment within the context of a black Christian community, with the novel supporting only those forms of amusement that transcend individualism and support a religiously oriented social sphere. Hence, music and inspired recitations reap the approval of the text's most conservative characters, while dramatic declamations are critiqued, particularly by the heroine's future husband, a minister. The central character, Megda, is both talented and universally liked, marking her as ideally suited to the task of influential community leader. Hence, any activity that does not explicitly further a Christian lifestyle is deemed worthless by Kelley. At a public performance by the local "Young People's Literary Society," Megda displays her abilities, first with a piano duet, which meets with universal approval. Next she participates in a recitation entitled "The Polish Boy." Expertly rendered, the recitation produces an outpouring of sympathy as Megda represents the vantage point of "a poor mother in her agony, love, fear and self-forgetfulness" who "pleads for the life of her boy."[17] In a similarly pathetic vein, Megda recites again, this time presenting "The Widow's Light," a piece rendered "in a subdued manner, which was just what was needed," according to the narrator (156).

But as Megda presents the role of Lady Macbeth, forgoing roles of the less fortunate for a dramatic, emotive display, the text notes that she serves as the "queen" in her group of young friends, wielding great influence. But, the text intimates, the portrait of Lady Macbeth accomplishes little good. It is neither inspiring nor socially useful, revealing merely an immature pursuit of personal recognition. The index to this belief appears in Mr. Stanley, the minister, who registers "a look of stern displeasure" as Meg is greeted with a "storm of applause" when she appears as a "tall, queenly woman" (159). As the audience interprets Meg's dramatic readings as "really something wonderful," Mr. Stanley becomes increasingly aloof (161). It is when Megda appears in a curtain call, bowing low, that she earns a "look of stern displeasure" that deepens to "one of sorrow and pain" at her pride (163). His response (along with that of a similarly minded friend) causes Megda to query, "Were the pleasures of the world so fleeting? Did it require something higher and nobler to satisfy?" (165). Despite the text's representation of Megda as talented, in this end-of-century-paradigm, her abilities do not attest to her uniqueness (and, hence, to her personal elevation, as with Jean Muir) or her misreading by a privileged social circle (as was the case with Wharton's Lily Bart), but to her worldliness and unwillingness to accept her role as a restrained, influential Christian leader, which Kelley suggests she could indeed be.

A more extended and, ultimately, more disturbing portrayal of personal, recreational pleasures appears in Harold Frederic's *The Damnation of Theron Ware* in what is, perhaps, the most prominent American treatment of *fin-de-siècle* aesthetic decadence. Frederic's central concern lies outside of Christian theology and its impact on communities (for Frederic held religion in no particular regard), despite the fact that his central character is a Methodist minister. The novel highlights personal failure and moral ineptitude over religious hypocrisy (which is also present in the text) as personal decline allows a previously zealous and visibly committed minister, Theron Ware, to privilege personal pleasure over community responsibility. As Frederic's novel traces Theron's moral decline, along the way, noting the way that the church makes use of individual charisma, but without lasting regard for the individual, Theron abandons his duty to his congregation and loses interest in his marriage. Ultimately, Theron's self-serving pursuit of personal superiority becomes too rarified, too personal, and too sexual, serving as proof of his corruption.

For Theron, the opposition between the personal and the communal stems from his religion's narrowness, combined with his own growing desire to pursue aesthetics, which his associates, Father Forbes (a Catholic priest) and Celia Madden (a seductive, red-headed aesthete) deploy so as to bewilder the relatively unschooled minister. And as Frederic makes clear, Theron's faith is built on a combination of enthusiastic ignorance and a need for external expressions of approval, not on real insight or devotion; he is motivated solely by outward appraisals of his worth. Yet the church is equally problematic as the site of Theron's quest for distinction. The Methodist church elders and congregation appear small-minded, as unable as Theron to set aside personal interests for any greater good. As the text progresses, Theron's naïveté turns to crass materialism, his religious convictions to arrogant skepticism, and his fervor into unskilled showmanship as the novel stresses the multiple ways that Theron abandons himself to pleasure. When he fancies himself to be growing wise, Theron rejects his communal duties and exclaims to the beautiful, cultured, Celia Madden, "I am not a Methodist Minister—please! . . . at least not today—and here—with you! I am just a man—nothing more—a man who has escaped from lifelong imprisonment, and feels for the first time what it is to be free!"[18]

Declaring that he will "smash" the bonds of convention, Theron pursues personal growth (as he sees it) at the expense of every other commitment, a pursuit made more problematic by the reader's knowledge that Celia (like his other would-be mentors), takes malicious pleasure in leading Theron into indecipherable realms of knowledge, which, she intimates, will make him more of a peer in her eyes. Because of Theron's insatiable desire for recognition, he begins to refer to his life as a "slavery—a double bondage," when speaking of his marriage and his ministry (261). At the height of his corruption, Theron, thinking of Celia, prays to the moon, which he sees as "our God . . . Hers and mine! You are the most beautiful of heavenly creatures, as she is of the angels on earth. I am speechless with reverence for you both" (263). Not only claiming to worship the moon in place of a Christian deity, Theron turns to a private, deeply flawed spirituality in place of the Methodism with which he is affiliated.

As the novel indicts self-indulgence, various striking entertainment scenes reveal the increasingly self-interested desires dominating Theron's life. In one of the most fantastic entertainment episodes in late nineteenth-century literature, Frederic situates a musicale in the private apartments of Celia Madden, where low lighting, Greek columns, and naked statuary initially shock Theron. But the sensationalism of the episode does not end there. Celia proceeds to smoke cigarettes, to uncoil her mane of luxuriant red hair, to slip into a "shapeless, clinging drapery, lustrous and creamy and exquisitely soft," and to perform the piano works of Chopin, the tumultuous strains of which completely unsettle the musically inexperienced Theron (198). As Celia claims to be "Hellenizing" Theron, she continually plays to his desires, giving him "sparkling half-winks" and a "roguish smile" (197). At the conclusion of the emotional recital, Theron remarks that her playing has been a "revelation" to him and that it is something that he will remember "to [his] dying day" (201). The problems announced by such a scene are multiple. First, Theron's adulation is voiced in the language of sacrilege, revealing his inability to separate artistic enthusiasm from religious fervor. Then too, Theron's supposed journey of self-improvement appears but a fallacy, for his responses to his so-called aesthetic education appear emotional rather than intellectual and, worst of all, oriented toward his desire for Celia's approval rather than toward "art." Although he craves recognition as a man of the world, he remains Celia's dupe. Finally, too, Celia's efforts to tantalize Theron appear limitedly personal, for her designs are nearly incomprehensible, except as pure mischief.

If the story of Theron Ware is strangely unfulfilling, it is because it inverts a familiar narrative pattern where self-improvement engenders uplift, then recognition. A narrative encompassing ability to acceptance constitutes a story that would likely have been told fifty years earlier, when Celia Madden would have been sincerely invested in Theron's strides and Theron himself

capable of affecting a larger social milieu. But Frederic robs his characters
of the merits previously attached to such a tale. Responding to a characteristically modern distrust of personal motivation (and voicing a sentiment
not unlike that fueling pageants, drills, and community entertainments),
Frederic produces a text that remains critical of the selfishness that dominates Theron's life. The avid pursuit of personal interests, Frederic suggests,
leads to a dislocation from community and family and, in the end, to moral
disintegration. At the same time, Frederic's novel fails to uphold the vision
of an integrated community, for it also convincingly indicts the hypocri-
sies and narrow-mindedness associated with Methodism, Catholicism, and
small-town values—the vehicles that could provide unity.

As both Frederic's and Kelley's admittedly different novels attest, instead
of indicating the worthiness of hereto unrecognized figures possessed of a
profound, if untapped potential, individuals with presumed abilities come
to represent a threat to social unity. Earlier, individual abilities had indicated
the coming into being of a social tier composed of individuals possessed of
unique abilities and profound personal agency. By the century's turn, however, there is no group logic that justifies the exercise of individual talents. If
talents are not directed toward the unification of the community, but to the
distinction of the individual, they appear dubious rather than transformative, decadent rather than dynamic.

Myths of a Familiar Past

While the period's fictions indict the type of individualism that they link to
moral stagnation and personal decline, entertainment guide books struggle
to locate larger, collective values associated with play time. As part of their
goal in highlighting a unified American experience via narrative entertainments, many entertainment forms focus on the past at a moment when citing
national unity appeared problematic, if not impossible to claim. Helping to
raise the consciousness of contentious difference within the national sphere
were authors such as Zitkala-Ša, who wrote of the conflicts posed by the jux-
taposition of her Sioux background and her white education. In addition,
there were Abraham Cahan (whose stories of ghetto impoverishment among
New York Jews began to appear in print during the 1890s), Sui Sin Far (the
first Eurasian to write about her U.S. experiences) and Charles Chesnutt,
Pauline Hopkins, Frances Harper, and Anna Julia Cooper (who produced fictions that drew attention to the hopeful future of black Americans, while
demonstrating race-based inequities inherited from slavery and Reconstruction). Given the recent divisiveness of an incomplete and difficult period of

Reconstruction, along with the institution of racial segregation (via *Plessy v. Ferguson* in 1896), it was clear that America was deeply and internally divided by 1900. Additional complications also threatened to divide the nation's population, among them the woman question, debates over Southern lynchings, the treatment of Native Americans, and proposed restrictions on immigration.

Somewhat unsurprisingly, at this historical juncture, entertainment forms of all sorts were characterized by split impulses between personal and communal, past and present. In the Playground Reform Movement, where parks and other city spaces were set aside for city children's leisure hours, there was an obvious nostalgia for "a lost, magic space of 'real outdoors'" that echoed tensions surrounding the perceived loss of an American frontier, announced by Frederick Jackson Turner in 1893.[19] With the urbanization of the landscape and the loss of what Turner cast as the formative frontier "experience" (an experience, in his eyes, capable of assimilating various forms of difference), came a modern lifestyle that appeared vastly different from the one that many adult Americans had known. Consequently, as William Gleason contends, the playground's space emerged as "the culture's most vital space," even as the Playground Reform Movement was itself fueled by opposing goals, one being the regard for individual experiences with the land, and the second being a desire to inculcate children with a sense of communal affiliations, which could further the assimilation of many poor and immigrant children.[20]

Part of what shaped prevailing attitudes toward leisure time was an undeniable sense that the national landscape—both physical and demographic—was changing dramatically. Richard Slotkin has argued that just as the public became conscious that the frontier was no more, the mythologizing of the West as a grand, national experience began.[21] Moreover, as an emblem of the American experience, the fictionalized, mythic West offered a convenient means of defining a formative Americanism, despite the fact that many Americans had never been there; however, they could all experience the myth.

Narrative, commemorative entertainment practices attempted a similarly unifying, nationalizing narrative as they sought to define some imagined moment of past solidarity, even if that moment had to be invented rather than recalled. Just as the mythologizing of the West conjured a broad, all-encompassing category of American experience, so too did the representation of American history, specifically of a break between the nineteenth and twentieth centuries, which was frequently invoked by recitations, group enactments of the past, and "old-time" entertainments. Purposefully broad, these stories entailed the dissemination of a distant, inexact past. From Puritan settlers to woodsmen to nineteenth-century members of the rising middling classes, key figures in recitations herald an imagined collective experience, one that projected white, rural, and middling values onto an increasingly diverse nation. Publicly circulating images of an imagined, collective past promised to unite participants and spectators. In this sense, commemorative forms of entertainment were invested in presenting myths as an all-inclusive, revisionist history where personal advancement and community building mutually reinforced one another. By acting out an idealized communal past, participants could uphold a vision of widespread harmony, which could be reenacted so as to include all participants in a coherent public vision of neighborhood and nation. The resulting narratives of national unity are essentially nostalgic, depicting a "historical decline and loss, involving a departure from some golden age of 'hopefulness.'"[22] Infused with suggestions about the loss of "personal wholeness and moral certainty," the "collapse of values" in the present, as well as perceived losses of "personal authenticity and emotional spontaneity," these texts treated the collective past as redemptive.[23]

Entertainment forms that took up historical narratives, particularly recitations, frequently attempted to represent the story of the nineteenth-century past as the antithesis of progressive modernity. This tactic involved contrasting an insular history with a sophisticated present. Casting the past as deeply personal and full of anomalous events, these narratives evoke a sympathetic nostalgia, keeping the past in public view for the purposes of contrast with the present. An entertainment such as "An Old Time Social" requires that guests appear in quaint costumes.[24] For the event, the "rooms should be decorated in 'old-time' style; old straight-backed cane-seated chairs, and claw-foot tables." Dried apples and pumpkins are advocated as decorations, as well as a grandfather clock and an "old-style" fireplace set. In addition, "old fashioned favorites" such as Blind Man's Buff and Forfeits are to be played.[25]

"Old-styled" entertainments, a particular subgenre of recitation appearing throughout entertainment manuals of the century's turn and beyond, also treat the past as laughably unpolished. The spelling bee in "An Old School Social" and various "pathetic" reminiscences require participants to "tell what event of your childhood made the most lasting impression on your mind." In "A Memory Social," where anecdotes about the past are brought to life, participants are to "recite the first poem ever committed to memory."[26] Directions for "An Old Time School Exhibition" (an evening theme party) suggest that "the interest in old-time manners and customs has become so universal that any representatives of the same will be welcomed most cordially by the majority of the people" who attend parties.[27] Here guests are to dress "in the costume of long ago" and are directed toward a room with "old-time story books," schoolroom benches, and "rough clapboard" seats. Each should take "some quaint old baptismal name" such as "Prudence," "Patience," "Deliverance," "Charity," "Hepzibah," "Elijah," or "Elected." Thus characterized, players take parts in a mock school recitation, which will be performed before an assembled school committee, where some speakers are urged to forget their pieces, others to "fail utterly," and all behave in a caricatured "old timey" way (119) (fig. 20). In the "historical" ethnography provided by such pieces, the past is rendered as devoid of any profound social consciousness and appears hopelessly insular, odd, and in the end, laughable.

This pronounced trend in caricaturing the past is satirized by Edith Wharton in *Hudson River Bracketed* (1929), where the protagonist's grandparents indulge in nostalgic play, which functions as a contrast to a troublingly complex present.

> They were a magnificent-looking couple, too, and when the Old Home Weeks began to be inaugurated throughout the land, Mr. and Mrs. Scrimser were in great demand in tableaux representing The Old Folks at Home. Mrs. Scrimser spinning by the kitchen hearth, and his grandpa (with his new set [of teeth] removed, to bring out his likeness to George Washington) leaning on a silver-headed crutch-stick, his nutcracker chin reposing on a spotless stock. But grandma liked better figuring as the Pioneer Wife in a log cabin, with grandpa (the new set in place again) garbed in a cow-puncher's rig, aiming his shot-gun through a crack in the shutters, and the children doing Indian warwhoops behind the scenes.[28]

Despite the images of wholesome heritage displayed here, Wharton's framing narrative calls attention to the dissonances between the comfortingly nostalgic, homespun backwardness of the "Old Folks" scene and protagonist Vance Weston's ultramodern, inconsistent elders. As Vance soon discovers, his grandfather is conducting an affair with his own teen girlfriend. Later, his grandmother, whom he once deemed mysterious and spiritual, becomes little more than a con artist, working as an evangelical enthusiast who capitalizes on her grandson's fame as a writer. The point of Wharton's deft tableau is clear; modern elders merely play at the appearance of stalwart and reliable family leaders of the past. Clearly, however, the grandparents of the 1920s are so far removed from reliable leaders that they can both invoke the images of old time stability and subvert old-time values at the same time. As Wharton's

Fig. 20. "Hi Holler," representing "An Old Time School
Exhibition" from *Popular Amusements for In and Out
of Doors* (1902). Courtesy, The Winterthur Library:
Printed Book and Periodical Collection.

tableau of "old time" entertainments suggests, "historical" representations
not only caricatured the past, but stood in relief to the relative complexity
of the present, where there were no similarly simple, straightforward narratives.

In part, recitation's status as an entertainment had the effect of bely-
ing the importance of entertainment's serious cultural work in narrating a
break between past and present as performed narratives smoothed over dissonances between cultural inheritances and individual dynamism. Raphael
Samuel terms the past a "plaything of the present" as he describes the staging
of history through the various media of popular culture, an act that resulted
in a rendering of history that is as dynamic and purposeful as it is entertain-

ing.[29] Based on Samuel's observation, it is possible to view the entertainment genres of the century's turn as fetishizing the nineteenth-century past, putting it on display, but also undercutting past accomplishments through caricatured representations. If the nostalgic recitations of the old-time past sound silly, self-conscious, or pathetic, they nevertheless reflect a moment when turn-of-the-century Americans felt the need to distinguish themselves from their ancestors, yet without necessarily asserting a pronounced faith in the present. As T. J. Jackson Lears has written, "It was not so much that late Victorians reacted consciously against modern culture as that they began half-consciously to perceive its limitations and contradictions, its failure to live up to its claims of perpetual progress and perfect autonomy."[30] A conceptual break with the past, as produced through nostalgic renderings of recent history, reveals the kind of "crisis of cultural authority" that Lears describes, although the nostalgia produced through entertainment is not so much distrustful of the past (as Lears would posit) as problematically indebted to it.

Somewhat ironically, popular entertainment forms such as pageants and recitations resembled past activities much more than present-day innovations. There was, for example, very little of modern technology visible in recitations, in contrast to kinetoscopes and nickelodeons or the filmic trends of the century's turn and beyond.[31] Nor did most forms of pageantry entail mechanized innovations. Earlier, methods of home entertainment had reflected some of the latest technological innovations, as in tableaux with elaborate lighting, special effects, and photorealistic scenes. In part, what was missing in the early twentieth-century remnants of the parlor tradition was the visible incorporation of new methods and innovative technologies. Claims to a trajectory of progress, then, were primarily voiced through narratives.

As an emblematically modern speaker who voiced his discontent with the past, Henry Adams describes a difficulty charting his relationship to the dawning twentieth century, exploring tensions similar to those in narrative entertainments.[32] Writing in *The Education of Henry Adams* (1907) at length about the supposed failure of his nineteenth-century education to prepare him for twentieth-century life, Adams presents himself as searching for paradigms through which to interpret new, technological innovations. At one point in the chapter entitled "The Dynamo and the Virgin," Adams depicts himself as crossing a dangerous chasm between centuries by narrating the break between them, forging comparisons between an older force experienced through religion and a newer, more technological articulation of power in the electric generator. In order to claim any dynamism of his own,

Adams envisions himself as a writer and historian who shapes the tale of dissonant values, taking narrative control over an institutional, technical age. Narrative entertainment forms such as recitations attempt a similar story-telling control as they link the centuries by portraying the nineteenth century's legacy in relation to the present. The problems that they face in forging "historical" connections are similar to those that Adams attempts to resolve: how to chart both the present and the past's dynamism. These goals, in fact, are deeply incongruent, as the tensions and inconsistencies riddling turn-of-the-century entertainments reveal.

Adams's dilemma, which he solves by meditating on the difficulty of explaining connections between the nineteenth-century past and the twentieth-century present, was, in the end, only partially possible to articulate through entertainment forms. Rather than emphasizing dissonant values and changing lifestyles, for example, entertainment forms work to present their narratives of the past as simple and accessible, as idealized, ideological bridges between unmentionable chasms. But recitations and pageants meanwhile claim importance for their participants by depicting the formative nineteenth century as parochial, distant, and naive, although populated with successful individuals. Only by presenting an exaggerated, deeply critical version of recent history could the leisure practices that were themselves rooted so firmly in past traditions draw attention to their progressive modernity—a tactic similar to Adams's insistence on the flaws of his nineteenth-century education.

From 1850 to 1900, the ways in which home, and increasingly, civic entertainment forms claimed to empower their participants changed dramatically. Previously, the physical play of the mid-nineteenth century suggested a visible break with gentility's traditions, hence the agency promoted by leisure activities was immediately visible. But as entertainment's forms became more congruent with notions of gentility and compatible with an emerging professionalism, physical disruption faded from popular home entertainments and their descendants. Instituting a very different form of disruption (one that also claimed a type of agency for its participants), narrative entertainments hinted that one of the most vital activities of a new century lay in radically reinventing the story of the past. One of the ironies surrounding mythologizing entertainments is that while they shaped history by claiming narrative power, the stories produced were not particularly dynamic. Their lack of spontaneity, however, is deceiving, for these stories nevertheless exercise a profound cultural work through their obvious caricatures of bygone decades, which remain at odds with entertainment's ostensible homage to an authentic past.

Selective Individualism and the "Memory Piece"

Producing an official history of the recent past, treating it as enjoyably predictable in its familiarity, personal-sounding "memory pieces" (or first-person narratives) transformed an individual memory into the history of an age, revealing the early twentieth century's predilection for converting the personal to the communal. These tales of the small-town boy who reaches success through steady principle—involving unchanging sites from childhood —inflect the past with the familiarity of memory. By invoking the history of a locality, "memory pieces" display personal anecdotes in order to create the impression of a collective, archetypal past. In this type of performance, a larger middle-class history is implied, for individuals' narratives become anecdotes for a larger swath of triumphantly formative, socioeconomic success. The blending of memory and history, so important to the era's recitation pieces, allowed personal narratives to intersect with recognizable and streamlined subjects suitable for institutional occasions at schools and clubs. Even while presenting a narrative of the past as deeply personal, memory pieces encouraged reciters to appropriate someone else's story, creating a personal tale that transcended the individual who related it. What resulted was a generic, dislocated, and supposedly personal memory that circulated as an indicator of communal experience.

While recitations hint at the entirety of the historical project that they take up, the full consequences of the "memory piece" are best contextualized through fiction, where these narratives appear as set pieces of nostalgic memory. Relying upon a first-person story of Jim Burden's youth, Willa Cather's 1918 novel, *My Ántonia*, becomes, in essence, a performance of stylized nostalgia, an elaborate memory piece that builds on Jim Burden's youth intertwined with observations about the loss of the open, free western lands.[33] The elaborate crafting of Jim's narrative is as subtle as it is deliberate, for Jim is a highly selective narrator in a story that at first seems deceptively straightforward as he emphasizes a simpler, less problematic past. In Jim's story, as in many recitations and memory pieces, the past give rise to images of a simpler, fictionalized moment when the landscape was wilder, where the people more honest, and where opportunity was everyone's. Revealing his deepest tendencies as a narrator, Jim latches onto a quote from Virgil, "*Optima dies . . . prima fugit*"—"the best times fly first"—his epigraph and Cather's announcement of the nostalgic qualities of Jim's extended memory piece.

Throughout his personal recollections, Jim consistently seeks out the positive version of events, simple stories that help him evoke an attractively streamlined past. As a corporate lawyer for a railroad company, Jim embodies the technological present as he narrates a tale in which old-time values are harnessed to his modern experience. Yet the telling of his story is punctuated with curious omissions, all in the service of reminding readers of Jim's crafting of his tale, for Jim's narrative self-fashioning is obvious, as in his insistence that simple workers are beautified by the dignity of their labor. Looking at the landscape, Jim evokes the obvious symbol of "a great black figure . . . a plough . . . left standing in the field. . . . Magnified across the distance by the horizontal light, it stood out against the sun, was exactly contained within the circle of the disc; the handles, the tongue, the share—black against the molten red. There it was, heroic in size, a picture writing on the sun."[34] Creating a striking image of heroic manual labor in a mechanized era, Jim blatantly renders the agrarian past a mythological icon.

Faced with university intellectualism and a brilliant instructor, the adolescent Jim finds himself caught between vivid images of his old life and the mental activities of the new one. At the university, Jim characterizes this contest between agrarian and professional, past and present, as a moment of retrospection, claiming:

> While I was in the very act of yearning toward the new forms . . . my mind plunged away from me, and I suddenly found myself thinking of the places and people of my own infinitesimal past. They stood out strengthened and simplified now, like the image of the plough against the sun. They were all I had for an answer to the new appeal. (875)

This "new appeal" of the intellectual, institutional present allows Jim to embrace the authenticity of farm labor. Only by vividly imagining the past as the site of a mythic struggle with the elements can Jim retain its values. In his situation, Jim Burden is emblematic of the early twentieth-century American, the one who "moved ahead" to the city, to a professional life. Stories of the past, like the one implicit in Jim Burden's plough story and like the recitation pieces of the period, reveal an interest in retaining some small fragment of a rapidly receding past in order to honor that past as well as contain it via self-consciously personal performances.

The potential appeal of such narratives is obvious, but as Jim tells his tale, Cather exposes the difficulties and the occasional self-induced blindness necessary to construct such an unnatural, nostalgic tale.[35] Notably, the stories that Jim foregrounds are those that highlight the seemingly indisputable values of self-reliance and perseverance, interests that allow him to privilege the successes of Lena Lingard, Tiny Soderball, and, eventually, Ántonia over the more troubling stories of failure, oppression, and limitation prevalent in so many immigrant lives. Throughout, the narrative is concentrated on Jim's fondest memories, among them the "Country Christmas" chapter, where Jim transforms the story of an impassable snowstorm into a tale about the values of self-reliance, homemade gifts, and the simple beauties of a Christmas tree, a story that asserts a middle-class complacency which, in turn, allows Jim to critique the complaining immigrant, Mrs. Shimerda, for her lack of self-reliance, her poor domestic management, and her un-American preferences.

In Jim's preferred narratives, we see the complacency of an affluent, protected young man, one who will never work as a manual laborer, who has never known poverty, and who has little ability to imagine the hardships daily faced by immigrant women such as Ántonia. His impatience with Ántonia most strikingly displays his failure to understand her bravado once she leaves school to labor in the fields and her desire for social freedom as a young "hired girl." Jim likewise disregards her overwhelming desire to be loved, which leads to a hasty engagement and, later, to a child born out of wedlock. Here, as elsewhere, Jim is distanced from the deeply personal stories that he tells, for his nostalgia is tied to his role as a viewer and to the episodes that he has witnessed from his position of economic security. Jim's distance from the events that he records accounts for the text's strange dissonances as it tells a story both personal and generic, individualized but also significantly removed from its narrator.

Ironically, despite the complexities that Jim's narration exemplifies, Cather's novel was widely critiqued as too simplistic for its modern readers of 1918.[36] It is therefore interesting to speculate that a critical resistance to the novel may have stemmed from its apparent likeness to other, less literary appearances of the "memory piece" in popular circulation. Yet Cather's text, more obviously than recitations, invites readers to question the completeness of Jim's tale and to glimpse these alternative stories that challenge the ideologies that Jim complacently brings to the text. Told by other narrators and recorded by Jim, three inset tales—all extraneous to the central action of the plot—contrast with the restrictions of Jim's nostalgia. In contrast to Jim's favored success stories, the Peter and Pavel tale (the story of the tramp who commits suicide in the threshing machine) and the history of Blind d'Arnault (the black pianist) collectively suggest that success is not contingent on individual effort, as Jim so firmly believes.[37] Peter and Pavel commit a horrible deed in their Russian village, throwing a bride and groom to ravenous wolves in order to save themselves, and they continue to be haunted by their deed, even in a new land. Unable to begin life afresh, they appear doomed by their past actions, with Pavel gasping out the haunting story on his death-bed. For these two immigrants, it is clear that there will be no miraculous beginning in a new country, no place where their work predicts success. Similarly unable to succeed, to take advantage of the possibilities of a new life in the West (which Jim positions as a test of Americanness), the tramp and Blind d'Arnault are crushed by life, forever severed from success. One takes his life rather than face daily competition and the other is fated to remain, via a portrait with pointed racial inflections, a pianist who plays "barbarously and wonderfully," a primitive without the ability to acquire polish or finesse (832).

Notably, these are the stories that Jim treasures as oddities and secrets rather than profound truths. Jim can imagine, as he does of Peter and Pavel's story, that "the wolves of the Ukraine had gathered that night long ago, and the wedding party been sacrificed, to give us a painful and peculiar pleasure" (751). Unable to recognize or acknowledge the unsettling hegemony implicit in these stories, Jim reflects on them only briefly. Instead of acknowledging stories of unfairness, marginalization, or lack of opportunity, he privileges the successes he comprehends: of Frances Harling, the savvy businesswoman (whom grandfather respects), of the domestication of Ántonia (of which Jim approves), of Tiny Soderball's economic success (proof of a hired girl's grit and ambition), and even of Coronado's supposed success in reaching Nebraska (this being a pet belief of Jim's). Jim characteristically glosses over uncomfortable tales: the story of Wick Cutter's attempted attack upon Ántonia (which ends with a glib comment about the Cutter marriage rather than about the near rape), his own relation with Lena Lingard (where there is a suggested intimacy and some teasing about marriage), and Jim's relationship with his scholarly mentor, Gaston Cleric (a tale riddled with erotic overtones).

Careful not to disrupt the simplicity of the story that he wishes to tell, Jim studiously avoids complications, particularly the complications that reflect on inequity, failure, and profound personal tension. Repeatedly, Jim's storytelling solution is to return to the "simpler" past. Most startling of all are his revisionist stories about his feelings for Ántonia, who is initially intertwined with Jim's competitive attitudes toward immigrants' encroachment upon the American West and his ambivalent, youthful sexuality. Indeed, it is only when Ántonia has borne a child out of wedlock that Jim announces that, "I'd have liked to have you for a sweetheart, or a wife, or my mother or my sister—anything that a woman can be to a man" (910). Given the patent absurdity of such retrograde wishes, situated as they are in the unchangeable past, Jim's desires bespeak a narrative need to erase dissonance. Rather than justifying his choices in the past or the present, Jim searches for a neutral, uncontested narrative of his relationship with Ántonia, ultimately finding it in the movements of the celestial bodies. As he prepares to leave Nebraska and Ántonia, a parting which will last twenty years and during which he voices disappointment in her hard, humble life, he notices the sun and moon, hanging on opposite sides of the sky. "For five, perhaps ten minutes," Jim narrates, "the two luminaries confronted each other across the level land, resting on opposite edges of the world. . . . I felt the old pull of the earth, the solemn magic that comes out of those fields at nightfall. I wished I could be a little boy again, and that my way could end there" (910). Constructing a story where his agency is erased, where he and Ántonia inhabit separate paths like the celestial bodies, Jim invokes a metaphor that explains an inevitable modernity, one experienced rather than chosen. According to this story, Jim is propelled by larger forces, which have set him on his particular path in life—one removed from his childhood friends and from the great western landscape of his youth—to life in New York City, to an unfulfilling marriage, and to corporate law.

While narratives like Jim's create an attractive, personal rendering of the past that seems immediate and satisfying, it is important to consider that such a zeal to codify and simplify history was not without its consequences. Such stories position nineteenth-century history as social, familial, nurturing, local, secure, but also predictably familiar. Memory pieces thus emerge as narratives that attempt to remind readers and auditors of a common set of tropes that fill in for the personal experience of the past, thereby supplying the same "memories" for a wide array of readers and listeners.

In the following anonymous poem, listed among a group of "Old Quotations" from Nellie M. Mustain's *Popular Amusements* (1902), a text containing many recitation pieces, a similar balance between personal and institutional stories appears in a poem about an old schoolhouse.

The old schoolhouse is altered now; its benches are replaced
By new ones, very like the same our pen-knives had defaced;
But the same old bricks are in the wall, the bell swings to and fro,
Its music just the same, dear Tom, 'twas twenty years ago.[38]

Here, although the interior fixtures of the old schoolhouse have altered, the structure's function, exterior, and sounds are all frozen in time. The speaker's memories of the place are similarly arrested. In his mind, the schoolroom is unchangeable, belonging to a recognizable past. The poem also dwells on the discrepancies between past and present, experience and history. Notably, too, the speaker soliloquizes before an imagined audience member (Tom), further personalizing the piece. In its attempts to transform the "old schoolhouse" into an object of nostalgia, this recitation evokes a rendering of the past that sounds like a memory, but which is transmitted in a written, repeatable text. By eliding memory's effect and history's evaluative stance, such pieces allowed speakers and listeners to assert a value judgment about long-ago days, labeling them "true" and "simple," honest and straightforward.

Selections such as the recitation piece "Grandmamma's Story" describe the old-time values of the past as they locate their story in the days of close family bonds, isolated towns, and trustworthy citizens—the days of personal experience and individual reward. This memory piece begins with the scenario of grandchildren begging for a story "strange and true," after which the old lady tells a "simple story" in a "straight" fashion that pleases her little listeners. The tale is about a "village, long ago" where there lived a "merry-hearted, honest lad" who works to support his mother. Little Lubin, being "brave," soon aspires to make his fortune in London "and work till he grew rich" for his mother's sake. After taking a tearful goodbye, Lubin arrives in the great city, where he is abused for being a homeless vagrant until a protector defends him and gives him a job, being impressed by Lubin's desire to support his mother. At the end of her tale, Grandmamma reveals herself to be Lubin's mother and Lubin to be the children's father. Her final words remind the children to "love your parents while they're here / God ne'er forgets the happy child who loves its parents dear."[39]

Only after "Grandmamma's" story has been narrated in its entirety does the speaker reveal that the events took place only a generation earlier. By dwelling on formative events in the past, this memory piece suggests that those scenes of long-ago triumph have afforded present-day listeners a legacy of comfort and security in a story of a socioeconomic heritage that embraces more than one family lineage. Here we also see a success story featuring a self-made man in a personal but emblematic story reminiscent of a Horatio Alger hero. Such pieces set up a complex relation between individual achievement and a period when many professional workers established the dominance of middle-class values. In the scenario created by the poem, listeners (here the self-made man's children) owe their comfortable position in life to the events of "long ago" days and to a father who struggled and prospered. By positioning the past as energetic and dynamic, but simultaneously as "ancient" or "long ago," such pieces create a comfortable distance between a formative, simpler past and a technological, professional present. This text, like Jim Burden's tale, selectively narrates a break between generations, seeking a formative connection to the past as well as a conveniently streamlined vision of the modern present as a sophisticated, yet respectful inheritor.

Conclusion: The Consequences of Representing the Past

Like their predecessors in the history of entertainment forms, memory pieces —even when most enthralled with the past—permit speakers the apparent agency of crafting a vision of the past, of shaping a compelling narrative about how to understand a formative middling American experience of life. Through popular entertainment forms such as memory-based recitations and mock imitations of nineteenth-century cultural life, participants in leisure pursuits controlled the representation of the past, revealing a vexed relation between nineteenth- and twentieth-century lifestyles. Part of the anxiety fueling such narratives is apparent in the entertainment forms that inherited the parlor's traditions, or recitations, pageants, and historical representations. As scripted, practiced, and largely institutional performances, they lacked a performative dynamism visible in earlier forms of home entertainment. Moreover, they eschewed individualism (in the present), locating narratives of personal success in a past portrayed as worthy of nostalgic remembrance, yet also hopelessly insular, a site of homogenized experience, yet out of sync with the present, a time when locating shared values presented an ongoing challenge.

In both fascinating and troublesome ways, the resulting narrative contrasts between the past and the present projected stasis onto the past, for recitations and memory pieces produce arrested images, whether of the plough against the sun or the scene of a woodland pastoral or the days of a poor boy's struggle to obtain work. Commemorating the past, even when presenting stories of individual success, meant pictorializing it, robbing it of urgency in the interest of claiming the dynamic qualities of the present. As they struggled, often ambivalently, to reconcile personal dynamism with a new, communally oriented century, middle-class Americans faced the challenges of self-representation, invoking ideals of agency, competition, and accomplishment through entertainment forms, as they had for the past seventy years of entertainment's narratives.

Epilogue

Throughout this study I have composed a narrative of home entertainment's development in relation to a middle class's gradual and, often, reactionary understanding of itself as a class, a trajectory that encompasses internally contradictory impulses and trends. We have seen, for example, that home entertainment was both an everyday enterprise and, at specially crafted moments, an extraordinary one as well. It had the capacity to host occasions of unique self-expression and individuation, even under the auspices of socially conscripted behaviors. It was defined by rules, but not determined by them. Both imaginatively escapist and the site of some of the most elaborately constructed labor in nineteenth-century social life, entertainment's activities reveal a capacity for questioning conventional behaviors, yet were themselves scripted, practiced, and repeatedly performed. Ever inviting us to participate, to highlight the dynamic self, home entertainments offered an appeal that remains difficult to resist.

Another set of contradictions forms the basis of home entertainment's complexity, particularly its dual roots in both texts and performances. As I have argued, the textual transmission of home entertainment contained idealized representations of its practices, intersecting with actual events that are no longer accessible to us, except through texts. These are texts, then, that remind us of the interplay between practice and representation, a condition essential in constructing the category of leisure as both an arena of activity and as a set of directions about the methods and consequences of such activities. Thus the textual representation of home entertainment becomes more than an ancillary narrative in the story of home entertainment's primacy in the nineteenth century; it is inseparable from the whole enterprise of leisure activity, encompassing its existence and cultural deployment. That the texts representing home entertainments were to become in turn significant vehicles of leisure pleasure, whether in the novel or the guide book, should not surprise us. They not only captured the power, the potential of home entertainments, but also invited vicarious participation, highlighting the agency of reading about play, the ability to imagine oneself as taking part in physical, dynamic, and potentially transformative ways.

As the texts encircling home entertainment worked to produce images of vital as well as interactive platforms for an energetic class with a treasure trove of activities with which to occupy their play time, they also sought to set parameters around middle-class belonging. Thus, while home entertainments drew vigorously from popular public amusements (theatricals and minstrelsy, for example), they upheld the home's potential to neutralize the extremist impulses found in public displays. In fact, most forms of home entertainment, while alluding to elaborate preparations, go out of their way to obscure references to performative professionalism (acting for a living), to talent (as it might apply to professionalism), and to performance-based ambitions. Instead, they attempt to inscribe entertainment forms as reflective of the broader, more diffused goals of a rising class, treating entertainment as more of a metaphor for ongoing, lifelong labor than a social setting infused with staged or theatrical ambitions. At its best, it was to promote the notion of authentic identity that was heightened by (but never to be replaced with) clever presentation.

Textual accounts of home entertainments offered new possibilities for exploring the concept of discretionary time, arguing implicitly that the deployment of free time became an increasingly important index of American identity. The loose master narratives of home entertainment suggest that one's performative abilities were to be treated casually, without the complications of "skill" and "talent." In other words, home entertainments cast individual abilities as unique, but, somewhat paradoxically, normative for a class. Instead, the notion that entertainment's activities intersect with other daily activities and with moderately genteel ambitions enabled entertainment guide books to encourage the tacit recognition that pleasurable rewards should not supplant notions of work. Even when considering the work of preparing leisure activities, the project of keeping work on view was one of home entertainment's recurring concerns. One might posit that the migration of home entertainment to the classroom and among schoolchildren was, in part, a development that highlighted the labors necessary to produce the late-century entertainment forms such as memorization and recitation. Among nervous schoolchildren, the preparations involved in these activities would be especially visible. In this sense, home entertainment's inheritors faced the goal that also propelled mid-nineteenth-century forms of leisure—showcasing arduous preparations, exhibiting a desire for cultural belonging.

* * *

As I was completing an earlier version of this project, a reader of the manuscript presented me with a cover of the *New Yorker*, which pictured what the late Victorians would have described as a "well-appointed" living room, populated with contemporary children at play. One child is seated at an institutional-looking computer with a hulking, intrusive monitor. Another goggle-adorned child is absorbed by a virtual reality game. Locked into their separate zones of activity, the children occupy the same room, but clearly not the same conceptual dimension. Above the mantelpiece there is a family portrait from bygone days, featuring three youngsters posing while at play. Clutching a hoop, rolling stick, and doll, the children play actively, and as the picture suggests, collectively. The message of the illustration is clear: technological play disallows social interaction. Moreover, it occupies the children on a virtual rather than an interactive level. Whereas the eighteenth- or nineteenth-century children appear placid, calm, and essentially agreeable, the modern youngsters are strained, excitable, and unsocial—perfect candidates for Ritalin and other forms of corrective parental intervention. Their future of immaturity and unsociability appears assured.

The implied narratives about the simpler past, about the unnecessary complications infusing contemporary forms of leisure, hint at a familiar anxiety about the value of leisure pursuits. The illustration implies that there is little social benefit to be found in technological play, despite the virtual prowess that it may be said to foster. It additionally hints that in a technological age, when computer-generated entertainments occupy youth, sociability has emerged not only as a lost art, but also as an unusually arduous form of work for those who have ordinarily spent their leisure hours in individualized pursuits. The virtual world, by contrast, is configured as easier, more fantastic, and more indulgent. At stake here, as in the larger evolution of home entertainment, is a reconfiguration of how to assess the labor demanded by changing venues of leisurely pursuits. As in the mid-nineteenth century, there remain profound and anxious questions about where these spatial and conceptual innovations will lead and concerns about whether the physical, interactive, and sociable aspects of entertainment can be retained.

Certainly home entertainment forms captivated audiences because they offered pleasure to those who partook and those who viewed, along with elaborate means of justifying leisure pursuits. In addition, because play was representable—visual, interactive, and richly symbolic—it could be woven into narratives in ways that work could not. Over the seventy years of leisure practices that I cover, home entertainments evolved so as to reveal changing understandings of participants' identities as individuals whose relation to the public sphere continued to change, where the middling classes were represented as individuals, or rather, individuals enmeshed in a complex set of ideological boundaries.

In their earliest manifestations, home entertainments allowed for participation on a personal, physical level, where participants could assess their own contributing labors. Repeatedly, such entertainments illustrated the work of becoming, of transforming, of shaping raw materials into products that exposed the labors of production, the fissures and rents in the "final" product. Gradually, however, the work of production became less visible, a less vital component of the enterprise encompassed by home entertainment. As play transformed into display, increasingly concealing the work of preparing tableaux vivants or of casting and rehearsing a private theatrical, there were fewer opportunities for performers and audiences to exchange roles, to experience firsthand the production as well as the interpretation of entertainment. Recitations, like pageants, were imagined as seamless spectacles for audiences who would be undisturbed, as they were entertained and, as with nostalgic recitations, privileged and saluted.

Even today, among entertainment forms where the labor of engagement is intangible and invisible, there are ongoing contestations about ways to evaluate leisure time, including its agency. There is the fear of being positioned as a passive spectator on whom culture acts, co-opted by the passivity of some leisurely activities or avoiding active forms of recreation entirely, thereby eschewing the personal bonds that accompany such play.[1] Of computer game aficionados and role-playing Internet activities we hear questions. ("Are players really in charge, actively participating, even though they appear passive?") Entertainment's intersection with labor continues to puzzle. ("Does interaction with computers during leisure time compete with social impulses?") Equally questionable is one's ability to interpret effort and success in the virtual age. ("Is play time sociable if the other players are unknown and unknowable?") These unresolved quandaries, though expressed and contextualized somewhat differently today, were also the kinds of questions accompanying nineteenth-century home leisure practices.

Yet interactive entertainments continue to appear in new avenues, new media, with the most visibly engaged performances appearing in scenarios where the link to the traditions of the nineteenth-century parlor are particularly visible. Among them are spectacles of interactive contest (*Survivor,* for example, and its various imitators), improvisations (*Whose Line Is It Anyway?*), and knowledge contests (trivia-based games of all sorts), where competitive performances expose the potential to tap into the hidden potential of unusual abilities. Such contests remain attractive because they suggest that, behind the scenes, individuals devote themselves to accumulating knowledge and entering into a lifelong cultural preparedness filled with countless hours of study, consideration, and absorption—labors that are later validated by performative triumphs in scenes of accomplishment that remind us of the type of work which, in the mid-nineteenth century, was idealized in its intersection with leisure time. Not only did the nuances of work during leisure hours suggest the continued possibilities of upward ascent, but references to individualized labors helped to support the concept of individual subjectivity through the richness of the personal life—a personal depth and profundity visible from even the merest glimpses captured during social activities. Through the seemingly most ancillary and ephemeral of pursuits, home entertainments allowed for the impression of a rich and varied life that easily spanned public and private contexts, where the individual's resources, once revealed publicly, were continually surprising. Those personal accomplishments showcased in both contemporary and nineteenth-century home entertainment practices continue to suggest that leisure differs significantly from everyday, professional labors, thereby granting leisure a specialized niche that remains separate and reactive to identities based on remunerative forms of work. In this sense, the enduring work infusing nineteenth-century leisure time called for an ideal form of socially engaged activity: laborious as well as entertaining, practical as well as escapist, engaged as well as engaging.

Notes

Introduction

1. See Stuart M. Blumin's discussion of terminology about status in *The Emergence of the Middle Class: Social Experience in the American City, 1760–1900* (New York: Cambridge University Press, 1989), pages 1 and 240–49. Because I stress transformations of identity, I treat the middle class as an emerging or mutating identity, using terms such as "the middling classes" rather than a "middle class," for until the late nineteenth century, there was little visible evidence of a single middle tier.

2. "A Few Friends," *Godey's* (April 1864), 375.

3. *Godey's* (April 1864), 376.

4. *Godey's* (May 1864), 470.

5. See Karen Halttunen, *Confidence Men and Painted Women: A Study of Middle-Class Culture in America, 1830–1870* (New Haven, CT: Yale University Press, 1982). Halttunen notes the mid-century rise of both entertainment and etiquette books. In addition to this rise in publications on home entertainments, it must be noted that many games were likely played somewhat earlier, especially in larger cities and among fashionable participants. The mid-century inscription and circulation of these trends, however, would have encompassed rural readers, upwardly striving social initiates, and various generations of players, thereby circulating entertainment practices more widely than their initial appearance in the 1820s and '30s would suggest. Also see Mary Chapman, *"Living Pictures": Women and Tableaux Vivants in Nineteenth-Century Fiction and Culture* (Cornell University, Ann Arbor: UMI, 1993) and "'Living Pictures': Women and Tableaux Vivants in Nineteenth-Century Fiction and Culture," *Wide Angle* 18.3 (July 1996), 22–52. Chapman places the beginning of an interest in tableaux vivants with an 1831 performance at Park Theatre in New York City ("Living Pictures," 25).

6. Miss Marguerite Merton, "Tableaux," *Godey's* (June 1846).

7. "Ella Moore's Letters from the City," *Godey's* (June–November, 1860) and "A Few Friends," *Godey's* (April–December, 1864). "Ella Moore's Letters" were later reprinted in their entirety as "Letters of Tableaux" in the entertainment guide book, *The Book of Tableaux and Shadow Pantomimes* (New York: Dick and Fitzgerald, 1869),

attributed to Sarah Annie Frost (with no mention of Ella Moore). Frost notes, "The following letters, published in Godey's Lady's Book, having been found useful to those arranging tableaux, are introduced here in their original form, as they were written from actual tableaux, which the writer had seen performed" (31).

8. "Ella Moore's Letters," *Godey's* (August 1860), 185.

9. "Ella Moore's Letters," *Godey's* (November 1860), 471.

10. See Chapman's dissertation for a discussion of the Howells and Alcott family interests in home entertainment. Writing of his experiences in Brooklyn around the 1830s, Furman describes an array of entertainments, among them sleighing, skating, and holiday revelry. See Gabriel Furman, "Winter Amusements in New York in the Early 19th Century," New York Historical Society Bulletin 23.1, Jan 1939, 12.

11. Frost (later known as Shields) was a regular contributor to *Godey's* during the 1850s and '60s, and her name appears on both fictional works and dramatic pieces, particularly acting charades. These same charades later appear in various Dick and Fitzgerald guide manuals.

12. Many of my references to circulation numbers, particularly in chapter seven, come from a perusal of guide books. A number of these texts, however, are not indexed on databases such as the National Union Catalogue or World Cat, and in many cases, when records are available, they are discrepant with one another and with copyright dates within actual books. As cheap, anonymous, and popular guide books, many entertainment manuals were not collected as part of research collections, except in rare instances. Many of the books that I have read have been housed in the general collections of many libraries. The John Nietz Old Textbook collection at the University of Pittsburgh, where this project began, is one of the few collections that catalogues entertainment guide books alongside pedagogical texts.

13. The texts directing and recording home entertainments fail to mention such tumultuous events as war, rioting, or economic catastrophes. Partly because they were guide books, encouraging the broad adoption of a social practice and partly because entertainment books promoted a vision of the middling classes as financially and socially secure (thus having ample free time), they promote a vision of participants as able to control the events of their immediate environments.

14. I also recall de Certeau's argument: "The presence and circulation of a representation . . . tells us nothing about what it is for its users. We must first analyze its manipulation by users who are not its makers. Only then can we gauge the difference or similarity between the production of the image and the secondary production hidden in the processes of its utilization." Michel de Certeau, *The Practice of Everyday Life*, trans. Steven Rendall (Berkeley: University of California Press, 1984), xiii. An attention to the "secondary production" of a social practice allows me to consider the ways that the meaning(s) of the momentary interactions of play differ from the significance of play as a textual production, or more loosely put, to understand a set of practices like those encompassing home entertainment as both temporal and textual.

15. See Halttunen, *Confidence Men and Painted Women*, Chapman, *"Living Pictures"* (diss.), and J. Jeffrey Franklin, *Serious Play: The Cultural Form of the Nineteenth-*

Century Realist Novel (Philadelphia: University of Pennsylvania Press, 1999). In Franklin's study of entertainment trends in Victorian English literature, he asserts that "play functioned as a lynch-pin concept within the discursive infrastructure by which Victorian society represented itself to itself" and that "play served a connective or bridging function" (4). Also see Patrick Beaver's *Victorian Parlor Games* (Wigton, Leicester: Magna Books, 1995) and Donna R. Braden's "'The Family That Plays Together Stays Together': Family Pastimes and Indoor Amusements, 1890–1930," in *American Home Life, 1880–1930*, ed. Jessica H. Foy and Thomas J. Schlereth (Knoxville: University of Tennessee Press, 1994), which provide overviews of various types of parlor games and their rules.

16. The "parlor" games that I will be describing were obviously intended, at some point in their inception, to be played in a family's parlor; which parlor they were played in, however, is infrequently noted in novels or entertainment manuals. The relative sophistication of play, its physical requirements, and the number, social standing, and age of the guests would have determined the exact settings for home entertainments, including doorways, sitting rooms, and even garrets.

17. Studies of middle-class culture on which I have relied tend to stress the ritual and material markers of status. Those that treat material culture include Kenneth Ames's *Death in the Dining Room & Other Tales of Victorian Culture* (Philadelphia: Temple University Press, 1992), Richard L. Bushman's *The Refinement of America: Persons, Houses, Cities* (New York: Alfred A. Knopf, 1992), and Mary M. Ryan's *Cradle of the Middle Class: The Family in Oneida County, New York, 1790–1865* (New York: Cambridge University Press, 1981). For studies that deal with ideologies of labor and leisure, see Thomas Schlereth, *Victorian America: Transformations in Everyday Life, 1876–1915* (New York: Harper Collins, 1991), Burton J. Bledstein's *The Culture of Professionalism: The Middle Class and the Development of Higher Education in America* (New York: Norton, 1976), and Samuel Haber's *The Quest for Authority and Honor in the American Professions, 1750–1900* (Chicago: University of Chicago Press, 1991). Those works that attend to ritualized class-specific behavior and emphasize the desires for order and pattern, particularly in regard to manners and genteel behavior include Halttunen's *Confidence Men and Painted Women*, John F. Kasson's *Rudeness and Civility: Manners in Nineteenth-Century Urban America* (New York: Hill and Wang, 1990), and Stephen Nissenbaum's *The Battle for Christmas* (New York: Vintage Books, 1997). In addition, Martin J. Burke's *The Conundrum of Class: Public Discourse on the Social Order in America* (Chicago: University of Chicago Press, 1995) and Stuart M. Blumin's *The Emergence of the Middle Class* usefully attend to taxonomies of class, and to the frequently contested classifications associated with class in U.S. culture.

18. Edward W. Said, *The World, the Text, and the Critic* (Cambridge, MA: Harvard University Press, 1983), 15.

19. See Joseph Litvak, *Caught in the Act: Theatricality in the Nineteenth-Century English Novel* (Berkeley: University of California Press, 1992), which focuses on a type of subjective performativity that is closely linked with notions of the theatrical display.

20. Thorstein Veblen, *The Theory of the Leisure Class* (New York: Modern Library, 1934), 9.

21. See Schlereth.

22. William A. Gleason, *The Leisure Ethic: Work and Play in American Literature, 1840–1940* (Stanford, CA: Stanford University Press, 1999), ix. Gleason's text represents a fascinating study of the concepts of work and leisure; whereas I concentrate on the strategies of enacted entertainments, Gleason stresses the "ethics" and labor-intensive dimensions of leisure time and argues that "one might shape a satisfying sense of self primarily through one's leisure activities instead of one's job" (1).

23. See Eric Lott, *Love and Theft: Blackface Minstrelsy and the American Working Class* (New York: Oxford University Press, 1993). Whereas Lott's work with the minstrel tradition highlights scenarios of performance, studying the enactments of various minstrel routines within the dynamics of advertising, sales, and the history of specific minstrel troupes, this type of work is not within the scope of my project. Because home entertainments were public in the textual sense, but privately enacted, we have no coherent sense of how the assignments of key acts to games or scenes may have reflected on the practices of play. Nor are there advertising strategies to examine or public responses to the activities.

24. De Certeau, xiv–xv. The scholarship that I invoke, by scholars such as Karen Halttunen, Richard L. Bushman, and Stuart M. Blumin, has propelled me to unearth the complexities of the middling classes by resisting tempting globalizations. These scholars portray a class that was not yet a class, a group that didn't yet know what to affiliate with—something evolving, but toward an uncertain and unmarked end. Blumin carefully traces the emergence of the term "middle class" throughout his study, treating the vocabulary of class as a sign of class consciousness, noting that terms surrounding "middling" Americans were used earlier and more pervasively than terms about a middle class.

Chapter 1

1. This activity was also known as "Graceful Lady," "The Horned Ambassador," and "The Handsome Gentleman." See *Family Pastime, or Homes Made Happy* (New York: Bunce and Brother, 1855), Catherine Elsing, *The Book of Parlour Games* (Philadelphia: H. C. Peck & Theo Bliss, 1856), and *The Sociable, or One Thousand and One Home Amusements* (New York: Dick and Fitzgerald, 1858). "The Horned Ambassador" appears in *Fireside Games for Winter Evening Amusement* (New York: Dick and Fitzgerald, 1859), "The Graceful Lady" in *Family Pastime*, and "The Handsome Gentleman" in *The Book of Parlour Games* and *The Sociable*.

2. Lydia Maria Child, *The Girl's Own Book*, (1832; Chester, CT: Applewood Books, 1992), 26.

3. Child, 27.

4. *Fireside Games*, 22.

5. Karen Halttunen places the American concern with etiquette near the middle

of the nineteenth century, calling attention to the numbers of American etiquette manuals that were offered to readers between the years 1830 and 1860 (*Confidence Men and Painted Women*, 92). Also see Arthur M. Schlesinger, *Learning How to Behave: A Historical Study of American Etiquette Books* (New York: Macmillan, 1947). Schlesinger contends that American manners and etiquette guides depict a rise of concern over etiquette beginning a generation before the Civil War, or roughly the 1840s (26).

6. Typically, authors of etiquette books quoted Emerson very selectively, streamlining and consolidating Emerson's logic. In regard to manners, for example, Emerson certainly does indicate their importance, but he also conveys the tremendous complexity that they suggest in their American manifestations.

7. Ralph Waldo Emerson, "Behavior," *The Conduct of Life*, vol. 6 in *The Complete Works of Ralph Waldo Emerson*, Centenary Edition (New York: Houghton Mifflin, 1903–04), 169–70.

8. Emerson, 170.

9. Emerson, 176, 186. See Julie Ellison, "The Gender of Transparency: Masculinity and the Conduct of Life," *American Literary History* 4.4 (Winter 1992). Ellison argues that Emerson's vision of cultural life entails the notion of a "true friend," or a natural man, who is both revealed and partially concealed by the apparatus of mannered behavior. For Emerson "manners were a form of emotional expression as well as emotional control or restraint" (585).

10. See Norbert Elias, *The Civilizing Process: The History of Manners and State Formation and Civilization*, trans. Edmund Jephcott (Cambridge, MA: Oxford University Press, 1994). Notably, Emerson's theory of manners is not shared by Elias, who links manners to the elites, casting in relief Emerson's deep investment in upholding the primacy of the middle class.

11. Pierre Bourdieu, *In Other Words: Essays Towards a Reflexive Sociology*, trans. Matthew Adamson (Stanford, CA: Stanford University Press, 1990), 11.

12. Kasson, 6.

13. Sarah Annie Frost, *Dramatic Proverbs and Charades* (New York: Dick and Fitzgerald, 1866). This script also appeared in several entertainment guide books, particularly in *Dramatic Proverbs and Charades* (1866) and *The Parlor Stage* (1866).

14. Frost, *Dramatic Proverbs*, 63.

15. See Bledstein, who writes that "In the nineteenth century, Americans who shared middle-class pretensions wanted respectability, orderliness, control, and discipline. But they also celebrated their own energy, their capacity for booming, boosterism, and the lust for power" (54).

16. Bledstein, 54.

17. Bledstein, 54–55.

18. Bushman, 289–290.

19. George Henry Sandison, *How to Behave and How to Amuse: A handy manual of etiquette and parlor games* (Historical Publishing Company, 1895).

20. Pierre Bourdieu, *The Logic of Practice*, trans. Richard Nice (Stanford, CA: Stanford University Press, 1980), 119.

21. See Blumin, chapters six and seven; see Haber, section two.

22. See Richard Butsch, *The Making of American Audiences: From Stage to Television, 1750–1990* (New York: Cambridge University Press, 2000). Butsch argues that working-class amusements were more interactive and participatory than genteel forms of leisure, citing the attendance at the public theaters, where working-class audiences, he claims, were frequently rowdy and vocal in their responses to stage actions. This account, however, focuses solely on responses to public performances, where the middling sorts behaved with much more restraint.

Home entertainments reveal, however, that there were forms of middling entertainment that were interactive, suggesting that interaction is not uniformly an indicator of class lines. Early entertainment manuals for children from the late eighteenth and early nineteenth centuries, however, define working-class amusements as bear baiting, dog fighting, drinking, gambling, and boxing.

23. See Victor Turner, *From Ritual to Theatre: The Human Seriousness of Play* (New York: Performing Arts Journal Publications, 1982). This history of the work-play continuum in preindustrial societies versus a greater distinction between work and leisure in postindustrial societies appears in Turner's account. He also defines liminoid spaces as hosting "industrial leisure genres [that] can repossess the character of 'work' though originating in a free time arbitrarily separated by managerial fiat from the time of 'labor' " (33).

24. "A Few Friends," *Godey's* (May 1864), 468.

25. Michael Newbury, "Healthful Employment: Hawthorne, Thoreau, and Middle-Class Fitness," *American Quarterly* 47.4 (Dec. 1995), 682.

26. Newbury, 685, 681.

27. See Bushman. What resulted among working populations, Bushman asserts, was a "vernacular gentility," or a livable, modest means of enacting what Bushman terms "refinement."

28. See Burke, *The Conundrum of Class,* particularly chapters four and five, on the rhetoric of what Burke terms "a reconcilable class conflict" in Jacksonian America (108).

29. See Paul Boyer, *Urban Masses and Moral Order in America, 1820–1920* (Cambridge, MA: Harvard University Press, 1978), for a discussion of the flight to suburbs.

30. Butsch writes that public theaters in Jacksonian America were "a rich soup of intense political participation by gentry, merchants, and artisans, all patrons of the same public houses," a situation that changed near the mid century as theaters worked to attract middle-class women as their core audience (43).

31. See *Fireside Games.* A comment in the preface makes it clear that parlor game-playing activities were distinct from manners. The text briefly lectures readers on the necessity of being a "good sport" during play, so as to make play enjoyable for all participants.

32. *Family Pastime,* 4.

33. Blumin, 109. Blumin writes of the artisans who became nonmanual businessmen during the nineteenth century. His chapter three, on merchants, details the vast

varieties of occupations that he locates under the general canopy of middle-class work.

34. Rebecca Harding Davis, "Life in the Iron Mills," in *Provisions: A Reader from Nineteenth-Century American Women*, ed. Judith Fetterley (Bloomington: Indiana University Press, 1985), 318.

35. Rebecca Harding Davis, 315.

36. See Bledstein.

37. Bushman, xiii. Also see Blumin, who lists the white-collar positions of businessmen and clerks, bookkeepers, bankers, accountants, shorthand writers, and copyists.

38. Elsing, *The Book of Parlour Games*, 29.

39. See Child, *The Girl's Own Book*. Additional "trade games" such as "The Flour Merchant" and "The Apprentice" require players to act out laboring scenarios; others, such as "Of What Trade Is Our Favorite?" entail eventual selection of one occupation.

40. Bledstein, 92.

41. Bourdieu, *The Logic of Practice*, 66.

42. See *Family Pastime*, 14–15.

43. See Halttunen (*Confidence Men and Painted Women*), who contends that parlor entertainments such as tableaux vivants constituted yet another form of genteel performance (184). Yet this is only one type of entertainment form, and not the prevalent form of the mid-century, from the directions of entertainment guide books.

44. See John G. Cawelti, *Apostles of the Self-Made Man* (Chicago: University of Chicago Press, 1965), particularly chapter one, "Natural Aristocracy and the New Republic."

45. Many early nineteenth-century entertainment manuals were reprinted from English texts or produced simultaneously for English and American readers, including Samuel Tizzard's *The New Athenian Oracle or Ladies' Companion* (Carlisle, PA: P. Loudin, 1806) and Alfred Eliott's *Playground and the Parlour: A handbook of boy's games, sports, and amusements* (London and New York: T. Nelson and Sons, 1868). Other guide books mention French influences; some even claim to have been translated from the French, as in the case of Elsing's *The Book of Parlour Games*, which was published in Philadelphia.

46. See Sybil Rosenfield, *The Temples of Thespis: Some Private Theaters and Theatricals in England and Wales, 1700–1820* (London: Society for Theatre Research, 1978).

47. Frost was born in Philadelphia in 1837 and died in 1886. She was the author of parlor entertainment manuals and plays, many published by Dick and Fitzgerald. She also published stories and advice columns in *Godey's Lady's Book*. For more information on Frost see Gwen Davis and Beverley A. Joyce, *Drama by Women to 1900: A Bibliography of American and British Writers* (Toronto: University of Toronto Press, 1992).

48. Sarah Annie Frost, *New Book of Dialogues for Juveniles* (New York: Dick and Fitzgerald, 1872).

49. Mrs. Russell Kavanaugh, *Original Dramas, Dialogues, Declamations, and Tableaux Vivans* (Louisville, KY: John P. Morton and Company, 1867).

50. George Arnold, *Parlor Theatricals; or Winter Evenings' Entertainment* (New York: Dick and Fitzgerald, 1859).

51. Arnold, 62.

52. Arnold, 63.

Chapter 2

1. Victor Turner, 36.

2. Susan Warner, *The Wide, Wide World* (New York: Feminist Press, 1897), 510. Henceforth, quotations from *The Wide, Wide World* will come from this edition and will be indicated by in-text citations.

3. See Nina Baym, *Novels, Readers, and Reviewers: Responses to Fiction in Antebellum America* (Ithaca, NY: Cornell University Press, 1984). As Baym has contended in her discussion of *The Wide, Wide World*, adults—not children—comprised the primary audience for the text. Also see Susan S. Williams, "'Promoting an Extensive Sale': The Production and Reception of *The Lamplighter*," *New England Quarterly* 69.2 (June 1996). Williams argues that *The Lamplighter* was marketed to adults, with an abridged edition available for children (180).

4. See Arnold Van Gennep, *The Rites of Passage* (Chicago: University of Chicago Press, 1960). These moments, according to Van Gennep, form the basis of an individual's relation to ritualized behavior. As such, childhood is at once an individual experience and a recognizable stage relating to a collective identity.

5. See Harvey Green, "Scientific Thought and the Nature of Children in America, 1820–1920," in *A Century of Childhood, 1820–1920*, ed. Mary Lynn Stevens Heininger (Rochester, New York: The Margaret Woodbury Strong Museum, 1984) and see Joseph F. Kett, *Rites of Passage: Adolescence in America, 1790 to the Present* (New York: Basic Books, 1977). Green points to a recognition of childhood's uniqueness during the first decades of the nineteenth century, while Kett traces a gradual emergence of childhood (in various ways) to the late eighteenth and early nineteenth centuries.

6. See Eric Sundquist, "Exploration and Empire," and see Jonathan Arac, "Personal Narratives," both in *The Cambridge History of American Literature, Vol. 2, 1820–1865*, ed. Sacvan Bercovitch (New York: Cambridge University Press, 1995) for discussions of the ways that the Mexican-American War and its enactment of Manifest Destiny situated the United States in relation to its foreign policy and a new relationship with Great Britain.

7. Philippe Ariès, *Centuries of Childhood: A Social History of Family Life*, trans. Robert Baldick (New York: Vintage, 1962). Ariès also contends that childhood is linked to economic prosperity, leisure time, and gendered labor among the rising bourgeois classes. Under these conditions, Ariès argues, both time and energy could be devoted to the child. Mary Lou Stevens Heininger contends that by the mid-nineteenth century, childhood was coming to be understood as a phase of develop-

ment with its own particular behaviors and playful privileges. See Heininger's "Children, Childhood, and Change in America, 1820–1920" in *A Century of Childhood, 1820–1920*, ed. Mary Lynn Stevens Heininger (Rochester, New York: The Margaret Woodbury Strong Museum, 1984), where Heininger argues that changing attitudes toward children began to appear around 1820. Heininger specifically notes that "play was considered natural and desirable for children, but responsible parents were expected to channel its delights into paths of virtue and useful skill" (6).

8. Leslie A. Fiedler, *Love and Death in the American Novel* (Criterion, 1960), xviii–xix.

9. See Wai Chee Dimock, "Class, Gender, and a History of Metonymy," in *Rethinking Class: Literary Studies and Social Formations*, ed. Wai Chee Dimock and Michael Gilmore (New York: Columbia University Press, 1994), 57–104. Dimock asserts that authors such as Emerson and Thoreau engaged a rhetoric of reduction, telescoping one particular and valuable characteristic, setting it apart from others (59).

10. Nathaniel Hawthorne, *The Scarlet Letter* (Columbus: Ohio University Press, 1962). Harriet Beecher Stowe, *Uncle Tom's Cabin*, ed. Kenneth S. Lynn (Cambridge, MA: Harvard University Press, 1962). See Nina Baym, *Women's Fiction: A Guide to Novels by and about Women in America, 1820–70*, 2nd ed. (Urbana: University of Illinois Press, 1993). Women's novels trace what Baym refers to as the basic plot of much nineteenth-century women's fiction, wherein a young girl is typically orphaned or abandoned to make her way in a morally corrupt world by rising above it. Also see Beverley V. Voloshin, "The Limits of Domesticity: The Female Bildungsroman in America, 1820–1870," *Women's Studies* 10.3 (Fall 1984), Jane Tompkins, afterword to *The Wide, Wide World* (New York: Feminist Press, 1987), and Cynthia Schoolar Williams, "Susan Warner's *Queechy* and the Bildungsroman Tradition" *Legacy* 7.2 (Fall 1990), who have resisted classifying Warner's novel as a Bildungsroman.

11. See Elizabeth Ammons, "Stowe's Dream of the Mother-Savior: Uncle Tom's Cabin and American Women Writers before the 1920s," in *New Essays on Uncle Tom's Cabin*, ed. Eric J. Sundquist (Cambridge, UK: Cambridge University Press). As Ammons contends of Stowe's Eva, whom she compares to Hawthorne's Pearl, Eva is markedly unrealistic and, Ammons claims, is "consistently describe[d] as dreamy, buoyant, inspired, cloudlike, spotless"; in addition, Ammons notes, the text "flatly states that this child has an 'aerial grace, such as one might dream of for some mythic and allegorical being'" (168). Because Stowe has so problematized and critiqued notions of nationalistic development, she erases any narratives of development from Eva's life, presenting her as having already attained her fullest potential.

12. See Hortense J. Spillers, "Changing the Letter: The Yokes, the Jokes of Discourse: Or, Mrs. Stowe, Mr. Reed," *American Quarterly* 38.2 (1986). According to Spillers, Eva appears to possess a strangely adult "lush sensuality" attributed to her by Stowe's language (39, 42). Furthermore, Spillers contends, Eva's language, particularly her demand, "I want him," directed to her father and regarding Tom, indicates a "daring and impermissible desire" for Tom, a desire that Spillers positions as strangely

adult. As in the sexualized dimension of the bond between Ellen and John Humphreys, Eva's relation to Tom, as suggested through Stowe's description, reveals a child whose seeming innocence is layered with connotations, uncertain and unfinished suggestions of a more mature knowledge.

13. See Blumin and Bushman.

14. Cawelti, 50. Also see Martha Banta, *Failure and Success in America: A Literary Debate* (Princeton, NJ: Princeton University Press, 1978), and Richard M. Huber, *The American Idea of Success* (New York: McGraw-Hill, 1971).

15. Judy Hilkey, *Character Is Capital: Success Manuals and Manhood in Gilded Age America* (Chapel Hill: University of North Carolina Press, 1997), 49, 52.

16. Nancy Armstrong, *Desire and Domestic Fiction: A Political History of the Novel* (New York: Oxford University Press, 1987), 60–62.

17. Benjamin Franklin, *The Autobiography of Benjamin Franklin* (1791 in French; 1793 in English; Mineola, NY: Dover, 1996). Franklin writes of *Poor Richard's Almanac* that ". . . I consider'd it as a proper vehicle for conveying instruction among the common people, who bought scarcely any other books; I therefore filled all the little spaces that occurr'd between the remarkable days in the calendar with proverbial sentences, chiefly such as inculcated industry and frugality, as the means of procuring wealth, and thereby securing virtue; it being more difficult for a man in want, to act always honestly, as to use here one of those proverbs, *it is hard for an empty sack to stand upright*" (75).

18. I am borrowing Stuart M. Blumin's term from his discussion of social and trade organizations, which promoted a classless ideal, even while they reinscribed deep hierarchies that allowed their members to chart success (218–19).

19. Gabriel Furman, 12.

20. Michel Foucault, *The History of Sexuality: An Introduction*, trans. Robert Hurley (New York: Vintage, 1980), 92.

21. Arguing that social practices "give rise to spaces where moves are proportional to situations," de Certeau suggests that we should interrogate forms of social practice for their tactics, or their specific events and rules, before considering the schema to which those practices belong (22). At the mid century, the "tactics" of play that are most immediate are those that are also most unique—the performance of childhood by adults. I read these forms of play for their double-sided gestures as they hosted opportunities for mid-century, middling adults to occupy a social role that was adjacent to mannered gentility. By doing so, forms of mid-century play stretched and expanded the tactical boundaries of a middling, adult social experience.

22. See *Youthful Recreations* (Philadelphia: J. Johnson, c. 1810), *Remarks on Children's Play* (New York and Baltimore: Samuel Wood and Sons, 1819), Eliza Leslie, *The American Girl's Book; or, occupation for play hours*, 16th ed. (1831; New York: R. Worthington, 1879), Lydia Maria Child, *The Girl's Own Book*, Catherine Elsing, *The Book of Parlour Games, Family Pastime*, and *The Sociable*.

Here I invoke illustrations as late as the 1890s, in part because such drawings do not appear in guide books until the later nineteenth century. Whereas descriptions of physically active versions of adult play emerged at around 1850, those activities are pictured in later texts; this trend likely reflects late-century improvements in printing techniques more than it reflects the circulation of practices.

23. See Katherine C. Grier, *Culture and Comfort: People, Parlors and Upholstery, 1850–1930* (New York: Strong Museum, 1988) and Halttunen, *Confidence Men and Painted Women*. Grier points to the physical humor and jokes of the mid-century entertainment, and Halttunen's chapter six, "Disguises, Masks, and Parlor Theatricals: The Decline of Sentimental Culture," discusses the emergence of entertainment guides.

24. *Family Pastime*, 3.

25. Ledger D. Mayne, *What Shall We Do Tonight?, or Social Amusements for Evening Parties* (Philadelphia: Claxton, Remsen, and Haffelfinger, 1873), 5.

26. This 1879 copy from which this picture is drawn is a reprint of the original 1831 edition.

27. John Angelo Lewis, "Professor Hoffmann," *Parlor Amusements and Evening Party Entertainments* (1879; New York and London: George Routledge & Sons [ca. 1885]), 70.

28. See Steven Marcus, *The Other Victorians: A Study of Sexuality and Pornography in Mid-Nineteenth-Century England* (New York: Basic Books, 1964).

29. *Family Pastime*, 3–4.

30. See Braden, who refers to entertainment practices as voicing the logic that "the family that plays together stays together" in a reading of entertainment practices that appears to be based on their idealistic introductions.

31. See Nissenbaum, who charts the development of Christmas as a domestic holiday from its beginnings as an uproarious street celebration dominated by the lower classes. Highlighting carnivalesque behavior among the lower classes, Nissenbaum goes on to discuss the inclusion of children in a more familial version of the Christmas celebration instituted in the 1820s. My argument begins thirty years later.

32. *The Sociable*, 173.

33. *The Sociable* dates from 1858, but sections of the text were reprinted in other texts from the same publisher (Dick and Fitzgerald). *Fireside Games*, for example, of 1859, is a reprint of a section of the larger *Sociable*.

Chapter 3

1. Bourdieu, *The Logic of Practice*, 71.

2. Armstrong, 5.

3. Armstrong, 254.

4. Donald Walker, *Games and Sports* (London: Joseph Thomas, 1840), 6.

5. Rosemarie Garland Thomson, "Narratives of Deviance and Delight: Staring at Julia Pastrana, the 'Extraordinary Lady,'" in *Beyond the Binary: Reconstructing Cultural Identity in a Multicultural Context*, ed. Timothy B. Powell (New Brunswick, NJ: Rutgers University Press, 1999), 82. As she focuses on a real individual, Thomson ex-

plores the ways in which staring reinforces physical difference, invoking disability studies as a way to interrogate a "culturally fabricated narrative of the body," as a type of "minority discourse" (82). While Thomson's work is compelling, particularly in its treatment of staring, it discusses actual physical differences. By contrast, I am interrogating deliberate and temporal transformations, or playful rather than long-term social identities. Hence, in the world of nineteenth-century entertainment, there can be no "minoritization" of the type studied by Thomson.

6. Edgar Allan Poe, *The Complete Tales and Poems of Edgar Allan Poe* (New York: Vintage, 1975), 713. Hereafter, in-text citations to this 1844 story refer to this edition.

7. Eric Fretz, "P. T. Barnum's Theatrical Selfhood and the Nineteenth-Century Culture of Exhibition," in *Freakery: Cultural Spectacles of the Extraordinary Body*, ed. Rosemarie Garland Thomson (New York: New York University Press, 1996), 98.

8. See Mikhail Bakhtin, *Rabelais and His World*, trans. Helene Iswolsky (Bloomington: Indiana University Press, 1984).

9. Bakhtin, 66.

10. See Halttunen, *Confidence Men and Painted Women*, and Ames for discussions of the legibility of genteel bodies.

11. It is interesting to posit how images, memories, or other allusions to the Civil War intersected with grotesque performances, for certainly "damaged" bodies may have seemed too real for some forms of grotesque play, yet entertainment texts continue to describe grotesque effects after the war.

12. See T. J. Jackson Lears, "From Salvation to Self-Realization: Advertising and the Therapeutic Roots of the Consumer Culture, 1880–1930," in *The Culture of Consumption: Critical Essays in American History, 1880–1980*, ed. T. J. Jackson Lears and Richard Wightman Fox (New York: Pantheon Books, 1983). Lears has argued that the ultimate task of advertising is the conceptual altering of the self, with product-based slogans and ideologies ultimately reflecting on the potential consumer.

13. See Chapman's *"Living Pictures"* for a discussion of beheaded women in tableaux vivants; Chapman argues that these spectacles symbolically silenced and immobilized women in response to unfeminine behaviors.

14. Winslow Homer, "The Bluebeard Tableau," *Harper's Bazar* (September 5, 1868).

15. See Chapman, *"Living Pictures."* I am indebted to Chapman for calling my attention to this illustration. Chapman's work on tableaux vivants in American culture points to a long history of misogyny as revealed in the entertainment form.

16. Ralph W. Emerson, "The American Scholar," in *The Selected Writings of Ralph Waldo Emerson*, ed. Brooks Atkinson (New York: Modern Library, 1940), 45–63.

17. See James W. Cook, Jr., "Of Men, Missing Links, and Nondescripts: The Strange Career of P. T. Barnum's 'What is It?' Exhibition," in *Freakery: Cultural Spectacles of the Extraordinary Body*, ed. Rosemarie Garland Thomson (New York: New York University Press, 1996), and R. G. Thomson, "Narratives of Deviance and Delight," where Thomson explores the history of Julia Pastrana, a hirsute Mexican In-

dian woman who was displayed as a "Nondescript" as well as an "Ape Woman," and "The Ugliest Woman in the World" (83).

18. See Ames, 193. Contending that parlor suites enforced genteel behavior, Ames notes that the physical conditions of the ordinary parlor encouraged "static sitting" and rigid self-control.

19. Caroline L. Smith, *The American Home Book of Indoor Games, Amusements, and Occupations* (Boston: Lee and Shepard, 1872), 202–3.

20. "A Few Friends," *Godey's* (April 1864), 374.

21. *Family Pastime*, 3–4.

22. See Peter Stallybrass and Allon White, *The Politics and Poetics of Transgression* (London: Methuen & Company, 1986).

23. Bakhtin, *Rabelais and His World*, 89.

24. See Nissenbaum.

25. *The Sociable*, ii.

26. See Child. The text wishes its readers, the "little ones especially," a "merry Christmas and a happy New-Year," having been published just before the holidays.

27. C. L. Smith, 219.

28. See C. L. Smith. This copy is from the State Historical Society Library of Wisconsin.

29. See Robert W. Rydell, "The Culture of Imperial Abundance: World's Fairs in the Making of American Culture," in *Consuming Visions: Accumulation and Display of Goods in America, 1880–1920*, ed. Simon J. Bronner (New York: W. W. Norton & Company, 1989) on the "imperial fetish" at the turn of the century's worlds fair, including the treatment of "non whites" as "natural resources" (116). Also see Simon J. Bronner, "Object Lessons: The Work of Ethnological Museums and Collections," in *Consuming Visions: Accumulation and Display of Goods in America, 1880–1920*, ed. Simon J. Bronner (New York: W. W. Norton & Company, 1989) on the hierarchies invoked by nineteenth-century "ethnological collections," with their implied national and racialized hierarchies.

30. Robyn Wiegman, *American Anatomies: Theorizing Race and Gender* (Durham, NC: Duke University Press, 1995), 22.

31. See John Nietz, *Old Text Books* (Pittsburgh: University of Pittsburgh Press, 1961). Nietz describes the "attitudes" of geography texts toward their subjects, chronicling the texts' interests in religion, reform, sports, and race and nationality. As Nietz notes, the Caucasian race was woven into narratives of superiority, while peoples of color, particularly those of the black race, were often described as "ignorant" or "degraded" (216).

32. See Edward W. Said, *Culture and Imperialism* (New York: Alfred A. Knopf, 1993).

33. See Tom E. Terrill, *The Tariff Politics and American Foreign Policy, 1874–1901* (Westport, CT: Greenwood Press, 1973), and David M. Pletcher, *The Diplomacy of Trade and Investment: American Economic Expansion in the Hemisphere, 1865–1900*

(Columbia: University of Missouri Press, 1998), especially chapter five on the United States' relations with Haiti. Also see Jackson Lears, "Beyond Veblen: Rethinking Consumer Culture in America," in *Consuming Visions: Accumulation and Display of Goods in America, 1880–1920*, ed. Simon J. Bronner (New York: W. W. Norton & Company, 1989) for a discussion of the "exotic" displays that were marketed to the mid-century middling classes, including P. T. Barnum's Iranistan villa and fashions such as the "Turkish shawl, the Castilian cloak and the Echarpe Orientale" (77).

34. Eric Lott, *Love and Theft*, 39–40. As Lott and other scholars have shown, minstrelsy rose to prominence in Jacksonian America, gradually coming into being as a respectable social event by the 1840s. Thus the precedent of deliberate and "amusing" events set by minstrelsy would have inflected the construction of race in entertainment guide books. For more on the time frame of minstrelsy's popularity, see Butsch.

35. Lott, 76.

36. Eliott, *Book of Parlour Games*, 198. The are various versions of this game, but this 1868 entertainment manual describes the activity as an "amusing pastime . . . modeled after the old nursery tale of 'The House that Jack Built,'" emphasizing the "simplicity" of the game.

37. Eliott, 199.

38. Among these types of books, "Yankee," "Negro," "Irish," and "Dutch" speech patterns are often mimicked in phonetic form.

39. Frank Bellew, *The Art of Amusing* (New York: Carleton, 1866).

40. Bellew, 99.

41. *Evenings at Home: The Juvenile Budget Opened*, 2nd ed. (Philadelphia: A Bartram, 1802). This text was first published in Dublin (1794) and London (1795–96).

42. *Evenings at Home*, 16.

43. *Evenings at Home*, 22.

44. *What Shall We Do Tonight?*, 215.

45. *What Shall We Do Tonight?*

46. See Gillian Avery, *Behold the Child: American Children and Their Books, 1621–1922* (Baltimore: Johns Hopkins University Press, 1994). According to Avery, tales from the Arabian nights appeared in English as early as 1712, presented in chapbook form.

47. Miss Marguerite Merton, "Tableaux," *Godey's* (June 1846), 277.

48. Merton, 278.

49. The tale of Bluebeard first appeared in Charles Perrault's fairy tales, published in France in 1697 as *Tales of Mother Goose*. Perrault's tale is said to have been based loosely on the life of Comorre the Cursed, a sixth-century Breton chief. Interestingly, however, the version of the tale presented in parlor games transforms Bluebeard into a figure with a suggested Arabian heritage, thereby racializing his crimes.

50. Sarah Annie Frost, *Amateur Theatricals and Fairy Tale Dramas* (New York: Dick and Fitzgerald, 1868).

51. Frost, *Amateur Theatricals*, 173.

Chapter 4

1. Bourdieu, *The Logic of Practice*, 67.

2. This emphasis on a woman's world coincides with Nancy Armstrong's argument in *Desire and Domestic Fiction* that a modern subjectivity was focalized through the woman's experience. Home entertainment scenes particularly revolve around women because, on the most practical level, the domestic overseeing involved in entertainment was feminized, but also because of the social precariousness that the woman's experience made visible.

3. See Cathy N. Davidson, *Revolution and the Word: The Rise of the Novel in America* (New York: Oxford University Press, 1986). Also see Jane P. Tompkins, *Sensational Designs: The Cultural Work of American Fiction, 1790–1860* (New York: Oxford University Press, 1985), and Michael Denning, *Mechanic Accents: Dime Novels and Working-Class Culture in America* (New York: Verso, 1987), as well as more recent work by Isabelle Lehuu, *Carnival on the Page: Popular Print Media in Antebellum America* (Chapel Hill: University of North Carolina Press, 1992), and Shelley Streeby, *American Sensations: Class, Empire, and the Production of Popular Culture* (Berkeley: University of California Press, 2002). From Tompkins to Denning, scholars have illustrated the profound cultural work exercised through the popular nineteenth-century novel, a primary source of entertainment, helping us understand the politically infused potential of harnessing sites of pleasure. With both the novel and the entertainment scene in the novel counting as forms of entertainment, discretionary time became the scene of rare opportunities for exploiting the destabilizing, unsettling, lasting effects of pursuing pleasure.

4. Said, *The World, The Text, and The Critic*, 16, 21.

5. See Litvak, *Caught in the Act*. As Litvak points out, these types of performances are imbued with highly theatrical strains in nineteenth-century literature as they call attention to the distinctions between individual characters and their greater worlds (31). Also see Nina Auerbach, *Private Theatricals* (Cambridge, MA: Harvard University Press, 1990). Auerbach has explored the "private theatricals" of universal experience, or narratives that repeatedly draw attention to the key moments of individual life.

6. Mikhail Bakhtin, *The Dialogic Imagination*, ed. Michael Holquist, trans. Caryl Emerson and Michael Holquist (Austin: University of Texas Press, 1981), 84. Bakhtin describes the chronotope as a device signaling "the intrinsic connectedness of temporal and spatial relationships that are artistically expressed in literature." The chronotope, which distinctly "expresses the inseparability of space and time," also reaches outward to the larger narrative, responding to "movements of times, plot, and history" (84). Bakhtin's formulation usefully explains the ways that representations of time and space lend entertainment scenes their power of concentrated detail.

7. Other studies that focus on the chronotope include Suzanne Rosenthal Shumway, "The Chronotope of the Asylum: Jane Eyre, Feminism, and Bakhtinian Theory,"

in *A Dialogue of Voices: Feminist Literary Theory and Bakhtin,* ed. Karen Hohne and Helen Wussow (Minneapolis: University of Minnesota Press, 1994), and Michael V. Montgomery, *Carnivals and Commonplaces: Bakhtin's Chronotope, Cultural Studies, and Film* (New York: Peter Lang, 1993). Both studies imagine the chronotope as a recurrent setting, whether in the novel or in regard to a film's setting.

8. Raymond Williams, *The English Novel from Dickens to Lawrence* (New York: Oxford University Press, 1970). Williams describes the ideological transformations of the 1840s as revealed through a "crisis of experience," calling attention to the increased value placed on individual experience over adherence to established social norms—a trend congruent with Bronte's portrait of Jane (11). Also see F. M. L. Thompson, *Rise of Respectable Society: A Social History of Victorian Britain, 1830–1900* (Cambridge, MA: Harvard University Press, 1988), and E. P. Thompson, *The Making of the English Working Class* (New York: Pantheon Books, 1964) for more information on the transformations in class in nineteenth-century England.

9. Samuel Tizzard, vi.

10. A Descendant of Cleobulina, An Ancient Composer of Enigmas, &c. [*sic*], *The Sphinx, or Allegorical Lozenges* (London: W. Darton, 1812), 2.

11. See Jonas Barish, *The Antitheatrical Prejudice* (Berkeley: University of California Press, 1981).

12. See Russell Lynes, *The Lively Audience: A History of the Visual and Performing Arts in America* (New York: Harper & Row, 1985), Bruce McConachie, *Melodramatic Formations: American Theatre and Society, 1820–1870* (Iowa City: University of Iowa Press, 1992), Michael Baker, *The Rise of the Victorian Actor* (Totowa, NJ: Rowman and Littlefield, 1978), David Grimsted, *Melodrama Unveiled: American Theater and Culture 1800–1850* (Berkeley: University of California Press, 1987), Benjamin McArthur, *Actors in American Culture 1880–1920* (Philadelphia: Temple University Press, 1984), and Robert C. Allen, *Horrible Prettiness: Burlesque and American Culture* (Chapel Hill: University of North Carolina Press, 1991).

13. The Brothers Mayhew [Augustus and Henry] *Acting Charades or Deeds Not Words* (London: Henry Vizetelly, 1850), v–vi.

14. The Brothers Mayhew, v–vi.

15. William Makepeace Thackeray, *Vanity Fair* (New York: Signet, 1989), 456.

16. Charlotte Brontë, *Jane Eyre,* ed. Richard J. Dunn (New York: W. W. Norton, 1987). See Litvak, who notes that "this assertion of 'ignorance' comes heavily charged with performative potential . . . it provides her with the leading role in a far more important, if more covert, play" (53).

17. See Mark M. Hennelly, "Jane Eyre's Reading Lesson," *ELH* 51.4 (Winter 1984). Hennelly contends that the importance of reading is asserted in the novel's discussions of romance. Hennelly traces allusions to reading throughout the details of Jane's romance with Rochester, "linking hermeneutics and love" in an attempt to control the sympathies of the reading audience (708).

18. Many scholars of Brontë's novel focus on the so-called supernatural or "psychic" connection between Jane and Rochester. See Angela Hague, "Charlotte Bronte

and Intuitive Consciousness," *Texas Studies in Literature and Language* 32.4 (Winter 1990), and J. Jeffrey Franklin, "The Merging of Spiritualities: *Jane Eyre* as Missionary of Love," *Nineteenth-Century Literature* 49.4 (Mar 1995).

19. See Armstrong, 193. This scheme, as Armstrong argues, is calculated to increase Jane's desire for Rochester and, simultaneously situate Jane as the "original object of desire" for Rochester.

20. George Eliot, *Daniel Deronda* (New York: Oxford University Press, 1988), 44.

21. Eliot, 44.

22. Eliot, 49, 50.

23. Louisa May Alcott, "Behind a Mask, or a Woman's Power," in *Alternative Alcott*, ed. Elaine Showalter (New Brunswick, NJ: Rutgers University Press, 1989), 101. Hereafter, in-text citations refer to the same edition.

24. Chapman argues that tableaux vivants were often associated with pure thinking and the cultivation of virtue ("Tableaux," 29). Clearly here, Alcott is working with a different set of nuances surrounding Jean Muir's active tableaux.

25. See Martin Meisel, *Realizations: Narrative, Pictorial, and Theatrical Arts in Nineteenth-Century England* (Princeton, NJ: Princeton University Press, 1983).

26. "Tableaux Vivans" *Harper's Monthly* 27 (Oct. 1863), 698–704.

27. Chapman similarly emphasizes Jean's agency, noting, "Jean shows how an object of the gaze can manipulate and return the gaze; by knowingly constructing herself as spectacle she is able to control the male gaze of her employers" ("'Living Pictures,'" 40).

28. See Judith Fetterley, "Impersonating 'Little Women': The Radicalism of Alcott's *Behind a Mask*," *Women's Studies* 10.1 (1983). Fetterley argues that Alcott's thriller challenges the normative role of a "domestic" little woman.

29. See Karen Halttunen, "The Domestic Drama of Louisa May Alcott," *Feminist Studies* 10.2 (Summer 1984), Elaine Showalter's introduction to *Alternative Alcott*, ed. Elaine Showalter (New Brunswick, NJ: Rutgers University Press, 1988), and Madeleine B. Stern, introduction to *Behind a Mask: The Unknown Thrillers of Louisa May Alcott*, ed. Madeleine Stern (New York: William Morrow & Company, Inc., 1975).

30. See Barbara Welter, "The Cult of True Womanhood: 1820–1860," in *The American Family in Socio-Historical Perspective*, 3rd ed., ed. Michael Gordon (New York: St. Martin's Press, 1983), Nancy Cott, *The Bonds of Womanhood: "Woman's Sphere" in New England 1780–1835* (New Haven, CT: Yale University Press, 1977), and Ryan, *Cradle of the Middle Class*. A self-consciousness about dramatic ability appears closely linked to mid-century women's rising control over domestic space, documented by historians such as Welter, Cott, and Ryan.

31. Sarah Annie Frost, *Stratagem*, in *Dramatic Proverbs and Charades* (New York: Dick and Fitzgerald, 1866).

32. Mrs. Mark Peabody, *Poor Cousins, Beadle's Dime Dialogues, No. 26: Original Minor Dramas, Exhibition Pieces, School Dialogues, Etc., Humorous Laughable and "Taking" for all grades of characters and all ages* (New York: Beadle and Adams, 1880).

33. Peabody, 9.

34. Peabody, 9.

35. Peabody, 11.

36. See Susan Siefert, *The Dilemma of the Talented Heroine: A Study of Nineteenth-Century Fiction* (Montreal: Eden Press, 1978). Siefert argues that nineteenth-century novels devalued women's talents in favor of the less conventional quality of good judgment; here, however, the abilities of the female actors are presented as both transgressive and practical with their dramatic skills, which, unlike the piano playing, drawing, and singing explored by Siefert, had not been domesticated until the advent of parlor play.

37. See Showalter's introduction to *Alternative Alcott*. Showalter claims that Judith "had become an icon of the vengeful and castrating woman for nineteenth-century artists" (xxx). Mary Chapman additionally argues that nineteenth-century versions of the story "sexualized and depoliticized Judith's story, seeing her act of violence in terms of castration rather than political assassination" ("'Living Pictures,'" 41).

Chapter 5

1. Bourdieu, *The Logic of Practice*, 66–67.

2. Thornstein Veblen, *The Theory of the Leisure Class* (New York: The Modern Library, 1931). For discussions of the trends toward material accumulation in relation to the late nineteenth-century home, see Jean-Christophe Agnew, "A House of Fiction: Domestic Interiors and the Commodity Aesthetic," in *Consuming Visions: Accumulation and Display of Goods in America, 1880–1920*, ed. Simon J. Bronner (New York: W. W. Norton & Company, 1989), Ames, *Death in the Dining Room*, Michael Barton, "The Victorian Jeremiad: Critics of Accumulation and Display," in *Consuming Visions: Accumulation and Display of Goods in America, 1880–1920*, ed. Simon J. Bronner (New York: W. W. Norton & Company, 1989), Grier, *Culture and Comfort*, and Lears, "Beyond Veblen."

3. See Miles Orvell, *The Real Thing: Imitation and Authenticity in American Culture, 1880–1940* (Chapel Hill: University of North Carolina Press, 1989).

4. See Grier, chapters two and three.

5. Pauline Hopkins, *Contending Forces: A Romance Illustrative of Negro Life North and South* (New York: Oxford University Press, 1988), 108.

6. See Charles W. Chesnutt, *The House Behind the Cedars* (New York: Penguin Books, 1993), and *The wife of his youth, and other stories of the color line* (Ann Arbor: University of Michigan Press, 1968).

7. Henry James, *The Tragic Muse* (New York: Augustus M. Kelley, 1970), I, 18.

8. Veblen, 104–5.

9. Veblen, 336.

10. Agnew, 141.

11. See William Leach, "Strategists of Display and the Production of Desire," in *Consuming Visions: Accumulation and Display of Goods in America, 1880–1920*, ed. Simon J. Bronner (New York: W. W. Norton & Company, 1989), 101. Also see Leach,

Land of Desire: Merchants, Power, and the Rise of a New American Culture (New York: Pantheon Books, 1993), and Jennifer Scanlon, *Inarticulate Longings: Ladies Home Journal, Gender, and the Promises of Consumer Culture* (New York: Routledge, 1995). As Agnew has argued, a late-century "commodity aesthetic" was so strong that it entailed seeing the world as filled with "transactionable goods," entailing the collapse, through purchases, of boundaries between "the self and the commodity world" (135).

12. Mary Elizabeth Wilson Sherwood, *Home Amusements* (New York: Appleton and Company, 1884), 21. Sherwood also published periodical articles as M. E. W. S., and later published many books under her married name, Mrs. John Sherwood.

13. Mrs. John Sherwood, *The Art of Entertaining* (New York: Dodd, Mead, and Co., 1892), 272–73.

14. See Banta, *Imaging American Women: Idea and Ideals in Cultural History* (New York: Columbia University Press, 1987), Chapman, *"Living Pictures"*, and Judith Fetterley, "'The Temptation to Be a Beautiful Object': Double Standard and Double Bind in *The House of Mirth*," *Studies in American Fiction* 5.2 (1977).

15. "Living Pictures," *The Critic* (April 8, 1893), 227.

16. Mrs. John Sherwood, "Some Society Tableaux," *Cosmopolitan* 24 (Jan. 1898), 235. Although the event actually took place in 1875, in commemoration of the Centennial, Sherwood's article did not appear until 1898.

17. Sherwood, "Society Tableaux," 236–38.

18. Sherwood, "Society Tableaux," 238–39.

19. William F. Gill, *Parlor Tableaux and Amateur Theatricals* (Boston: J. E. Tilton, 1867), 5.

20. See Grace Ann Hovet and Theodore R. Hovet, "Tableaux Vivants: Masculine Vision and Feminine Reflections in Novels by Warner, Alcott, Stowe, and Wharton," *American Transcendental Quarterly* 7.4 (Dec. 1993). The Hovets argue that the "transparency" of the female form and psyche was a common effect of tableaux vivants; they argue that Emerson's discussions of vision reflect a similar sense of feminine transparency (as the object looked upon), as penetrated by a powerful male gaze that looks through the feminine object. Mary Chapman similarly argues that period tableaux vivants obstructed a sense of individuality and "point to a crisis in signification that was most frequently articulated in terms of the legibility of woman" (*"Living Pictures,"* 197).

21. Herman Melville, "The Paradise of Bachelors and the Tartarus of Maids," *The Piazza Tales and Other Prose Pieces, 1839–1860*, ed. Harrison Hayford et al. (Chicago: Northwestern UP and Newberry Library, 1987), 335.

22. Frost, *Book of Tableaux*, 12.

23. See Lawrence W. Levine, *Highbrow/Lowbrow: The Emergence of Cultural Hierarchy in America* (Cambridge, MA: Harvard University Press, 1988).

24. See Hildegard Hoeller, *Edith Wharton's Dialogue with Realism and Sentimental Fiction* (Gainesville: University of Florida, 2000), for a study of Wharton's use of the sentimental tradition.

25. Charles Harrison, *Theatricals and Tableaux Vivants for Amateurs* (London: A. Bradley, 1882), 120.

26. See William B. Dillingham, "Frank Norris and the Genteel Tradition," in *Critical Essays on Frank Norris,* ed. Don Graham (Boston: G. K. Hall and Company, 1980).

27. Frank Norris, *The Pit: A Story of Chicago* (New York: Doubleday, Page & Co., 1903), 7. Hereafter, in-text citations refer to this edition.

28. Agnew defines the term as "a way of seeing the world in general, and the self and society in particular, as so much raw space to be furnished with mobile, detachable, and transactionable goods," leading to the dissolution of boundaries between self and goods (135).

29. This role was made famous by Sarah Bernhardt, who starred in Victorien Sardou's *Theodora* in 1884.

30. Depicted in a 1690 play by Jean Racine entitled *Athalie* and a 1733 oratorio by Handel entitled *Athalia,* the titular character was the daughter of Jezebel and Queen of Judah as well as an idol worshiper and usurper to the throne.

31. Carmen was made famous by Georges Bizet's opera of the same name (1875), which depicts the titular character as headstrong, self-actualized, seductive, and promiscuous, making her a particularly controversial woman's role when the opera was first produced.

32. For a discussion of the various cultural and social pursuits of high society New York in Edith Wharton's day, see Maureen E. Montgomery, *Displaying Women: Spectacles of Leisure in Edith Wharton's New York* (New York: Routledge, 1998).

33. See Levine. The middle-class culture traced throughout this study, however, cannot be considered simply a middlebrow or mediocre "middle" culture. According to Levine's formulation, the middlebrow was not labeled or marginalized until roughly the turn of the century, or the period of Wharton's novel.

34. Edith Wharton, *The House of Mirth* (New York: Penguin Classics, 1985), 108–9. Hereafter in-text citations refer to this edition.

35. For an extended discussion of the style attributed to Reynolds's painting, see Melanie Dawson, "Lily Bart's Fractured Alliances and Wharton's Appeal to the Middlebrow Reader," *Reader* 41 (Spring 1999), 1–30.

36. See Cynthia Griffin Wolff, *A Feast of Words: The Triumph of Edith Wharton* (New York: Oxford University Press, 1977). Wolff notes that Selden's belief that he has seen the "real" Lily Bart is in part related to his own feelings for Lily, not necessarily to the scene he views, claiming that "the 'real' Lily—the only Lily he tolerates— is the beautiful idealized memory he carries of her" (131–32).

37. Rosedale's admiration for Lily Bart notably aligns her with the works of the old masters, for as he exclaims after Lily's tableau, "My God, . . . if I could get Paul Morpeth to paint her . . . the picture'd appreciate a hundred per cent in ten years" (158).

38. See Judith Fryer, "Reading Mrs. Lloyd," in *Edith Wharton: New Critical Essays,* ed. Alfred Bendixen and Annette Zilversmit (New York: Garland Publishing, 1992), Kirsten Holmstrom, *Monodrama, Attitudes, Tableaux Vivants: Studies on Some Trends in Theatrical Fashion 1770–1815* (Stockholm: Almqvist and Wiksell, 1967), and

Jack McCullough, *Living Pictures on the New York Stage* (Ann Arbor, MI: UMI Research Press, 1983).

39. "Living Pictures," Velvet Skin Soap Advertisement, *McClure's* 4 (April 1895).

40. Lily shows what Martha Banta terms her "outline" (a term Banta presents as representing moderately sexualized attitudes) simultaneously awing and alienating her viewers. Banta writes that "whatever the social and economic causes for the distance kept between virginity and promiscuity in turn-of-the-century America, unrestrained sexuality was not the look that displayed itself the best before the general public. *Outline, silhouette, design, shape,* and *pose* are . . . the terms most applicable. . . ." (622).

Chapter 6

1. Helen E. Hollister, *Parlor Games for the Wise and Otherwise* (Philadelphia: The Pen Publishing Company, 1900).

2. Hollister's text remained in print from 1887 to 1922. Although Hollister's text sold well enough to necessitate multiple printings and those printings span a respectable period, the success of this older-styled parlor games manual is somewhat of an enigma in the turn-of-the-century entertainment market.

3. Beatrice Tukesbury, "Emma Sheridan Fry and Educational Dramatics," *Educational Theatre Journal* 16 (Oct. 1964), 341.

4. Tukesbury, 341.

5. A. Minnie Herts, "The Children's Educational Theatre," *Atlantic Monthly* 100 (Dec. 1907).

6. Herts, 800.

7. Herts, 801.

8. Evelyne Hilliard, Theodora McCormick, and Kate Oglebay, *Amateur and Educational Dramatics* (New York: The Macmillan Company, 1917), 2.

9. Catherine Miller Balm, *Stunt Night Tonight!* (New York: Harper and Brothers, 1928), 13. Some editions list Catherine Atkinson Miller as the author.

10. Concerns about children and the movies were particularly prevalent in the early twentieth century, spawning concerns seen in Edgar Dale, *How to Appreciate Motion Pictures,* (1933; New York: Arno Press, 1970), and in the Payne Fund studies. See Garth Jowett, *Children and the Movies: Media Influence and the Payne Fund Controversy* (New York: Cambridge University Press, 1996).

11. See Harvey Green, *Fit for America: Health, Fitness, Sport, and American Society* (Baltimore: Johns Hopkins University Press, 1986).

12. See T. J. Jackson Lears, *No Place of Grace: Antimodernism and the Transformation of American Culture, 1880–1920* (New York: Pantheon Books, 1981) and Bledstein.

13. See Walter Benn Michaels, *Our America: Nativism, Modernism, and Pluralism* (Durham, NC: Duke University Press, 1995) and Priscilla Wald, *Constituting Americans: Cultural Anxiety and Narrative Form* (Durham, NC: Duke University Press, 1995).

14. See Gail Bederman, *Manliness and Civilization: A Cultural History of Gender and Race in the United States, 1880–1917* (Chicago: University of Chicago Press, 1995), and see Kett. Bederman addresses fears of effeminacy among young American men near the century's turn; Kett explores definitions and fears surrounding emerging ideas of adolescence.

15. Mary Dawson and Emma Paddock Telford, *The Book of Entertainments and Frolics for All Occasions* (Philadelphia: David McKay, 1911).

16. George B. Bartlett, *New Games for Parlor and Lawn: with a few old friends in a new dress* (New York: Harper & Brothers, 1882), iii. Additionally, the activities are reprinted from the pages of *Harper's Young People, Youth's Companion,* and *Wide Awake,* according to the preface, iii.

17. Jessie H. Bancroft, *Games: Revised and Enlarged Edition of Games for the Playground, Home, School, and Gymnasium* (New York: Macmillan Company, 1937), 68.

18. Balm, 13.

19. Sinclair Lewis, *Main Street* (New York: Library of America, 1992).

20. Lewis, 53. Hereafter, in-text citations refer to this edition.

21. This activity seems to be a version of "Hunt the Slipper," a much earlier parlor game. The game's familiarity here suggests that Carol's reforms are dated.

22. See Melanie Dawson, *From Carnival to Nostalgia: The Play of Cultural Literacy in the Nineteenth-Century Parlor,* Appendix A (diss., University of Pittsburgh, 1991), for a list of Penn's publishing record, including a list of reprinted books.

23. In 1939 Penn Publishing was bought by Max Salop, owner of Harlem Book Company and Tudor Publishing Company. After the purchase of Penn, Tudor continued to print texts under the Penn imprint for a short time. Scholars have pointed to the significance of Dick and Fitzgerald as well as Beadle and Adams as publishing forces. See Madeleine Stern, "Dick and Fitzgerald," in *Publishers for Mass Entertainment in Nineteenth-Century America,* ed. Madeleine B. Stern (Boston: G. K. Hall & Co., 1980), and Albert Johannsen, *The House of Beadle and Adams and its Dime and Nickel Novels: The Story of a Vanished Literature* (Norman: University of Oklahoma, 1950).

24. Delsarte poses functioned both as therapeutic exercises and as graceful "attitudes" that made their way into physical, presentational entertainments. They originated with François Delsarte, a French musician and actor. His codified movements, initiated as a means of analyzing and interpreting bodily gestures, gradually gained attention as tools for creating aesthetic poses in tableaux and other physical presentations. The Delsarte system upheld relaxed physical composure, or an ease in public as well as private—in short, an attractive ideal for middle-class women. Genevieve Stebbins was the first to bring Delsarte to American women in *Delsarte System of Expression* (New York: Edgar S. Werner, 1885).

25. *The 1897 Sears, Roebuck Catalogue* (New York: Chelsea House, 1968).

26. A number of Dick and Fitzgerald texts also appear in the Sears catalogues, particularly in the earlier 1890s; in general, the Dick and Fitzgerald texts are more oriented to ethnic and minstrel humor. While Dick and Fitzgerald seems to have sur-

vived the 1890s intact, the company does not display a significant increase in its turn-of-the-century holdings, as did Penn.

27. Penn took over the texts published by small firms such as P. Garrett & Company, the National School of Elocution and Oratory, and the E. L. Kellogg Company—all companies with established authors among their ranks.

28. Among the established authors that Penn acquired, Phineas Garrett published under the P. Garrett and Company imprint, Alice M. Kellogg, Amos M. Kellogg, and C. S. Griffin under the Kellogg imprint, and Mrs. J. W. Shoemaker and Charles M. Shoemaker under the National School of Elocution and Oratory.

29. My accounting includes only those of Penn's entertainment texts of ninety or more pages.

30. Such texts include: *Eureka Entertainments: containing a wide variety of new and novel entertainments suitable to all kinds of public and private occasions* (Philadelphia: Penn 1907 [repr. through 1923]), Alexander Clark, *Schoolday Dialogues: A Collection of Original Dialogues and Tableaux Designed for School Exhibitions, Literary Societies, and Parlor Entertainments* (Philadelphia: Penn 1897 [repr. through 1925]), and William M. Clark, *Sterling Dialogues: A Choice Collection of Original Dialogues for Day-Schools, Sunday-Schools, Lyceums, Anniversaries, Holidays, Etc.* (Philadelphia: Penn 1898 [repr. through 1929]).

31. Selections include: John H. Bechtel, *Select Speeches for Declamation: chosen from the leading writers and speakers of all ages and nations and adapted in length and variety for use in schools and colleges* (Philadelphia: Penn 1898 [repr. through 1927]), Mrs. J. W. Shoemaker, *Choice Dialogues: a collection of new and original dialogues for schools and social entertainment* (Philadelphia: Penn 1896 [repr. through 1924]), Amos M. Kellogg, *Practical Recitations: short pieces for school entertainment for children of thirteen years* (Philadelphia: Penn 1918 [repr. through 1925]), and Alice M. Kellogg's *How to Celebrate Washington's Birthday in the Schoolroom: helps for the primary, grammar, and high school* (Philadelphia: Penn 1911 [repr. through 1915]).

32. These texts include: E. C. and L. J. Rook, *Young Folks' Entertainments* (Philadelphia: Penn, 1889 [repr. through 1929]), E. C. and L. J. Rook, *Child's Own Speaker* (Philadelphia: Penn 1895 [repr. through 1927]), and Clara J. Denton's *Little People's Dialogues: designed for young people of ten years* (Philadelphia: Penn, 1902 [repr. through 1926]).

33. Among such texts are: Charles C. Shoemaker, *Holiday Entertainments* (Philadelphia: Penn 1889 [repr. through 1929]), Sara S. Rice, *Holiday Recitations for Reading and Recitations: specially adapted to Christmas, New Year, Valentine's Day, Washington's Birthday, Easter, Arbor Day, Decoration Day, Fourth of July, and Thanksgiving* (Philadelphia: Penn 1892 [repr. through 1920]), and Alice M. Kellogg, *Primary Recitations: short, bright selections for Thanksgiving, Washington's Birthday, Arbor day, May day, Bird day, Memorial day, Flag day, closing exercises, nature recitations, patriotic and general occasions* (Philadelphia: Penn 1907 [repr. through 1925]).

34. Notable texts include: Clara J. Denton, *Little People's Dialogues: Easy Enter-*

tainments for Young People (Philadelphia: Penn 1892 [repr. through 1927]), C. S. Griffin's *Little Primary Pieces for Wee Folks to Speak* (Philadelphia: Penn 1912 [repr. through 1927]), and E. C. and L. J. Rook's *Child's Own Speaker,* and *Young Folks' Recitations* (Philadelphia: Penn, 1925).

35. See Gordon L. Weill, *Sears, Roebuck, U.S.A.: The Great American Catalog Store and How It Grew* (New York: Stein and Day, 1977), and Boris Emmet and John E. Jeuck, *Catalogues and Counters: A History of Sears, Roebuck and Company* (Chicago: University of Chicago Press, 1950) for discussions of the early Sears catalogues. Both texts point to the significant rural population in the year 1880 as a factor in the catalogue company's success; close to 72 percent rural, the country readily embraced a merchandiser who came to the doorsteps of its consumers.

36. In 1899, in an effort to cut costs, the Sears catalogue (number 108) appeared without a book department. The next year, however, books reappeared in the catalogue, a type of market reversal not unusual in the corporation, where comprehensiveness was often more important than the profits of individual departments (Emmet and Jeuck, 8). Also see Louise E. Asher and Edith Heal, *Send No Money* (Chicago: Argus Books, 1942). Asher and Heal contend that the book and stationery department in the catalogue usually ran at a loss, since there were few sales of the literature classics; "how-to" books, the Bible, and sex manuals fared better (64–65).

37. *Decorum: a practical treatise on Etiquette and dress of the best American society* (New York: Union Publishing House, 1882), and Richard A. Wells, *Manners, Culture, and Dress of the Best American Society* (Springfield, MA: King, Richardson, and Co., 1893).

38. Sherwood, *Art of Entertaining.*

39. Maude C. Cooke, *Social Etiquette or Manners and Customs of Polite Society* (Philadelphia: National Publishing Co., 1896), *Correct Social Usage,* 12th rev. ed. (New York: New York Society for Self-Culture, 1909), and Frances Stevens and Frances M. Smith, *Health, Etiquette and Beauty: a handbook for popular use* (New York: A. L. Burt, 1889).

40. See Schlereth. The craze in athleticism expressed in college sports, competitive teams, and general fitness resulted in a broadening array of entertainments outside of the home. In addition, growing numbers of clubs and educational organizations drew Americans to associate with their civic-minded neighbors.

41. See Karen Halttunen, "From Parlor to Living Room: Domestic Space, Interior Decoration, and the Culture of Personality," in *Consuming Visions: Accumulation and Display of Goods in America, 1880–1920,* ed. Simon J. Bronner (New York: W. W. Norton & Company, 1989).

42. Gertrude Stein, *How to Write* (New York: Dover Publications, 1975), 388.

43. Jürgen Habermas, *The Structural Transformation of the Public Sphere: An Inquiry into a Category of Bourgeois Society,* trans. Thomas Burger with Frederick Lawrence (Cambridge, MA: MIT Press, 1993), 30, 45. In-text citations refer to the same edition.

44. Edith Wharton and Ogden Codman, Jr., *The Decoration of Houses* (London: B. J. Batsford, 1898), 124–25.

45. Emma Whitcomb Babcock, *Household Hints* (New York: D. Appleton & Company, 1884).

46. Babcock, 95.

47. Carol Ryrie, Brink, *Caddie Woodlawn* (New York: Alladin Paperbacks, 1990), 181. The novel was composed in 1935, but is set during the days during and after the Civil War, reflecting Brink's claim that she is telling the story of her grandmother's youth.

48. Brink, 182.

49. Brink, 187.

50. Carolyn Steedman, *Strange Dislocations: Childhood and the Idea of Human Interiority, 1780–1930* (Cambridge, MA: Harvard University Press, 1995), 5.

51. Steedman, 97.

52. Pierre Nora, "Between Memory and History," trans. Marc Roudebush, *Representations* 26 (Spring 1989), 7–25, 8.

53. See Nora.

54. See Susan Stewart, *On Longing: Narratives of the Miniature, the Gigantic, the Souvenir, the Collection* (Baltimore and London: John Hopkins University Press, 1984). In her suggestion that child bodies, as miniature bodies, represent deflated forms of authority, Stewart offers a means to address the evocation of the past through the child performer.

55. Alice Cary, "Pictures of Memory," in *Choice Readings for Public and Private Entertainments,* ed. Robert McLean Cummock (Chicago: A. C. McClurg and Co., 1920). The text was first published in 1878.

56. Cary, 245.

57. Henry Davenport Northrop, *Young People's Speaker, being a choice treasury of new and popular recitations, readings, dialogues, original and adapted comedies, tableaux, etc.* (J. R. Jones, 1895).

58. Richard Harding Davis, "The Boy Orator of Zapata City," in *The Reciter's Treasury of Prose and Drama,* ed. Ernest Pertwee (London: George Routledge and Sons, 1904).

59. Richard Harding Davis, 50.

60. Richard Harding Davis, 57.

61. Richard Harding Davis, 57.

62. Marc Dolan, *Modern Lives: A Cultural Re-reading of "The Lost Generation"* (West Lafayette, IN: Purdue University Press, 1996), 17–18.

Chapter 7

1. Charlotte Perkins Gilman, *Herland* (New York: Pantheon Books, 1979).

2. Gleason, 174. Here I am countering Gleason's argument that Gilman's novel

Herland reveals a "complicity" with a spirit of play, for I find that the spirit of play is exactly what the novel calls into question as it positions competitive leisure activities as nostalgically personal, but nevertheless fails to allow the novel's characters to feel satisfied with these new spectacles. In my reading then, "play" has not been redefined to include pageants; rather, it has been called into question as a value.

3. See Charlotte Perkins Gilman, *The Living of Charlotte Perkins Gilman* (written in 1935; Madison: University of Wisconsin Press, 1990) for a discussion of the activities that Gilman herself enjoyed (79). Gilman's competitive spirit was expressed in mind games, puzzles, and other contests, both solitary and communal. Given Gilman's own passion for "physical culture," the exercises, like the pageants of the fictive land, could be viewed as richly engaging activities, rewarding for enthusiastic participants, which the critical male explorers are not.

4. Boyer, 253.

5. The Cokesbury Press, for example, published E. O. Harbin's *Phunology: a collection of tried and proved plans for play, fellowship, and profit, for use in the home, church, and community organizations for a wholesome program of recreation* in 1923, while *The Christian Herald* printed Emma J. Gray's *Fun for the Household* in 1897.

6. Amos R. Wells, *Social—To Save* (Boston and Chicago: United Society of Christian Endeavor, 1895), 2.

7. Wells, *Social—To Save*, 3.

8. See Paula M. Kane, *Separatism and Subculture: Boston Catholicism, 1900–1920* (Chapel Hill: University of North Carolina Press, 1994). Kane contends that Boston churches and schools of the turn of the century and in the early twentieth century evaluated various dramatic activities while the craze for community plays, or little theater, was sweeping the country.

9. Amos R. Wells, *Social Evenings: a book of games and pleasant entertainments* (Boston and Chicago: United Society of Christian Endeavor, 1894), 1–2.

10. Jane Addams, *Twenty Years at Hull House* (New York: Signet, 1961), 239, 243.

11. Kenneth L. Heaton, *Character Building Through Recreation* (Chicago: University of Chicago Press, 1929), xiii.

12. Helen Ferris, *Producing Amateur Entertainments: Varied Stunts and Other Numbers with Program Plans and Directions* (New York: E. P. Dutton & Company, 1921).

13. J. C. Elsom and Blanche M. Trilling *Social Games and Group Dances: a collection of games and dances suitable for community and social use* (Philadelphia: J. R. Jones, 1919), 16.

14. Banta, *Imaging American Women*, 654–55.

15. See David Glassberg, *American Historical Pageantry* (Chapel Hill: University of North Carolina Press, 1990). Glassberg's study of the pageantry movement highlights the perceived need for communities to assimilate immigrants, and to forge group identities that would overshadow individuality.

16. Games-oriented guide books such as those by "Professor Hoffmann" (John Angelo Lewis, *Parlor Amusements*) were written under pseudonyms and invoked the

title "doctor" as a kind of euphemism. Many late nineteenth-century and turn-of-the-century advice texts offered authors credentialing via academic titles, church affiliation, or club memberships.

17. Emma Dunham Kelley, *Megda* (New York: Oxford University Press, Schomburg Library, 1988), 154.

18. Harold Frederic, *The Damnation of Theron Ware* (New York: Penguin Books, 1986), 250. Hereafter referred to with in-text citations.

19. Gleason, 99.

20. Gleason, 100.

21. See Richard Slotkin, *The Fatal Environment: The Myth of the Frontier in the Age of Industrialization, 1800–1890* (New York: Athaneum, 1985).

22. Bryan S. Turner, "A Note on Nostalgia," *Theory, Culture, and Society* 4.1 (Feb. 1987), 150.

23. Bryan Turner, 150–51.

24. See Jay Mechling, "The Collecting Self and American Youth Movements," in *Consuming Visions: Accumulation and Display of Goods in America, 1880–1920*, ed. Simon J. Bronner (New York: W. W. Norton, 1989). Mechling writes, "Dressing American children in buckskin or tan drill was a sudden impulse of the late nineteenth century," and he goes on to link these practices to scouting and other programs promoting child socialization (255).

25. Nellie M. Mustain, *Popular Amusements for In and Out of Doors* (Chicago: Lyman A. Martin, 1902), 44.

26. Mustain, 43.

27. Mustain, 119.

28. Edith Wharton, *Hudson River Bracketed* (New York: D. Appleton and Company, 1929), 7.

29. Raphael Samuel, *Theatres of Memory* (New York: Verso, 1994), 429. Also see Samuel's chapter fifteen, "Dreamscapes," for a discussion of the resurgence of interest in photography at the moment of its apparent decline in the face of new technologies. Samuel's suggestion that, at the moment when art forms are outdated, they are inscribed with a newfound sense of value is much like the attitude toward the recitations that I am describing here.

30. Lears, *No Place of Grace*, 26.

31. See Butsch, chapters ten through fifteen.

32. See Henry Adams, *The Education of Henry Adams* (Boston: Houghton Mifflin, 1973).

33. This interpretation of Cather's novel challenges one of the prevalent strains in the scholarly work on *My Ántonia* by pointing to its overtly constructed nature. Many scholars have insisted on the novel's veracity as a frontier text and as an accurate representation of premodern life, building on an interpretive trend initiated by the novel's first reviewers. I am no less insistent that we read the novel for its realism, situating Jim Burden's narrative impulses as overlapping with common entertainment trends.

34. Willa Cather, *Early Novels and Stories* (New York: Library of America, 1987), 865–66. Hereafter, in-text citations refer to this edition.

35. See Jean Schwind, "The Benda Illustrations to *My Ántonia:* Cather's Silent Supplement of Jim Burden's Narrative," *PMLA* 100.2 (1985), 51–67.

36. See John J. Murphy and Kevin A. Synnott, "The Recognition of Willa Cather's Art," in *Critical Essays on Willa Cather*, ed. John J. Murphy (Boston: G. K. Hall, 1984) for a discussion of Cather's early reception.

37. See Michael Peterman, "Kindling the Imagination: The Inset Stories of *My Ántonia,*" in *Approaches to Teaching Cather's* My Ántonia, ed. Susan J. Rosowski (New York; MLA, 1989). Peterman points to the same chapters that I discuss here, but whereas Peterman reads these stories as important vehicles of the tie between Jim and Ántonia, I analyze them here as a nonintrusive reminder of Jim's narrative tendencies.

38. Mustain, 21.

39. Ellis Davidson, *The Happy Nursery: a book for mothers, governesses, and nurses, containing games, amusements, and employments for boys and girls* (London: Cassell, Petter, and Galpin, 1870), 150–53.

Epilogue

1. See Robert Putnam, *Bowling Alone: The Collapse and Revival of American Community* (New York: Simon & Schuster, 2000). In part, this is the anxiety that Putnam's study asserts as it highlights continuing fears about the disintegration of social bonds in leisure pursuits. Putnam reports, for example, that there are now fewer strong communal affiliations in recreational groups than in previous decades. Putnam's thesis is made stronger by suggestions that suburban living, technological work, and the impact of the virtual world have resulted in a more individualistic society, one oriented away from group activities, and a milieu where individuals eschew traditional bonds for less meaningful, and possibly less enduring forms of recreation. Part of what has made Putnam's study so influential is the assertion that shifts in leisure life help us chart an altered social landscape.

Selected Bibliography

(For a complete list of all sources, including literary and archival works, see chapter notes.)

Agnew, Jean-Christophe. "A House of Fiction: Domestic Interiors and the Commodity Aesthetic." In *Consuming Visions: Accumulation and Display of Goods in America, 1880–1920,* edited by Simon J. Bronner, 133–55. New York: W. W. Norton & Company, 1989.

Allen, Robert C. *Horrible Prettiness: Burlesque and American Culture.* Chapel Hill: University of North Carolina Press, 1991.

Ames, Kenneth L. *Death in the Dining Room & Other Tales of Victorian Culture.* Philadelphia: Temple University Press, 1992.

Ariès, Philippe. *Centuries of Childhood: A Social History of Family Life,* translated by Robert Baldick. New York: Vintage, 1962.

Armstrong, Nancy. *Desire and Domestic Fiction: A Political History of the Novel.* New York: Oxford University Press, 1987.

Asher, Louise E., and Edith Heal. *Send No Money.* Chicago: Argus Books, 1942.

Auerbach, Nina. *Private Theatricals.* Cambridge, MA: Harvard University Press, 1990.

Avery, Gillian. *Behold the Child: American Children and Their Books, 1621–1922.* Baltimore: Johns Hopkins University Press, 1994.

Baker, Michael. *The Rise of the Victorian Actor.* Totowa, NJ: Rowman and Littlefield, 1978.

Bakhtin, Mikhail. *The Dialogic Imagination,* edited by Michael Holquist and translated by Caryl Emerson and Michael Holquist. Austin: University of Texas Press, 1981.

———. *Rabelais and His World,* translated by Helene Iswolsky. Bloomington: Indiana University Press, 1984.

Banta, Martha. *Failure and Success in America: A Literary Debate.* Princeton, NJ: Princeton University Press, 1978.

———. *Imaging American Women: Idea and Ideals in Cultural History.* New York: Columbia University Press, 1987.

Barish, Jonas. *The Antitheatrical Prejudice.* Berkeley: University of California Press, 1981.

Barton, Michael. "The Victorian Jeremiad: Critics of Accumulation and Display." In *Consuming Visions: Accumulation and Display of Goods in America, 1880–1920*, edited by Simon J. Bronner, 55–71. New York: W. W. Norton & Company, 1989.

Baym, Nina. *Novels, Readers, and Reviewers: Responses to Fiction in Antebellum America.* Ithaca: Cornell, 1984.

———. *Women's Fiction: A Guide to Novels by and about Women in America, 1820–70.* 2nd ed. Urbana: University of Illinois Press, 1993.

Beaver, Patrick. *Victorian Parlor Games.* Wigston, Leicester: Magna Books, 1995.

Bederman, Gail. *Manliness and Civilization: A Cultural History of Gender and Race in the United States, 1880–1917.* Chicago: University of Chicago Press, 1995.

Blair, Karen J. *The Torchbearers: Women and Their Amateur Arts Associations in America, 1890–1930.* Bloomington: Indiana University Press, 1994.

Bledstein, Burton J. *The Culture of Professionalism: The Middle Class and the Development of Higher Education in America.* New York: Norton, 1976.

Blumin, Stuart M. *The Emergence of the Middle Class: Social Experience in the American City, 1760–1900.* New York: Cambridge University Press, 1989.

Bourdieu, Pierre. *In Other Words: Essays Towards a Reflexive Sociology,* translated by Matthew Adamson. Stanford, CA: Stanford University Press, 1990.

———. *The Logic of Practice,* translated by Richard Nice. Stanford, CA: Stanford University Press, 1980.

Boyer, Paul. *Urban Masses and Moral Order in America, 1820–1920.* Cambridge, MA: Harvard University Press, 1978.

Braden, Donna R. "'The Family That Plays Together Stays Together': Family Pastimes and Indoor Amusements, 1890–1930." In *American Home Life, 1880–1930,* edited by Jessica H. Foy and Thomas J. Schlereth, 145–61. Knoxville: University of Tennessee Press, 1994.

Brodhead, Richard H. *Cultures of Letters: Scenes of Reading and Writing in Nineteenth-Century America.* Chicago: University of Chicago Press, 1993.

Bronner, Simon J. "Object Lessons: The Work of Ethnological Museums and Collections." In *Consuming Visions: Accumulation and Display of Goods in America, 1880–1920,* edited by Simon J. Bronner, 217–54. New York: W. W. Norton & Company, 1989.

Burke, Martin J. *The Conundrum of Class: Public Discourse on the Social Order in America.* Chicago: University of Chicago Press, 1995.

Bushman, Richard L. *The Refinement of America: Persons, Houses, Cities.* New York: Alfred A. Knopf, 1992.

Butsch, Richard. *The Making of American Audiences: From Stage to Television, 1750–1990.* New York: Cambridge University Press, 2000.

Cawelti, John G. *Apostles of the Self-Made Man.* Chicago: University of Chicago Press, 1965.

Certeau, Michel de. *The Practice of Everyday Life,* translated by Steven Rendall. Berkeley: University of California Press, 1984.

Chapman, Mary. *"Living Pictures": Women and Tableaux Vivants in Nineteenth-Century Fiction and Culture.* Diss. Cornell University: Ann Arbor: UMI, 1993.

———. "'Living Pictures': Women and *Tableaux Vivants* in Nineteenth-Century Fiction and Culture." *Wide Angle* 18.3 (1996): 22–52.

Cook, James W., Jr., "Of Men, Missing Links, and Nondescripts: The Strange Career of P. T. Barnum's 'What Is It?' Exhibition." In *Freakery: Cultural Spectacles of the Extraordinary Body,* edited by Rosemarie Garland Thomson, 139–57. New York: New York University Press, 1996.

Cott, Nancy. *The Bonds of Womanhood: "Woman's Sphere" in New England, 1780–1835.* New Haven, CT: Yale University Press, 1977.

Cremin, Lawrence A. *American Education: The National Experience, 1783–1876.* New York: Harper & Row, 1980.

———. *A History of Education in American Culture.* New York: Henry Holt and Company, 1953.

Davidson, Cathy N. *Revolution and the Word: The Rise of the Novel in America.* New York: Oxford University Press, 1986.

Dawson, Melanie V. *From Carnival to Nostalgia: The Play of Cultural Literacy in the Nineteenth-Century Parlor.* Diss. University of Pittsburgh: Ann Arbor: UMI, 1997.

Denning, Michael. *Mechanic Accents: Dime Novels and Working-Class Culture in America.* New York: Verso, 1987.

Dimock, Wai Chee. "Class, Gender, and a History of Metonymy." In *Rethinking Class: Literary Studies and Social Formations,* edited by Wai Chee Dimock and Michael Gilmore, 57–104. New York: Columbia University Press, 1994.

Dolan, Marc. *Modern Lives: A Cultural Re-reading of "The Lost Generation."* West Lafayette, IN: Purdue University Press, 1996.

Elias, Norbert. *The Civilizing Process: The History of Manners and State Formation and Civilization,* translated by Edmund Jephcott. Cambridge, MA: Blackwell, 1994.

Ellison, Julie. "The Gender of Transparency: Masculinity and the Conduct of Life." *American Literary History* 4.4 (Winter 1992): 584–606.

Emerson, Ralph Waldo. "The American Scholar." In *The Selected Writings of Ralph Waldo Emerson,* edited by Brooks Atkinson. New York: Modern Library, 1940.

———. "Behavior." In *The Conduct of Life,* volume 6, *The Complete Works of Ralph Waldo Emerson,* Centenary Edition, 169–70. New York: Houghton Mifflin, 1931.

Foucault, Michel. *The History of Sexuality: An Introduction,* translated by Robert Hurley. New York: Vintage, 1980.

Franklin, J. Jeffrey. *Serious Play: The Cultural Form of the Nineteenth-Century Realist Novel.* Philadelphia: University of Pennsylvania Press, 1999.

Fretz, Eric. "P. T. Barnum's Theatrical Selfhood and the Nineteenth-Century Culture of Exhibition." In *Freakery: Cultural Spectacles of the Extraordinary Body,* edited by Rosemarie Garland Thompson, 97–107. New York: New York University Press, 1996.

Garvey, Ellen Gruber. *The Adman in the Parlor: Magazines and the Gendering of Consumer Culture, 1880s to 1910s.* New York: Oxford University Press, 1996.

Glassberg, David. *American Historical Pageantry.* Chapel Hill: University of North Carolina Press, 1990.

Gleason, William A. *The Leisure Ethic: Work and Play in American Literature, 1840–1940.* Stanford, CA: Stanford University Press, 1999.

Green, Harvey. *Fit for America: Health, Fitness, Sport, and American Society.* Baltimore: Johns Hopkins University Press, 1986.

———. "Scientific Thought and the Nature of Children in America, 1820–1920." In *A Century of Childhood, 1820–1920,* edited by Mary Lynn Stevens Heininger, 121–37. Rochester, NY: The Strong Museum, 1984.

Grier, Katherine C. *Culture and Comfort: People, Parlors, and Upholstery, 1850–1930.* Rochester, NY: The Strong Museum, 1988.

Grimsted, David. *Melodrama Unveiled: American Theater and Culture, 1800–1850.* Berkeley: University of California Press, 1987.

Haber, Samuel. *The Quest for Authority and Honor in the American Professions, 1750–1900.* Chicago: University of Chicago Press, 1991.

Habermas, Jürgen. *The Structural Transformation of the Public Sphere: An Inquiry into a Category of Bourgeois Society,* translated by Thomas Burger with Frederick Lawrence. Cambridge, MA: MIT Press, 1993.

Halttunen, Karen. *Confidence Men and Painted Women: A Study of Middle-Class Culture in America, 1830–1870.* New Haven, CT: Yale University Press, 1982.

———. "From Parlor to Living Room: Domestic Space, Interior Decoration, and the Culture of Personality." In *Consuming Visions: Accumulation and Display of Goods in America, 1880–1920,* edited by Simon J. Bronner, 157–89. New York: W. W. Norton & Company, 1989.

Heininger, Mary Lou Stevens. "Children, Childhood, and Change in America, 1820–1920." In *A Century of Childhood, 1820–1920,* edited by Mary Lynn Stevens Heininger. Rochester, NY: The Strong Museum, 1984.

Higham, John. *Strangers in the Land: Patterns of American Nativism, 1860–1925.* New Brunswick, NJ: Rutgers University Press, 1955.

Hilkey, Judy. *Character Is Capital: Success Manuals and Manhood in Gilded Age America.* Chapel Hill: University of North Carolina Press, 1997.

Holmstrhom, Kirsten. *Monodrama, Attitudes, Tableaux Vivants: Studies on Some Trends in Theatrical Fashion, 1770–1815.* Stockholm: Almqvist and Wiksell, 1967.

Hovet, Grace Ann, and Theodore R. Hovet. "Tableaux Vivants: Masculine Vision and Feminine Reflections in Novels by Warner, Alcott, Stowe, and Wharton." *American Transcendental Quarterly* 7.4 (Dec. 1993): 335–56.

Huber, Richard M. *The American Idea of Success.* New York: McGraw-Hill, 1971.

Huizinga, J. *Homo Ludens: A Study of the Play-Element in Culture.* Boston: Beacon Press, 1950.

Kasson, John. *Rudeness and Civility: Manners in Nineteenth-Century Urban America.* New York: Hill and Wang, 1990.

Kelley, Mary. *Private Woman, Public Stage: Literary Domesticity in Nineteenth-Century America.* New York: Oxford University Press, 1984.

Kerber, Linda K. "Separate Spheres, Female Worlds, Woman's Place: The Rhetoric of Women's History." *Journal of American History* 75.1 (June 1988): 9–39.

Kett, Joseph F. *Rites of Passage: Adolescence in America, 1790 to the Present.* New York: Basic Books, 1977.

Leach, William. *Land of Desire: Merchants, Power, and the Rise of a New American Culture.* New York: Pantheon Books, 1993.

Lears, Jackson, "Beyond Veblen: Rethinking Consumer Culture in America." In *Consuming Visions: Accumulation and Display of Goods in America, 1880–1920*, edited by Simon J. Bronner, 73–98. New York: W. W. Norton & Company, 1989.

———. "From Salvation to Self-Realization: Advertising and the Therapeutic Roots of the Consumer Culture, 1880–1930." In *The Culture of Consumption: Critical Essays in American History, 1880–1980*, edited by T. J. Jackson Lears and Richard Wightman Fox, 1–38. New York: Pantheon Books, 1983.

———. *No Place of Grace: Antimodernism and the Transformation of American Culture, 1880–1920.* New York: Pantheon Books, 1981.

———. "Strategists of Display and the Production of Desire." In *Consuming Visions: Accumulation and Display of Goods in America, 1880–1920*, edited by Simon J. Bronner, 99–132. New York: W. W. Norton & Company, 1989.

Lehuu, Isabelle. *Carnival on the Page: Popular Print Media in Antebellum America.* Chapel Hill: University of North Carolina Press, 1992.

Levine, Lawrence W. *Highbrow/Lowbrow: The Emergence of Cultural Hierarchy in America.* Cambridge, MA: Harvard University Press, 1988.

Litvak, Joseph. *Caught in the Act: Theatricality in the Nineteenth-Century English Novel.* Berkeley: University of California Press, 1992.

Lott, Eric. *Love and Theft: Blackface Minstrelsy and the American Working Class.* New York: Oxford University Press, 1993.

Lynes, Russell. *The Lively Audience: A History of the Visual and Performing Arts in America.* New York: Harper and Row, 1985.

McArthur, Benjamin. *Actors in American Culture, 1880–1920.* Philadelphia: Temple University Press, 1984.

McConachie, Bruce. *Melodramatic Formations: American Theatre and Society, 1820–1870.* Iowa City: University of Iowa Press, 1992.

McCullough, Jack. *Living Pictures on the New York Stage.* Ann Arbor, MI: UMI Research Press, 1983.

Marcus, Steven. *The Other Victorians: A Study of Sexuality and Pornography in Mid-Nineteenth-Century England.* New York: Basic Books, 1964.

Mechling, Jay. "The Collecting Self and American Youth Movements." In *Consuming Visions: Accumulation and Display of Goods in America, 1880–1920*, edited by Simon J. Bronner, 255–85. New York: W. W. Norton, 1989.

Meisel, Martin. *Realizations: Narrative, Pictorial, and Theatrical Arts in Nineteenth-Century England.* Princeton, NJ: Princeton University Press, 1983.

Michaels, Walter Benn. *Our America: Nativism, Modernism, and Pluralism.* Durham, NC: Duke University Press, 1995.

Montgomery, Maureen E. *Displaying Women: Spectacles of Leisure in Edith Wharton's New York.* New York: Routledge, 1998.

Montgomery, Michael V. *Carnivals and Commonplaces: Bakhtin's Chronotope, Cultural Studies, and Film.* New York: Peter Lang, 1993.

Newbury, Michael. "Healthful Employment: Hawthorne, Thoreau, and Middle-Class Fitness." *American Quarterly* 47.4 (Dec. 1995): 681–714.

Nietz, John. *Old Text Books.* Pittsburgh, PA: University of Pittsburgh Press, 1961.

Nissenbaum, Stephen. *The Battle for Christmas.* New York: Vintage Books, 1997.

Nora, Pierre. "Between Memory and History," translated by Marc Roudebush. *Representations* 26 (Spring 1989): 7–25.

Orvell, Miles. *The Real Thing: Imitation and Authenticity in American Culture, 1880–1940.* Chapel Hill: University of North Carolina Press, 1989.

Putnam, Robert. *Bowling Alone: The Collapse and Revival of American Community.* New York: Simon & Schuster, 2000.

Rosenfield, Sybil. *The Temples of Thespis: Some Private Theatres and Theatricals in England and Wales, 1700–1820.* London: Society for Theatre Research, 1978.

Rydell, Robert W. "The Culture of Imperial Abundance: World's Fairs in the Making of American Culture." In *Consuming Visions: Accumulation and Display of Goods in America, 1880–1920,* edited by Simon J. Bronner, 191–216. New York: W. W. Norton & Company, 1989.

Said, Edward W. *Culture and Imperialism.* New York: Alfred A. Knopf, 1993.

———. *The World, the Text, and the Critic.* Cambridge, MA: Harvard University Press, 1983.

Samuel, Raphael. *Theatres of Memory.* New York: Verso, 1994.

Schlereth, Thomas. *Victorian America: Transformations in Everyday Life, 1876–1915.* New York: Harper Collins, 1991.

Schlesinger, Arthur M. *Learning How to Behave: A Historical Study of American Etiquette Books.* New York: Macmillan, 1947.

Shumway, Suzanne Rosenthal. "The Chronotope of the Asylum: *Jane Eyre,* Feminism, and Bakhtinian Theory." In *A Dialogue of Voices: Feminist Literary Theory and Bakhtin,* edited by Karen Hohne and Helen Wussow. Minneapolis: University of Minnesota Press, 1994.

Siefert, Susan. *The Dilemma of the Talented Heroine: A Study of Nineteenth-Century Fiction.* Montreal: Eden Press, 1978.

Slotkin, Richard. *The Fatal Environment: The Myth of the Frontier in the Age of Industrialization, 1800–1890.* New York: Athaneum, 1985.

Stallybrass, Peter, and Allon White. *The Politics and Poetics of Transgression.* London: Methuen & Company, 1986.

Steedman, Carolyn. *Strange Dislocations: Childhood and the Idea of Human Interiority, 1780–1930.* Cambridge, MA: Harvard University Press, 1995.

Stevenson, Louise L. *The American Homefront: American Thought and Culture, 1860–1880*. New York: Twayne Publishers, 1991.

Stewart, Susan. *On Longing: Narratives of the Miniature, the Gigantic, the Souvenir, the Collection*. Baltimore and London: Johns Hopkins University Press, 1984.

Streeby, Shelley. *American Sensations: Class, Empire, and the Production of Popular Culture*. Berkeley: University of California Press, 2002.

Thompson, E. P. *The Making of the English Working Class*. New York: Pantheon Books, 1964.

Thompson, F. M. L. *Rise of Respectable Society: A Social History of Victorian Britain, 1830–1900*. Cambridge, MA: Harvard University Press, 1988.

Thomson, Rosemarie Garland. *Extraordinary Bodies: Figuring Physical Disability in American Culture and Literature*. New York: Columbia University Press, 1997.

———. "Narratives of Deviance and Delight: Staring at Julia Pastrana, the 'Extraordinary Lady.'" In *Beyond the Binary: Reconstructing Cultural Identity in a Multicultural Context*, edited by Timothy B. Powell. New Brunswick, NJ: Rutgers University Press, 1999.

———, ed. *Freakery: Cultural Spectacles of the Extaordinary Body*. New York: New York University Press, 1996.

Turner, Bryan S. "A Note on Nostalgia." *Theory, Culture, and Society* 4.1 (Feb. 1987): 147–56.

Turner, Victor. *From Ritual to Theatre: The Human Seriousness of Play*. New York: Performing Arts Journal Publications, 1982.

Wald, Priscilla. *Constituting Americans: Cultural Anxiety and Narrative Form*. Durham, NC: Duke University Press, 1995.

Warhol, Robyn R. *Gendered Interventions: Narrative Discourse in the Victorian Novel*. New Brunswick, NJ: Rutgers University Press, 1989.

Wiegman, Robyn. *American Anatomies: Theorizing Race and Gender*. Durham, NC: Duke University Press, 1995.

Williams, Raymond. *The English Novel from Dickens to Lawrence*. New York: Oxford University Press, 1970.

Index